Storage Area Network
Fundamentals

Meeta Gupta

Cisco Press

Cisco Press
201 West 103rd Street
Indianapolis, IN 46290 USA

Storage Area Network Fundamentals

Meeta Gupta

Copyright© 2002 Cisco Systems, Inc.

Published by:
Cisco Press
201 West 103rd Street
Indianapolis, IN 46290 USA

Printed in the United States of America 1 2 3 4 5 6 7 8 9 0

First Printing   April 2002

Library of Congress Cataloging-in-Publication Number: 2001092282

ISBN: 1-58705-065-X

Trademark Acknowledgments

All terms mentioned in this book that are known to be trademarks or service marks have been appropriately capitalized. Cisco Press or Cisco Systems, Inc. cannot attest to the accuracy of this information. Use of a term in this book should not be regarded as affecting the validity of any trademark or service mark.

Warning and Disclaimer

This book is designed to provide information about Storage Area Networks. Every effort has been made to make this book as complete and as accurate as possible, but no warranty or fitness is implied.

The information is provided on an "as is" basis. The author, Cisco Press, and Cisco Systems, Inc. shall have neither liability nor responsibility to any person or entity with respect to any loss or damages arising from the information contained in this book or from the use of the discs or programs that may accompany it.

The opinions expressed in this book belong to the author and are not necessarily those of Cisco Systems, Inc.

Feedback Information

At Cisco Press, our goal is to create in-depth technical books of the highest quality and value. Each book is crafted with care and precision, undergoing rigorous development that involves the unique expertise of members from the professional technical community.

Readers' feedback is a natural continuation of this process. If you have any comments regarding how we could improve the quality of this book, or otherwise alter it to better suit your needs, you can contact us through e-mail at feedback@ciscopress.com. Please make sure to include the book title and ISBN in your message.

We greatly appreciate your assistance.

Publisher	John Wait
Editor-In-Chief	John Kane
Cisco Systems Program Management	Michael Hakkert
	Tom Geitner
	William Warren
Acquisitions Editor	Amy Lewis
Production Manager	Patrick Kanouse
Development Editor	Ginny Bess Munroe
Senior Editor	Sheri Cain
Copy Editor	Cris Mattison
Technical Editor(s)	Craig Dennis
	Steve Dussault
	Ron Milione
Team Coordinator	Tammi Ross
Cover Designer	Louisa Klucznik
Composition	ContentWorks
Indexer	Brad Herriman
Proofreader	Dayna Isley

CISCO SYSTEMS

Corporate Headquarters
Cisco Systems, Inc.
170 West Tasman Drive
San Jose, CA 95134-1706
USA
http://www.cisco.com
Tel: 408 526-4000
          800 553-NETS (6387)
Fax: 408 526-4100

European Headquarters
Cisco Systems Europe
11 Rue Camille Desmoulins
92782 Issy-les-Moulineaux
Cedex 9
France
http://www-
europe.cisco.com
Tel: 33 1 58 04 60 00
Fax: 33 1 58 04 61 00

Americas Headquarters
Cisco Systems, Inc.
170 West Tasman Drive
San Jose, CA 95134-1706
USA
http://www.cisco.com
Tel: 408 526-7660
Fax: 408 527-0883

Asia Pacific Headquarters
Cisco Systems Australia,
Pty., Ltd
Level 17, 99 Walker Street
North Sydney
NSW 2059 Australia
http://www.cisco.com
Tel: +61 2 8448 7100
Fax: +61 2 9957 4350

**Cisco Systems has more than 200 offices in the following countries. Addresses, phone numbers, and fax numbers are listed on
the Cisco Web site at www.cisco.com/go/offices**

Argentina • Australia • Austria • Belgium • Brazil • Bulgaria • Canada • Chile • China • Colombia • Costa
Rica • Croatia • Czech Republic • Denmark • Dubai, UAE • Finland • France • Germany • Greece • Hong
Kong • Hungary • India • Indonesia • Ireland Israel • Italy • Japan • Korea • Luxembourg • Malaysia •
Mexico • The Netherlands • New Zealand • Norway • Peru • Philippines Poland • Portugal • Puerto Rico •
Romania • Russia • Saudi Arabia • Scotland • Singapore • Slovakia • Slovenia • South Africa • Spain Sweden
• Switzerland • Taiwan • Thailand • Turkey • Ukraine • United Kingdom • United States • Venezuela • Vietnam
• Zimbabwe

Copyright © 2000, Cisco Systems, Inc. All rights reserved. Access Registrar, AccessPath, Are You Ready, ATM Director, Browse with Me, CCDA, CCDE, CCDP, CCIE, CCNA, CCNP, CCSI, CD-PAC, *CiscoLink*, the Cisco Net*Works* logo, the Cisco Powered Network logo, Cisco Systems Networking Academy, Fast Step, FireRunner, Follow Me Browsing, FormShare, GigaStack, IGX, Intelligence in the Optical Core, Internet Quotient, IP/VC, iQ Breakthrough, iQ Expertise, iQ FastTrack, iQuick Study, iQ Readiness Scorecard, The iQ Logo, Kernel Proxy, MGX, Natural Network Viewer, Network Registrar, the Networkers logo, *Packet*, PIX, Point and Click Internetworking, Policy Builder, RateMUX, ReyMaster, ReyView, ScriptShare, Secure Script, Shop with Me, SlideCast, SMARTnet, SVX, TrafficDirector, TransPath, VlanDirector, Voice LAN, Wavelength Router, Workgroup Director, and Workgroup Stack are trademarks of Cisco Systems, Inc.; Changing the Way We Work, Live, Play, and Learn, Empowering the Internet Generation, are service marks of Cisco Systems, Inc.; and Aironet, ASIST, BPX, Catalyst, Cisco, the Cisco Certified Internetwork Expert Logo, Cisco IOS, the Cisco IOS logo, Cisco Press, Cisco Systems, Cisco Systems Capital, the Cisco Systems logo, Collision Free, Enterprise/Solver, EtherChannel, EtherSwitch, FastHub, FastLink, FastPAD, IOS, IP/TV, IPX, LightStream, LightSwitch, MICA, NetRanger, Post-Routing, Pre-Routing, Registrar, StrataView Plus, Stratm, SwitchProbe, TeleRouter, are registered trademarks of Cisco Systems, Inc. or its affiliates in the U.S. and certain other countries.

All other brands, names, or trademarks mentioned in this document or Web site are the property of their respective owners. The use of the word partner does not imply a partnership relationship between Cisco and any other company. (0010R)

About the Author

Meeta Gupta has a masters degree in computer engineering. The topic of networking is her first love. She is presently working at NIIT Ltd., where she designs, develops, and authors books on various subjects. She has co-authored books on TCP/IP, A+ Certification, Visual C#, ASP.NET, and PHP. She also has extensive experience in designing and developing ILTs. Besides writing, Meeta has had a two-year stint in training and instruction. She has conducted courses on C++, Sybase, Windows NT, UNIX, and HTML for audiences that range from students to corporate clients.

About the Technical Reviewers

Craig Dennis is currently an independent consultant, specializing in LAN/WAN installation and design for businesses in the Northern Virginia area. He is a Certified Cisco Systems Instructor and Design Professional (CCSI, CCDP). Craig is a coauthor of *CCNP Remote Access Exam Certification Guide* (published by Cisco Press).

Steve Dussault, CCIE #3073, is a senior consulting engineer for Networked Information Systems, a Cisco Systems Gold Partner. Steve also holds Cisco CCDP certification, CSS1 and Voice Access specializations, and Sun Microsystems. Steve designs and implements enterprise network solutions for Cisco customers worldwide. In his spare time, Steve teaches entry- and advanced-level scuba diving and enjoys the outdoors. Steve can be reached by e-mail at steve@awuwi.com.

Ron Milione is the chief technology officer for Global Centric Networks.

Dedication

This book is for Prashant. We love you a lot, and we still miss you terribly.

Acknowledgments

No man is an island, and no author writes a book alone. Many people contribute to a book, aside from the author. Thank you, Anita, for giving me the opportunity to write this book and for giving me support throughout the process. Thanks, Anisha, for juggling with my a's and the's. Thank you, Sunil, Priyanka, and Parul for putting my words into pictures. I couldn't have asked for a better graphics team.

A tremendous vote of thanks to Ginny Bess Munroe at Cisco Press for going through the drafts and patiently making corrections and suggesting changes. If this book comes out any better, blame it on Ginny. A big thanks to my technical editors, Craig Dennis, Steve Dussault, and Ron Milione, for guiding me where I faltered.

Last, but not least, thank you mom, daddy, and Vikas. You are my life-support system. Thanks for never complaining about the crazy hours I kept while writing this book.

Contents at a Glance

Contents

Introduction

During the last decade, a multitude of changes in computing technology and the globalization of business through the Internet has resulted in a tremendous growth in storage requirements. This has forced many organizations around the world to reassess the way they view their storage environment. Many applications, such as e-commerce, imaging, data warehousing, Enterprise Resource Planning (ERP), and Customer Relationship Management (CRM), fill storage media quickly. Data accessibility and availability for these applications has to be fast and efficient. Clearly, the ever-increasing information access requirements have had a profound effect on most data centers. As a result, many organizations are searching for cost-effective ways to ensure high data availability and reliability.

As organizations seek out cost-effective ways to manage the virtual explosion of information created by e-business and other initiatives, they are turning to storage area networks (SANs). SANs address today's most challenging business requirements: how to protect and access critical data, how to utilize computing resources more efficiently, and how to ensure the highest levels of business continuance.

SANs are networks within networks and their design separates server applications from data storage without sacrificing storage access times. They offer simplified storage management, scalability, flexibility, availability, and improved data access, movement, and backup. SANs also let numerous servers and applications access the data simultaneously. They minimize the need for specialized data storage servers and provide high-speed storage pools through a group of connected servers and high-speed workstations.

Goals and Methods

The most important and somewhat obvious goal of this book is to provide you with in-depth knowledge about storage networks. In fact, if the primary objective of this book was any different, then the book's title would be misleading; however, the methods used in this book help you to design, implement, and secure SANs and make you much more knowledgeable about how to do your job.

Who Should Read This Book?

According to a recent survey, more than 50 percent of IT organizations worldwide estimate that their storage requirements are growing by about 25–50 percent annually. Corporate IT expenditures also keep growing to match the increasing storage needs. This book targets IT professionals who are interested in finding solutions to their growing data storage needs and expenditures. Specifically, IT professionals and resellers who are seeking data storage solutions for data mining, online transaction processing, imaging, data warehousing, or any other highly data-intensive applications, will gain most from this book.

How This Book Is Organized

Although this book can be read cover-to-cover, it is designed to be flexible and to allow you to easily move between chapters and sections of chapters to cover just the material that you need more work with. Chapter 1 provides an overview of basic networking concepts and gives you a glance into the world of SANs. Chapter 2 gives you a thorough introduction to the concept of SANs. Chapters 3 through 5 discuss the Fibre Channel technology, on which SANs of today are based. Chapter 6 discusses the SAN topologies in detail, and Chapters 7 through 9 discuss the topics of implementation, security, and troubleshooting problems in a SAN. Chapter 10 discusses the upcoming iSCSI technology, and Chapter 11 discusses the future of SANs. If you intend to read each chapter, the order presented in the book is an excellent sequence to use.

Chapters 1 through 11 cover the following topics:

- Chapter 1, "Networking and Storage Concepts," serves as a review of basic networking concepts. Read it before you embark on the world of SANs.

- Chapter 2, "Introduction to Storage Area Networks," gives you an overview of the SAN technology. The chapter covers the evolution and benefits of storage networks, basic SAN components, and how data is accessed over a SAN.

- Chapter 3, "Fibre Channel Basics," provides in-depth coverage of Fibre Channel technology, which forms the backbone of any SAN-based storage network. This chapter also gives you detailed information on various Fibre Channel ports, the three Fibre Channel topologies, the five Fibre Channel layers, and the six classes of service available in Fibre Channel technology.

- Chapter 4, "Fibre Channel Products," introduces you to various Fibre Channel products, such as Host Bus Adapters (HBAs), common Fibre Channel connectors, Fibre Channel hubs, switches, bridges, routers, and storage devices.

- Chapter 5, "Fibre Channel Cabling," deals with Fibre Channel cabling. Here, you'll learn about copper-based and fiber-optic cabling and how to implement them in a SAN.

- Chapter 6, "SAN Topologies," focuses on the three Fibre Channel topologies—point-to-point, Fibre Channel-Arbitrated Loop (FC-AL), and switched fabric. You'll also learn about the advantages and disadvantages of each topology.

- Chapter 7, "Designing and Building a SAN," provides you detailed guidelines and best practices for the designing and implementation of SANs, while ensuring SANs' scalability, high-performance, stability, and resilience to disasters.

- Chapter 8, "Implementing SAN Security," deals with the implementation of security measures to prevent security breaches and compromise of mission-critical data stored in a SAN.

- In Chapter 9, "Problem Isolation and Management of SANs," you learn how to isolate problems in a SAN and how to effectively manage SANs. You also learn to isolate and troubleshoot problems, manage disasters, and manage an entire SAN.

- Chapter 10, "iSCSI Technology," covers the iSCSI technology in detail. Here, you learn about the reasons for the emergence of this technology, basic iSCSI concepts, and considerations and requirements for implementing the iSCSI technology.

- Chapter 11, "Future of SANs," discusses the future of storage networks. It gives you an overview of ongoing developments in the field of SANs and of storage technologies other than SANs.

- Appendix A, "RAID Technology and Fibre Channel Vendors."

In this chapter, you will learn about the following topics:

- Basic networking concepts and topologies
- Need for storage networks
- Storage devices and techniques
- Network attached storage (NAS) and storage area networks (SANs)
- SAN standards organizations

CHAPTER 1

Networking and Storage Concepts

This is the age of the Internet. But a few of us also realize that this is the Store Age—the age of mission-critical, data-intensive applications that have been fueled by the immense popularization of the phenomenon called the Internet. Also, the progress achieved by the multimedia industry has enabled the integration of storage-intensive data, such as audio and video, with common applications, thus making increased demands on the storage capacity. These applications have grown at such a rapid pace that today for many of us the term computing is synonymous with data management.

No matter if it's a large corporate organization sprawled across the globe or a small business, all are struggling to keep pace with the ever-growing amount of business data, which might be dispersed all over the network, especially if the network is a wide-area network (WAN). The current scenario has forced the IT industry to re-evaluate the strategy for managing the existing storage infrastructure and to accommodate the staggering amount of data in the future.

Basic Networking Concepts and Topologies

What is known as the Internet today started in early 1968 as a connection of four computers as a part of the project funded by the U.S. Department of Defense (DoD). This network was known as Advanced Research Project Agency Network (ARPANET).

With the realization that communication through networks is the fastest and cheapest way to communicate with other computers, many hardware and software vendors jumped on the bandwagon. Soon a wide range of hardware and software network products was available in the market. To avoid the incompatibility between various products and the monopoly of a product, a need for common standards of communication, which ensures that the inter-connected machines communicate successfully, was realized. These standards are known as *protocols*. Transmission Control Protocol/Internet Protocol (TCP/IP) is one of the most widely used protocols to date. Likewise, a theoretical model was developed that established a way to communicate about communication solutions for networks. This model is known as the *Open System Interconnect (OSI)* reference model. The following section discusses OSI.

OSI Reference Model

The contemporary seven-layer OSI model has evolved over the past several years. Figure 1-1 shows the OSI model. The main aim of the model was to establish open standards for current and future developments in the field of networking. This model does not exist physically. It is a theoretical model that serves as a guideline to help vendors develop compatible solutions. The model also helps in understanding complex network functions and in designing specialized and modular network products and solutions.

Figure 1-1   *The Seven Layers of the OSI Reference Model*

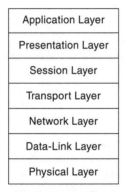

OSI Reference Model

As the name suggests, the seven-layer OSI model consists of seven layers, where each layer represents a specific group of tasks and a specific aspect of communication. The seven layers of the model in the order of the lowest layer to the highest layer are physical layer, data-link layer, network layer, transport layer, session layer, presentation layer, and application layer. The following sections describe each of these layers.

Physical Layer

The physical layer facilitates the transmission of data across a *transmission medium*. A transmission medium is a physical path over which data is transmitted in signals. Electrical and fiber optic cables and radio waves are some commonly used transmission media.

The physical layer converts the data passed over to it by the upper layers into a series of *bits*. A bit is the unit of communication in data networks. At a given time, it can contain only one of two valid values—1 or 0. 1 represents the presence of information, whereas 0 represents the absence of information. The bits are then placed over the transmission medium to be propagated to the receiver device or node in the form of a signal.

Signals that travel over the network transmission media are of two types—*analog* and *digital*. As shown in Figure 1-2, analog signals resemble a series of sine waves. Therefore, the state of the analog wave changes continuously and all the values in the range are included. Digital signals, on the other hand, are discrete in nature. This means that a digital signal can have only two states—1 or 0. Figure 1-3 depicts a digital signal.

Figure 1-2   *An Analog Signal*

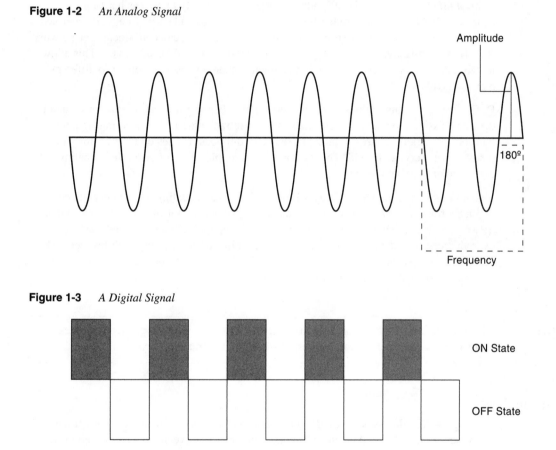

Figure 1-3   *A Digital Signal*

Most network devices—including computers—operate on digital signals. Some transmission media, such as telephone cables, can carry analog signals only. As a result, when a digital signal needs to be transmitted over an analog transmission medium, it needs to be converted into a corresponding analog signal. Modems are used for converting digital signals to analog and vice versa. Other transmission media, such as ISDN lines, carry digital signals. Therefore, there is no need to convert signals.

NOTE   You'll learn more about modems in the "Common Network Devices" section later in this chapter.

Data-Link Layer

The data-link layer is responsible for providing unique identification to the devices, such as computers, printers, and so on along a network, which is based on their *Media Access Control (MAC) addresses*. MAC addresses are also popularly known as hardware addresses. MAC addresses are hard-coded into the network adapter or network interface card (NIC) of a device and are used to uniquely identify each device in a local-area network (LAN). Also, this layer maps IP addresses to corresponding MAC addresses. This allows network devices on a LAN to communicate with other devices that belong to different networks (LANs).

During transmissions, frames might be corrupted or destroyed because of a noise burst on the transmission medium. These frames must be retransmitted. However, multiple transmissions of a frame can result in the presence of duplicate frames on the transmission medium. The services provided by the data-link layer play a significant role in dealing with corrupted or duplicate frames.

Besides organizing the physical layer bits into frames and dealing with damaged and duplicate frames, the data-link layer is also responsible for controlling data flow so that network devices, such as printers that operate at comparatively lower speeds, are not overwhelmed with data from the sender device while communicating with fast network devices such as switches. In addition, the data-link layer also plays an important role in error detection and notification of the detected errors to the upper layers.

NOTE   Although the data-link layer is responsible for detecting and notifying errors, it does not correct errors. Error correction is a responsibility of the transport layer.

Network Layer

Although MAC addresses are used to uniquely identify a device on a local network, MAC addresses are not effective when communication occurs between devices located in two separate networks. This is because MAC addresses are long in size (48 bytes). As a result, they generate a large amount of network traffic. Also, MAC addresses are vendor-specific, which means that they might not be compatible.

The network layer is responsible for providing unique identification to devices when communication occurs between two different networks or over the Internet. This network layer addressing scheme is known as *IP addressing*. An IP address is a 32-bit binary number, which is represented as a set of four octets. Following is an example of a valid IP address:

10010111.00001111.00011111.00010001

Although the example represents a unique IP address, it is inconvenient to remember. Therefore, an alternative *dotted decimal notation* is used. According to this notation, an IP address is denoted as four decimal-based integers separated by decimal points. Here, each integer represents a byte (or octet) that can range from 0 to 255. The corresponding dotted decimal notation of the IP address shown in the preceding example is the following:

151.15.31.17

An IP address consists of two parts. The first part is used to identify a network, and the second part represents the host address. How many octets specify the network address and how many represent the host address depends on the *IP address class*. The network layer supports five address classes: Class A, B, C, D, and E. Of these classes, A, B, and C are the most frequently used. The first (left-most) octet of a Class A address represents the network address, and the rest of the three octets denote the host address. Similarly, the left-most two octets of a Class B address represent the network address, and the rest represent the host address. In a Class C address, the first three octets denote the network address, and the right-most octet specifies the host address.

The most important responsibility of the network layer is to route data packets across internetworks to the specified destination network on the basis of IP addresses. This process is known as *routing*. The network layer is also responsible for determining all the possible routes to a destination network. After route discovery, this layer determines the shortest and fastest path to the destination network.

Transport Layer

Although the network layer locates the destination network and the data-link layer identifies the destination host in the network, the transport layer is responsible for delivering data from the sender to the recipient.

The transport layer deliveries are of two types. In *connection-oriented* data deliveries, the recipient acknowledges each set of successfully received data. The next set of data is not transmitted until the sender device receives a positive acknowledgment from the recipient. If the sender doesn't receive positive acknowledgment for a given set of transmitted data, it resends the corrupted batch. In case of *connectionless* deliveries, the sender does not take the onus of retransmitting data in case of data-loss or corruption.

In addition, the transport layer also organizes messages received from the higher layers into segments and provides error control and end-to-end data flow control. If packets arrive with delays or are lost over the internetwork during a transaction, only the sender and receiver nodes are involved in packet recovery. No other device or layer is involved in the process. This is known as *end-to-end flow control*. The transport layer also uses positive and negative acknowledgments to implement flow control.

Session Layer

The session layer is responsible for establishing, maintaining, synchronizing, and managing a *session* between two communicating entities on the network after a connection between them has been established. A session is the logical connection between the two communicating entities. The session layer also helps the application layer to identify the services available on the network and to connect to them. In addition, the session layer can start a connection request and coordinate access rights.

The session layer facilitates three types of dialogs between two communicating entities. These include *simplex*, *half-duplex*, and *full-duplex* dialogs:

- **Simplex dialogs**—In simplex dialogs, only one device is allowed to transmit. The rest of the devices involved in the session can only receive data. For example, broadcasts are simplex dialogs.

- **Half-duplex dialogs**—In half-duplex dialogs, both of the communicating entities can transmit and receive data. However, only one device can transmit at a time. For example, a network device transmits data and then receives data over the same transmission cable.

- **Full-duplex dialogs**—In full-duplex dialogs, the communicating entities can transmit and receive data simultaneously.

NOTE	A conversation over walkie-talkies is a good analogy of a half-duplex dialog. Similarly, a telephonic conversation is one of the best analogies of a full-duplex dialog.

Presentation Layer

The presentation layer is responsible for formatting and encrypting data into a format that the communicating entity can understand and process. Therefore, the presentation layer plays a significant role in facilitating data exchange between entities that run on different hardware and software platforms and that use different or incompatible data (file) formats.

The presentation layer is also responsible for encrypting data to ensure security of data while in transit. Encryption is a security method that prevents data from unauthorized access. This layer is also responsible for decrypting data received by a network entity and compressing and decompressing the data that the two communicating entities are exchanging.

Application Layer

In addition to supporting application and end-user processes, the application layer provides an interface between the network and the user. In other words, this is where interaction between a user and the network occurs. Thus, the application layer is also where network services reside. All network applications and services, such as e-mail, Telnet, FTP, and so on, are a part of this layer.

The OSI seven-layer model is a theoretical model. Therefore, you can neither see the layers nor use them. However, the seven layers help you to understand the transactions over the network and the functioning of various network devices. The next section describes the devices that you commonly use in a network.

Common Network Devices

You use several devices to build a network and to connect computers to the network. Some of the most important network devices are *media connectors*, *NICs*, *repeaters*, *hubs*, *modems*, *bridges*, *routers*, and *brouters*. These devices are discussed in the following sections.

Media Connectors

Media connectors, such as T-connectors, BNC-connectors, RJ-45, DB-15, and DB-25, provide network devices with a point of connectivity to the network's transmission medium.

NOTE   Media connectors function at the first layer, or the physical layer, of the OSI model.

Figure 1-4 depicts commonly used media connectors.

Figure 1-4   *Common Media Connectors*

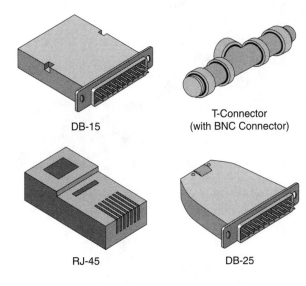

DB-15

T-Connector
(with BNC Connector)

RJ-45

DB-25

NICs

Compared to media connectors that are external connectivity devices, NICs are installed internally in the network devices. They are also known as network adapter cards or simply network cards. NICs provide network connectivity to a device and are also the source of the hardware address of a network device. They are attached to the transmission medium with the help of media connectors and drop cables, if necessary. Figure 1-5 depicts an NIC.

NOTE   NICs function at the second layer or the data-link layer of the OSI reference model.

Figure 1-5   *A Network Interface Card*

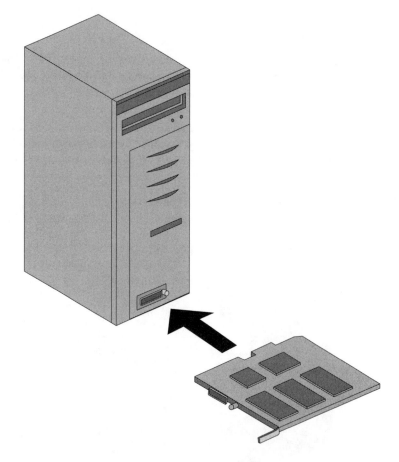

Repeaters

Each transmission medium has a maximum length beyond which the signals start to deteriorate significantly. For example, according to Ethernet specifications, cables cannot exceed a maximum length of 150 meters. *Repeaters* extend the length of a transmission medium effectively by amplifying the signal to its original strength. However, they are not intelligent devices. Intelligent devices can provide additional and complex functions, such as LAN emulation, in addition to forwarding signals. Therefore, intelligent devices also tend to amplify the disturbances, such as noise bursts that the transmission medium picks up from its environment. Figure 1-6 depicts a repeater.

Figure 1-6   *A Repeater*

Hubs

Hubs allow multiple network devices to be connected to them. As a result, they act as a central point of connection in a network. There are three types of hubs—passive, active, and intelligent. *Passive hubs* merely broadcast the signals received from a connected device to all the other devices connected to them. *Active hubs*, however, regenerate signals before broadcasting them to the connected devices. In addition to regenerating signals to their original strength, *intelligent hubs* forward the signals only to the intended recipient. This reduces unnecessary network traffic considerably.

Figure 1-7 depicts a hub.

Figure 1-7   *A Hub*

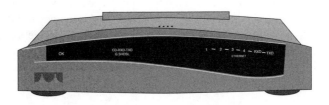

Modems

Computers operate on digital signals, but analog telephone lines, as the name suggests, can carry only analog signals. If a telephone line were directly connected to a computer, transmission would be impossible, because the two signals are incompatible. A modem (modulator-demodulator) acts as an interface between the two. The modem converts analog signals received from a telephone line into digital signals that a computer can process and vice versa.

NOTE   Modems, hubs, and repeaters function at the physical layer of the OSI model.

Figure 1-8 depicts a modem.

Figure 1-8   *A Modem*

Bridges

A bridge is a device that helps break a large network into smaller segments. It acts as a filter that effectively reduces network traffic by preventing frames meant for the same network segment from reaching other segments. A bridge also allows more than one conversation to occur simultaneously, thus increasing the overall performance of the network.

When a bridge is added to the network, it creates a table that consists of the hardware addresses of all the devices connected to it. On receiving a signal, the bridge checks the address of the destination device for which the signal is intended. If the recipient is located in one of the segments that is connected to the bridge, the bridge forwards the signal only to that particular segment. This reduces the amount of network traffic that is generated by the broadcasts. If the recipient is not a part of the connected segments, the signal is broadcast.

NOTE	Bridges function at the data-link layer of the OSI model.

Figure 1-9 depicts a bridge.

Figure 1-9   *A Bridge*

Routers

Routers are used to connect separate networks or logical divisions of a network known as *subnetworks*, or *subnets*. Routers function very much like bridges, but instead of connecting physical segments of a network, they connect the subnets or separate networks. During the communication between devices that are located on different networks or subnets, routers are responsible for determining the best path for the data to travel to the destination host. Figure 1-10 depicts a router.

Figure 1-10   *A Router*

Brouters

Brouters are a combination of routers and bridges. Therefore, they can handle communication within a network and between different networks or subnets. After receiving a packet, brouters check if the packet is meant for the local network. If the destination device is located in the local network, the packet is forwarded to the segment where the recipient is located. Otherwise, the packet is routed to the destination network. Figure 1-11 depicts a brouter.

NOTE	Routers function at Layer 3, or the network layer, of the OSI model. Brouters, however, can function at the second layer (the data-link layer) and the third layer (network layer) of the OSI model.

Figure 1-11   *A Brouter*

Network Topologies

The physical arrangement of a transmission medium in a network and the manner in which network devices are connected to the medium is known as the *network topology.* Common network topologies implemented in the present-day networks include the *bus, star, ring,* and *mesh* topologies.

Bus Topology

In the bus topology, all the network devices are connected to a common transmission medium in a multi-point connection. The common transmission medium of the network is also referred to as the *backbone.* Network devices can either be attached directly to the backbone by using T-connectors, or they can use short cables known as *drop cables.* The backbone must be terminated at both ends or else a signal will be infinitely reflected over it, disrupting the normal network operation.

Figure 1-12 shows the bus topology setup. This topology is the cheapest and easiest to build. However, this topology is not fault-tolerant, and it is difficult to troubleshoot problems in this topology because points of failure can be anywhere.

Figure 1-12   *Bus Topology Setup*

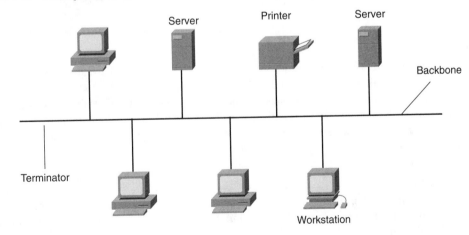

Star Topology

In the star topology, the hub forms the central point of connection for the network devices. The devices are connected to the hub through drop cables in a point-to-point connection. This topology, though slightly more expensive than the bus topology, is easiest to troubleshoot and reconfigure. It is also fault-tolerant. As a result, if a network device fails, the other network devices continue to function without being affected. However, if the hub fails, all the devices connected to it are affected. Figure 1-13 shows the star topology setup.

Figure 1-13   *Star Topology Setup*

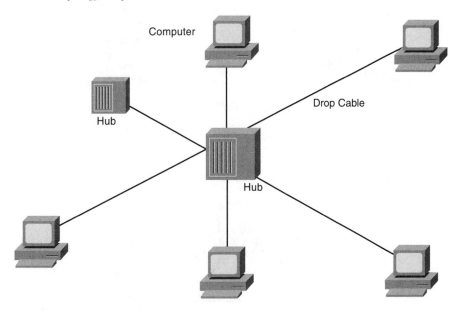

Ring Topology

In the ring topology, all the network devices, or nodes, are connected to their neighboring device to form a ring. This topology is extremely fault tolerant, especially in the case of a double ring. This is because the ring can automatically reconfigure itself logically to exclude the failed device. It is also easy to manage. However, it is expensive and difficult to physically reconfigure. Figure 1-14 depicts the ring topology setup.

Mesh Topology

All the network devices are connected to every other device on the network in a mesh topology. As a result, it is an extremely expensive topology. However, it is the most fault-tolerant topology. Due to the excessive use of cables, it is difficult to manage. Figure 1-15 shows the mesh topology setup.

Figure 1-14   *Ring Topology Setup*

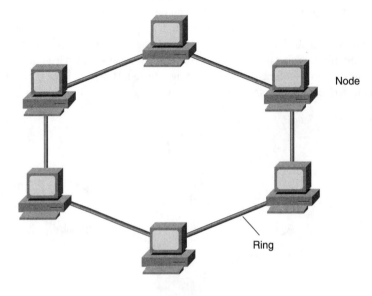

Figure 1-15   *Mesh Topology Setup*

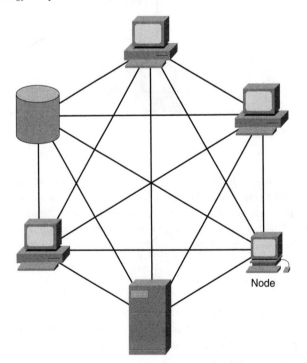

The nodes in each physical topology access the transmission medium in a different manner. The following section describes various MAC standards.

MAC Standards

Two or more signals being placed on a transmission medium at the same time should be kept to a minimum or not occur at all. If two or more signals are placed together on the transmission medium, the signals can collide and result in the corruption of both signals and the subsequent disruption of normal network functioning. Rules, known as *MAC standards*, control when a network device can transmit data. These rules prevent the corruption and disruption of network functioning.

Each physical topology is associated with its own media access method and standards. The common MAC standards include *contention*, *token passing*, and *polling*. These standards are discussed in the following sections.

Contention

With contention, when a device wants to transmit data, it has to compete with other devices to place its signal on the transmission medium. It is highly possible that two or more devices will attempt to place their signals on the medium simultaneously. If this happens, the signals collide and are destroyed. The destroyed signals cause excessive noise bursts over the transmission medium, which can disrupt normal network functions until all the signals are terminated. Contention is commonly used in the bus topology. Although a simple access method, contention is the slowest because the probability of collisions is high, which considerably reduces network productivity.

Token Passing

Token passing uses a special frame called a *token*, which continuously circulates in the network. If a device wants to transmit data, it captures the free circulating token and places the data in it. After the transmission is completed, the device releases the token. This access method is used in the ring topology. There is a lower possibility of collision in this topology. However, a node might have to wait for its turn to transmit data until the current node releases the token.

Polling

With the polling method, a primary device, also known as a master device, polls all the network devices at regular intervals to see if they need to transmit data. When a device has to transmit data, it requests the primary device to send a request frame when the primary device polls it. On receiving the request frame, the device places the data in the request frame and returns the packet to the primary device. The primary device subsequently forwards the frame to the intended recipient. This access method is commonly used by intelligent hubs in the star topology. Similar to token passing, the probability of collision or data loss is minimal in this topology. However, devices have to wait for their turn to transfer data.

The primary concern of a network is to deal with data. As the amount of data stored on a network increases, the need for storage management increases proportionally. The following section describes how storage networks can alleviate the problem of managing stored data and keep it safe at the same time.

The Need for Storage Networks

This is the age of mission-critical, storage-intensive applications that with the advent of the Internet and popularization of e-commerce have forced businesses to provide 24-hour, 7-days a week data availability to their customers. 24/7 worldwide data availability ensures that users can access data at any point of time. This means that the storage infrastructure must always be ready to handle transaction data. Some of the applications that need to deliver 24/7 services include the following:

- Online trading and transactions

> **NOTE** Popular online trading sites, such as Amazon.com, register a high number of hits and orders on a per-hour basis. All the user registration and order information needs to be stored, verified, and modified. This makes online transactions and trading storage-intensive.

- E-commerce transactions (B2B and B2C)
- Enterprise Resource Planning (ERP)
- Managing Information Systems (MIS)
- Data warehouse and data mining systems
- Web-based e-mail

> **NOTE** Details of the huge number of users using Web-based mail services, such as Hotmail and Yahoo, need to be stored and managed. This makes Web-based e-mail highly storage-intensive.

- Multimedia applications
- Internet downloads

These storage-intensive applications have posed unprecedented demands on the current storage infrastructure, which has been unable to keep up with the demand. According to industry analysts, the demand for data storage is predicted to increase from the current demand of 2000 terabytes (TB) to more than 150,000 TB by the year 2003. If this problem is not addressed soon, the future will be full of frequent server crashes and the loss of important, confidential business data.

Following are some of the most important contributing factors to the need for a better storage infrastructure:

- **Limited scalability supported by Small Computer System Interface (SCSI) devices**—Theoretically, present-day SCSI devices can support up to 15 other devices. However, in reality, a SCSI device cannot support more than four to five devices. Also, the large number of devices severely hampers the performance of the server. As a result, the ability of a SCSI-based server to support multiple storage devices is limited. With the ever-increasing amount of data, this doesn't prove to be a reliable and financially viable solution.

- **Inability for input/output (I/O) bandwidth of storage devices to keep up**— Although the capacity of storage devices has increased manifold, up to many terabytes, the I/O bandwidth of the devices has failed to keep up. Therefore, in spite of the availability of extremely large storage capacities, I/O operations are comparatively slow. This severely reduces the overall performance of a network, which can cause a business to lose in today's market of cutthroat competition.

- **High cost of distributed networks**—Today's networks span the globe and are distributed by nature. In this scenario, there's a high possibility that different parts of the internetwork can run on different platforms (hardware and software). In such cases, only highly trained and skilled personnel can handle the storage resource management. However, hiring personnel is expensive and can increase the cost of managing the network by a rough estimate of ten times the present cost.

- **Inconsistencies resulting from simultaneous access to data by multiple clients**— Data can be accessed simultaneously by multiple users. Each user gets a copy of the data, which can lead to conflicts and inconsistencies in the data while updating the data on the server or the database. This can cause problems, especially in the case of distributed applications such as ERP, where multiple copies of the data are created.

- **Excessive network traffic generated because of backups and data recovery**— While performing backup and recovery operations across a distributed network, an excessive amount of data traffic is generated, which can cause network shutdowns in extreme cases.

- **Increasing financial costs**—Managing storage resources in the current infrastructure is expensive. Yet these resources cannot cope with the staggering amount of data influx. Moreover, hiring competent and trained storage managers is a costly exercise.

The inability to manage huge amounts of business data generated on a daily basis and extremely expensive solutions that might prove to be obsolete in a matter of a year or so have created a lot of interest in the field of storage infrastructures. More businesses are adopting measures to combat data management. Storage devices such as optical storage devices, disk arrays, and tape libraries are some of the most popularly used solutions, although they might prove to be temporary solutions because of the exponential increase in the amount of data being handled on a daily basis.

Storage Devices and Techniques

Storage infrastructures form the basis of the reliable storage of business data. A wealth of storage devices exists that can be used to store huge amounts of data. These include *disks*, *disk arrays*, *tape libraries*, and *optical storage devices*, such as compact disks (CDs) and digital versatile disks (DVDs). The following sections discuss each of these.

CD Storage and Libraries

CDs provide the least expensive storage solution. However, a CD's storage capacity (up to a few gigabytes) is less than that of other storage devices. The more data, the larger the number of CDs. Therefore, if the amount of business data is gigantic, managing the number of CDs becomes tedious, if not impossible. A few types of CDs are available in the market that can be used based on the user requirement. These include the CD-R format that can be written onto only once and CD-RW that can be rewritten many times. A collection of CDs that contain business data is known as a *CD library*.

DVD Storage and Libraries

Although their physical size is similar to that of a CD, a single DVD can store from 4.7 GB and 8.5 GB to 17 GB of data. However, DVDs are more expensive than CDs. Because of their storage capacity and reliability, they have successfully replaced CDs. Similar to CDs, DVDs are available in many formats such as DVD-ROM (are read-only), DVD-R (can be rewritten once), and DVD-RAM and +RW (can be rewritten many times).

Disk Storage Systems

Disk storage systems form the hub of any storage infrastructure. They are high-performance, reliable storage devices that can store up to several terabytes of data. These devices can be used in a wide range of platforms, such as Unix, Windows, Macintosh, Linux, and so on.

They are also highly scalable because additional disk storage devices can be integrated into the existing infrastructure without the need of undergoing costly upgrades. IBM's 7133 Serial Disk System and FastT200 Storage Server are examples of disk storage systems.

Disk Arrays

A disk array is a set of high-performance storage disks that can store several terabytes of data. In addition, a disk array is considered to be highly reliable because even if several of its components fail, the device can continue to function. A single disk array can also support multiple points of connection to the network. As a result, the probability of unavailability of data stored on the array due to a single point of failure is practically eliminated. A disk array either can be a redundant array of independent disks (RAID) device or a non-RAID device. *RAID* is a method of distributing data across several storage disks. Six levels of RAID—Level 0 through Level 5—help in the efficient usage of available bandwidth. The RAID levels also provide efficient methods of data recovery in the case of server crashes.

NOTE   For detailed information on RAID and RAID levels, refer to Appendix A, "RAID Technology and Fibre Channel Vendors."

Tape Libraries and Subsystems

A tape library is a set of tape cartridges that store data. In addition to the tape cartridges, a tape library also consists of a tape subsystem and tape management hardware and software that operates the library. A tape subsystem is the hardware interface that enables communication between the host processor and the library. A tape library can store from 10 GB to 1 TB of data. The tape cartridges of a tape library can mount and dismount on their own, which makes the intervention of an operator unnecessary.

There are various storage techniques used in present-day networks to manage an ever-increasing amount of data. These include embedded storage, directly attached storage, and network attached storage.

As shown in Figure 1-16, embedded storage is a device that is embedded into the server. As a result, the capacity of storage is proportional to the server's capacity for accommodating the embedded storage devices (mostly in the form of high-capacity storage disks). Embedded storage has not proven to be an effective solution for storage problems because a huge amount of storage capacity is dependent on the server the devices are embedded in.

If the server fails, a huge chunk of data becomes unavailable to the users, which is not acceptable in today's scenario of e-commerce applications.

Figure 1-16   *Embedded Storage*

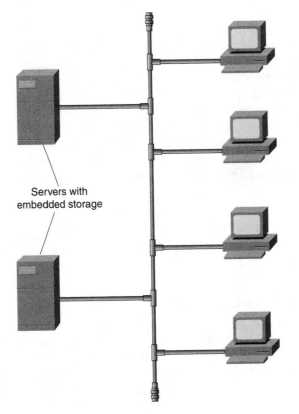

Servers with
embedded storage

Figure 1-17 shows a direct-attached storage (DAS) device as an external storage device that is connected directly to a server through the SCSI interface. A DAS either can be implemented as Just a Bunch of Disks (JBOD) or as a disk array. DAS devices are comparatively slower than embedded storage. Only a limited number of DAS devices can be attached to a server because the number of SCSI interfaces available to a server are limited. Also, if a server fails, a large chunk of data stored on it becomes unavailable to the users.

If the storage device is shared between two or more servers, access to the data becomes slower, although the potential problem of a single point of failure is eliminated (see Figure 1-18).

Figure 1-17   *DAS*

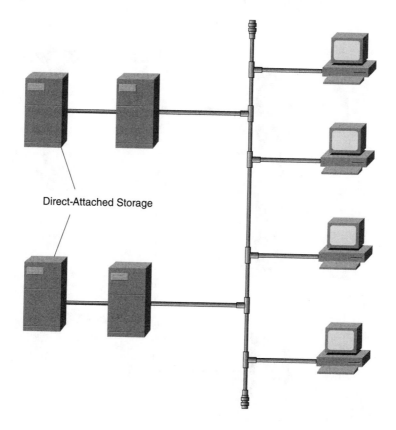

Direct-Attached Storage

As shown in Figure 1-19, a network-attached storage (NAS) device is directly connected to the network instead of being connected to a server. NAS implements the concept of shared storage and is highly platform-independent. It can communicate seamlessly with popular network environments, such as Unix, Windows, AIX, Macintosh, and so on.

Generally, a NAS device is a plug-and-play device, which when connected to the network starts functioning with minimal configuration. When a client requests data from the server, the server directs the information to the appropriate NAS device. The NAS device then extracts the required data and forwards it to the server, which in turn passes the data to the client. As a result, the interaction is slow and generates more network traffic. This makes NAS highly suitable for small- to medium-scale networks, but not for extremely large networks. However, the setup does ensure high availability and reliability of data along with improved network performance.

NAS is discussed in more detail in the following section.

Figure 1-18 *A DAS Device Shared Between Servers*

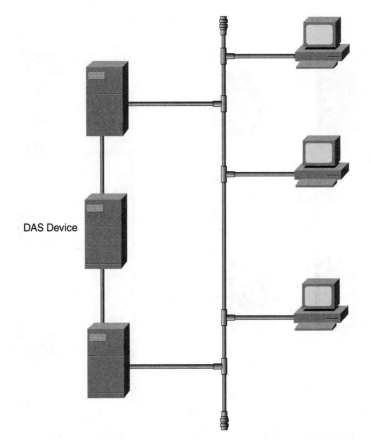

Figure 1-19 *NAS*

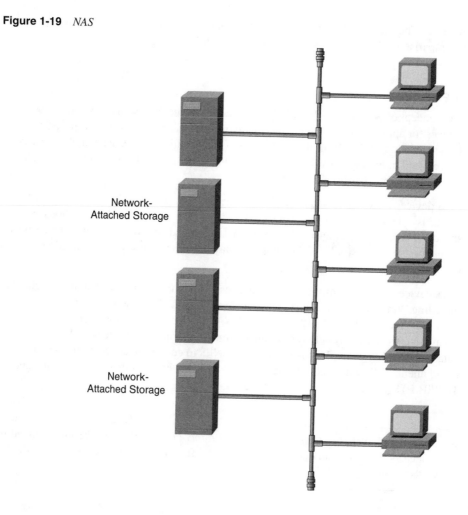

Network-
Attached Storage

Network-
Attached Storage

NAS and SAN

Data-intensive applications and the Internet resulted in a data boom. The amount of data that is being transacted has skyrocketed, which has sent businesses scrambling for reliable solutions that are comparatively low in cost and easy to manage. NAS is being touted as one of the best solutions for small- and medium-sized businesses because it effectively addresses the problem of data storage.

Storage area networks (SANs), the most recent storage solution technology in the market, were developed to deal with enormous amounts of data securely and reliably without hampering overall network performance. NAS and SANs are introduced in the following

sections. The focus of this book is on SANs, but as you'll see, NAS is worth mention, and a comparison of the two demonstrates the possibilities of SANs.

NAS Devices

The concept of NAS is simple. All business data is stored on resources, known as *NAS devices* (or appliances), which are physically separate from the general-purpose servers. This separation of data from the servers and its localization on specialized NAS devices, has resulted in increased overall network productivity, lessened storage-related problems, and lowered Total Cost of Ownership (TCO).

NAS devices were developed to address storage-related problems in real-time. A NAS device is a dedicated, high-performance, standalone storage device that functions at high speeds. It is generally a piece of hardware that is shipped with its own managing software. A network device is similar to the plug-and-play devices because you only need to connect it to the network, power it, and start using it.

NAS devices are platform-independent because they can support a wide range of clients, including Windows, Unix, Linux, Macintosh, and OS/2. They use various network protocols, such as HTTP, FTP, and TCP/IP. NAS devices also use file-sharing protocols such as Network File System (NFS) and Common Internet File System (CIFS) to manage data requests. For example, NAS devices use NFS to communicate with Unix- and Linux-based clients, IPX with NetWare-based clients, CIFS with Windows-based clients, and TCP/IP, FTP, and HTTP for Internet-based transactions.

NOTE	A new protocol, *Network Data Management Protocol (NDMP)*, is also being deployed in NAS devices. NDMP is an open network protocol for backing up data over multi-OS networks.

Advantages and Disadvantages of NAS Devices

In addition to providing data access to clients and backing up data, NAS devices can also handle tasks such as proxy, firewall, tape backups, and audio/video streaming. The other advantages of implementing NAS solutions on a network are the following:

- **Improved server performance**—Because data is stored separately from the server, the strain of file processing is eliminated from the server. As a result, the server only needs to process requests from its clients. The actual I/O, which consumes about 60% of CPU capacity, is performed by the NAS devices. This increases server efficiency and considerably reduces the time it takes to respond to client requests.

- **Increased reliability and data availability**—NAS devices operate independently of servers. Therefore, even if a server is down, data is available to the clients through other servers. This makes a network highly reliable and immune to server crashes.

- **Easy scalability**—NAS devices can be attached to a network during normal working hours. This can be done in a matter of a few minutes without having to interrupt the normal functions of a network.

- **Easy manageability**—Anyone can administer a NAS device because it configures itself automatically after being connected to the network. In case of problems, NAS devices can be remotely administered either with the help of standard Web browsers or third-party management tools.

- **Support to heterogeneous networking environments**—A NAS device can operate seamlessly in a heterogeneous environment that consists of various platforms, such as Windows, Unix, Linux, OS/2, and so on. It supports a wide range of protocols, such as TCP/IP, HTTP, and IPX.

- **Transparent backups**—Data stored on the NAS devices can be backed up without affecting other servers.

- **Increased network productivity**—The implementation of NAS solutions increases the productivity and the efficiency of the entire network. Reliable access to the data at all times improves client productivity. Servers show a marked improvement in their performance as the CPU-intensive I/O activities are performed by the NAS devices. Implementation of the NAS devices also simplifies the job of network administrators by allowing them to add additional storage to the network on-the-fly without having to bring down the entire network. Also, administrators can save time and effort on installation and on troubleshooting storage-related problems.

- **Reduced TCO**—By bringing down administrative and productivity costs, NAS solutions result in a marked reduction of TCO. Businesses can also reduce expenditures on skilled IT staffs that would be required for less effective systems of storage.

Although NAS works well in small- to medium-sized networks, it can prove to be highly insufficient in the case of large networks. Following are some of the disadvantages of NAS:

- **Excessive network traffic**—A request from a client is targeted at the server, which then passes it on to the corresponding NAS device. The NAS device then returns the requested data to the server. The server consequently forwards the data to the client. This is a long procedure and both the client/server interactions and server/NAS device interactions use network bandwidth.

- **Slow transactions**—Although NAS devices function at high speeds, the response time to client requests can increase during peak working hours when the number of clients requesting information is high.

- **Increased vulnerability**—Because NAS devices are directly attached to the network and can be easily accessed, they are vulnerable to malicious attacks. As a result, there is a great chance that confidential business data can be compromised.

Although NAS devices improve the overall network's performance, reduce the total cost of implementation, provide scalable solutions, and simplify manageability, they lose out in terms of the excessive network traffic that they produce, which leads to slower transactions. SANs have emerged as an answer to all the problems posed by NAS. The following sections discuss why many industry experts are so enthusiastic about the emergence of SAN technology.

SANs

As noted previously, *SANs* are a storage solution technology developed to handle enormous amounts of data. Figure 1-20 shows a typical SAN setup. As shown in the figure, the storage devices are directly connected to neither the servers nor the network clients. All the storage devices are interconnected to each other to form a separate network, which can be accessed only through the servers. This is a considerably secure setup because the storage devices are well hidden from the clients.

Figure 1-20 *Typical SAN Setup*

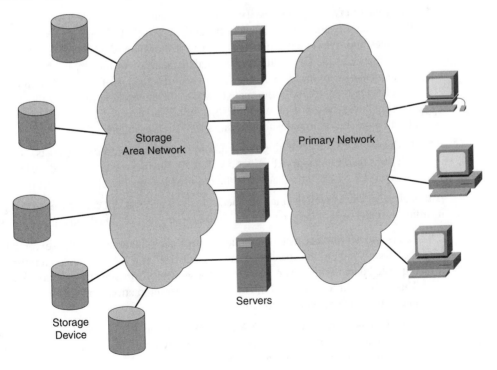

NAS Versus SANs

Many people tend to confuse NAS with SAN (probably because SAN is NAS spelled left to right). Although both technologies do share a few similarities, there are underlying differences, as highlighted in Table 1-1.

Table 1-1   *The Differences Between NAS and SAN*

NAS	SAN
Use the same cabling as the cabling on the network they are connected to.	Use high-speed connectivity such as a Fibre Channel, irrespective of the cabling used by the network they are connected to.
Use network protocols (TCP/IP, IPX/SPX, and so on) and file sharing protocols (CIFS, NFS, and so on) to communicate with the network.	Do not use any network protocols because data requests are not made over the LAN to which they are connected.
Are easy to install and maintain, resulting in lower TCO.	Need considerable expertise to install and manage. As a result, they are expensive.
The file system is located at the NAS device.	The file system is located at the network servers.
Can support heterogeneous clients seamlessly.	Special software is required to provide access to heterogeneous clients.
Are slow compared to SANs.	Are faster than NAS.

SAN Standard Organizations

Although fast emerging, the SAN technology is a relatively new technology. Most of the SAN solutions that are currently available in the market are standalone and cannot boast seamless compatibility. However, many vendors, industry associations, and standards organizations are working toward common industry standards to ensure interoperability between SAN devices, software, and solutions provided by various vendors. Some of these associations and standards bodies are actively involved in the development of a commonly accepted SAN technology. Standard organizations are SNIA, FCIA, ANSI, IETF, SCSITA, and InfiniBandTA.

The Storage Networking Industry Association (SNIA) is the primary organization for the development of SAN standards. As a forum of major SAN vendors (IBM, Brocade Systems, Jiro, Hewlett Packard, Fibre Alliance, and so on) and networking professionals, SNIA is responsible for developing and promoting efficient and compatible solutions in the market. In addition, SNIA is also committed to delivering widely accepted architectures, technical reference material, and industry-wide education on implementing the standards through various conferences. SNIA is also actively involved in developing NAS standards.

NOTE For more information on SNIA, refer to its Web site at www.snia.org.

In late 1999, two industry associations—Fibre Channel Community (FCC) and Fibre Channel Association (FCA)—merged to form FCIA (Fibre Channel Industry Association). As an international organization of Fibre Channel product vendors, industry professionals, system integrators, and consumers, this organization focuses on establishing a broad and successful market for the Fibre Channel infrastructure in the field of SAN. Similar to SNIA, FCIA is actively involved in developing a universal infrastructure for Fibre Channel, educating the industry (vendors and consumers) through conferences, and promoting interoperability among various Fibre Channel products.

NOTE For more information on FCIA, refer to its Web site at www.fibrechannel.com.

As an organization of various vendors of SCSI products, the SCSI Trade Association (SCSITA) focuses on the promotion of SCSI technology in the field of SANs. Similar to its sister organizations, SCSITA is actively involved in developing interoperable SCSI-related standards and educating the market about the advantages of implementing SCSI technology in SANs.

NOTE For more information on SCSITA, refer to its Web site at www.scsita.org.

The Internet Engineering Task Force (IETF) is one of the most important communities of the networking industry and is an active player in the evolution and implementation of formal standards related to SAN management.

NOTE For more information on IETF, refer to its Web site at www.ietf.org.

Rather than actively developing standards, the American National Standards Institute (ANSI) acts as a middleman between various organizations. The basic role of ANSI is to facilitate the development of SAN-related Fibre Channel standards by establishing consensus among organizations such as SNIA, FCIA, IETF, and so on that are actively involved in the development of SAN standards.

NOTE For more information on ANSI, refer to its Web site at www.ansi.org.

Founded by IBM, the InfiniBand Trade Association (InfiniBandTA) is currently working on the development of new I/O specifications to facilitate data transfers on switched Fabric technology.

NOTE For more information on InfiniBandTA, refer to its Web site at www.infinibandta.org or www.futureio.org.

Summary

In this chapter, you reviewed basic networking concepts, such as the seven-layer OSI reference model, commonly used network devices, common network topologies, and media access methods.

Due to the immense popularity of Web-based mail systems, e-commerce, and the common-place use of multimedia applications, the need for efficient storage, maintenance, and full-time availability of data has emphasized the inability of the current storage infrastructure to keep up with the demand. In addition, various storage devices, such as CD and DVD libraries, disk storage systems, disk arrays, and tape subsystems, are fairly expensive.

For a long time, NAS was being touted as the future solution because of its ability to adapt to future growth, reduced TCO, and easy manageability. However, a few disadvantages associated with the use of NAS technology inspired experts and industry organizations to look for better solutions. SANs have emerged as the latest storage solution technology in the market. The highlight of the SAN technology is that it can efficiently deal with enormous amounts of data, while ensuring security and reliability without hampering the overall network performance.

The industry and private networks are yet to realize the enormous potential of SANs. However, a few organizations are actively involved in developing SAN standards and benchmarking the performance of SAN products. Some of these organizations include SNIA, FCIA, ANSI, IETF, SCSITA, and InfiniBandTA.

In this chapter, you will learn about the following:

- Evolution and benefits of SANs
- SAN components and building blocks
- Data access over SANs

CHAPTER 2

Introduction to Storage Area Networks

Storage area networks are the future of enterprise storage, period. If your company is heading toward, or has already passed the terabyte mark in storage, it's a prime candidate for a SAN migration. If you are forecasting significant growth in storage requirements, you should develop your SAN strategy now.

—Excerpted from "Building a Storage Area Network," Dave Fetters
www.networkcomputing.com/1109/1109ws1.html

This is the age of e-commerce, online transactions, and overloaded databases. The amount of data that is transacted across a network on an hourly basis is staggering. The popularization of multimedia applications has contributed only more to the chaos. Even the most seasoned of network administrators are facing the brunt of this massive onslaught of data.

As you learned in the previous chapter, storage networks have emerged as the solution that most network administrators have been waiting for. In fact, storage networks offer much more than data management. In this chapter, you'll learn the basics of SAN, the technology behind it, its evolution, the history and advantages that have made it the best-of-the-breed solution, and the basic building blocks that make up a storage network.

Evolution and Benefits of SANs

In the pre-Internet era, storage management was not a big problem. Networks were small in size and businesses were just beginning to realize the potential that computer technologies and networks would have on their operations. The focus was on how to make data processing faster. Small Computer Systems Interface (SCSI) was born out of this need. As reliability and the popularity of computers and computer networks increased, the amount of data that had to be maintained on computers rose proportionately. At this time, storage was embedded in servers. However, a server's storage capacity was severely limited because it could handle only a finite number of storage disks. This limitation caused major bottlenecks when several users tried to access information simultaneously. This gave birth to separate storage devices such as Just a Bunch Of Disks (JBODs), disk arrays, and tape libraries. These storage devices could effectively store huge amounts of data. However, with the growth of server farms, administrators realized that the interactions with these

devices were extremely slow if too many users tried to access the same information from an individual server in the group.

NOTE   A *server farm* is a group of network servers that are located in physical proximity to each other and that provide services to network clients. Server farms serve to expedite the computing process by distributing the workload between individual servers in the group.

SCSI was already a proven technology and had made its mark as a high-speed interface to peripheral devices. Network engineers began to integrate the SCSI interface more and more into networking equipment to make the flagging data transactions faster. This proved to be an effective solution, and users were more than happy with it. However, the unprecedented growth of the Internet changed the entire equation.

As the number of transactions over the Internet increased phenomenally, business data that needed to be stored and managed grew in leaps and bounds. With the immense popularity of e-commerce, online trading, data warehousing, data mining, and multimedia technology, the storage infrastructure began to stumble and data management proved to be an administrator's worst nightmare. Although SCSI tried to keep up with the situation, the distributed nature of corporate networks posed another major problem. The devices connected to servers through the SCSI interface could not exceed a length of 25 meters, which severely limited the deployment of the devices and the network.

This limitation of SCSI gave rise to the concept of network-attached storage (NAS). Instead of being connected to the servers, these NAS devices were directly connected to the network. Storage-related problems were lessened for network administrators, and proved to be an effective solution until the following drawbacks were realized:

- Performance of NAS devices is severely limited by the available network bandwidth if the average data transfer rate is less than 100 Mbps.
- Network traffic increases considerably when NAS devices are used in a network. This is because NAS devices can be involved in bandwidth-intensive data transmissions, such as backups. Because they share the same transmission medium as the clients and other servers on the network, excessive network traffic is generated, which can bring down overall network productivity and performance.
- NAS devices are vulnerable to malicious attacks.
- NAS devices can be difficult to manage because they are separate entities and are not logically tied together.

For the preceding reasons, NAS also proved to be merely a stopgap solution. Both NAS and SCSI failed to manage large volumes of data being transacted on a daily basis, especially in large corporate networks. Meanwhile, work continued toward a better solution for

storage-management problems. Today, this solution is known as storage area networks (SANs). The entire concept of SANs was developed based on the following three factors:

- The solution had to be a stable, one that would work well despite the predicted increase in Web-based transactions and businesses.
- The solution had to help increase overall network productivity.
- The solution had to not only work with small- and medium-sized networks, but also with large corporate networks that span the entire globe.

You can visualize a SAN as a separate high-speed storage network within a local-area network (LAN). All the storage resources are interconnected to each other by using general network elements—routers, hubs, switches, and gateways—which help in eliminating distance-based restrictions posed by the SCSI interface. Figure 2-1 shows a typical SAN setup.

Figure 2-1   *The Storage Behind Network Servers*

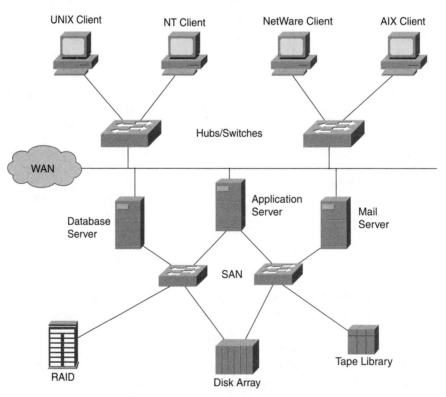

As seen in Figure 2-1, the SAN is the storage behind the network servers. All storage devices are interconnected to form a separate network behind the network servers, which is well hidden from general users. All servers can access all storage resources, when required. Clients

interact with servers over the LAN, whereas servers interact with storage devices over the SAN. Neither of these interactions (LAN and SAN) need to share network bandwidth, as was the case with earlier solutions such as NAS. This results in a marked increase in overall network productivity and satisfies one of the requirements for developing a workable solution.

One of the advantages of the SAN is its scalability. You can add new storage resources to the network dynamically. Moreover, because a storage device is not associated with any server, adding a new storage device does not lead to adding a corresponding server. This is a boon in disguise for most network administrators because they have to manage fewer devices. This results not only in fewer management headaches, but also brings down the total cost of the network.

Network performance also improves with SANs. Server/storage interactions do not use network bandwidth, which reduces network traffic considerably. This is because bandwidth-intensive bulk-data transfers, such as backups and database updates, occur within the SAN. As a result, traffic on the LAN, which is attached to the SAN, is not affected and users can continue with their normal work without having to feel the bandwidth pinch. Likewise, server performance is improved. Servers become free from data input/output (I/O) activities, which are highly CPU-intensive. As a result, servers can process client requests faster, which brings about a dramatic reduction in client response time.

Another advantage is improved data availability. In a SAN setup, multiple servers share access to the same data simultaneously. If a server becomes unavailable, other servers can take over, which results in improved data availability to the clients and high failovers. This helps in eliminating data-accessibility problems that arise due to a single point of failure (SPOF).

The Fibre Channel infrastructure, which forms the base of the SAN, guarantees fast data transfer rates (from 100 Mbps to 1.0625 Gbps). This data rate is faster than data exchange rates in LANs to which the SAN is connected. This is especially beneficial in the case of e-commerce where fast data transactions are important to online companies that are aiming to gain favor from users.

NOTE   Fibre Channel technology was developed by American Natural Standards Institute (ANSI) to support high data transfer rates (up to 1 Gbps). Fibre Channel offers flexible topologies, long-distance connectivity, and support to various existing media types (copper and fiber optic) and networking technologies, such as SCSI, IP, ATM AAL, and IEEE 802.2.

For detailed information on Fibre Channel technology, see Chapter 3, "Fibre Channel Basics," and Chapter 4, "Fibre Channel Products."

Because SANs are based on Fibre Channels and switched Fibre technology and can be accessed from anywhere in the network, there is a low probability of a SPOF. Also, being

separate from the primary network, SANs are less susceptible to data corruption. Both of these factors make them highly reliable.

In addition, Fibre Channel technology supports connectivity up to 10 kilometers. Because the underlying interface of the SAN is made up of Fibre Channels, the distance does not limit the physical placement of storage devices, as was the case with SCSI-based infrastructures, which when stretched to the maximum, can support no more than 30 meters of connectivity. Therefore, SAN storage can be allocated to an application even if the storage device is located on a remote site.

Managing storage as a central entity rather than on a per-device basis makes tasks related to storage management easier and less expensive. Resources aren't scattered across the network, but instead, they are consolidated on one network.

Transparent backups and restores are also advantageous with SANs. As any administrator knows, backups can be the cause of major network bottlenecks. Especially if they need to be done during normal working hours and if storage devices are distributed all over the network. In a SAN setup, the storage devices that need to be backed-up are separate from the primary LAN. This externalization of storage makes backup activities faster and transparent to the users who can continue their usual operations without feeling a bandwidth pinch. Similarly, data can be restored quickly and easily while the primary network is still operational.

SANs also allow cross-platform data sharing and can support a wide variety of platforms, including Windows, UNIX, Linux, Macintosh, OS/390, and so on. Besides multi-platform support, SANs also support multiple protocols, including Transmission Control Protocol/ Internet Protocol (TCP/IP) and Internetwork Packet Exchange (IPX). SANs also support storage protocols, such as Storage IP, Fibre Channel, and InfiniBand.

SANs are considered to be behind server storage as they are not visible to users. Therefore, storage resources can be accessed only through network servers in the SAN setup. Moreover, SANs support auditable security mechanisms to prevent unauthorized access to the data. If the servers are properly configured for secure access to storage resources, the probability of malicious, unauthorized access can be reduced substantially.

Finally, centralized management is far less expensive than the traditional model that consists of standalone servers and storage devices. Improved network performance, high data availability, and easy backups and restores also contribute to a reduced Total Cost of Ownership (TCO). Obviously, SANs meet the requirements of their development goals.

SAN Components and Building Blocks

A wealth of devices and components make up a SAN. These include the following:

- Servers
- Storage
- Interfaces

- Interconnects
- Fabric
- Software and applications

Of these components, SAN interfaces, SAN interconnects, and the SAN Fabric are considered to be the basic building blocks of a SAN because they directly influence the entire SAN architecture and performance. In one of his papers, Michael Peterson of Strategic Research Corporation described the relationship between these three components as a chained sequence of *"server-to-interface-to-interconnect-to-fabric-to-interconnect-to-interface-to-storage."* This concept is depicted in Figure 2-1.

Figure 2-2   *Correlation Between the SAN Fabric, Interconnects, and Interfaces*

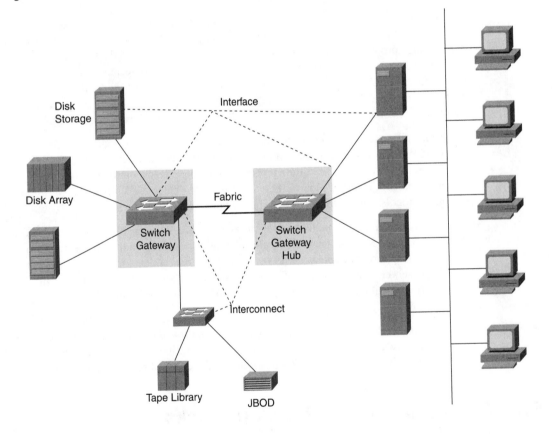

NOTE	Strategic Research Corporation is a market research organization in the field of storage networking.

Before even planning or building a SAN, an understanding of the various components or building blocks is important. You will now consider them in detail.

SAN Servers

Initially, SAN solutions supported a homogeneous server environment where the network consisted of servers with a common operating system. In a homogeneous environment, it is quite easy to connect these servers to the storage devices through the SAN and to share the data. However, a homogeneous environment is an unrealistic solution in the real world. This is because, over time, various corporate networks might have invested in a mix of servers according to their changing requirements.

The current SAN infrastructure can support heterogeneous server environments. The mix of various server platforms supported includes versions of UNIX, Linux, Windows NT, Windows 2000, versions of NetWare, OS/390, AIX, Solaris, and HP-UX. The problem in using heterogeneous server platforms is that the file systems of the major server platforms, such as IBM mainframes, Windows NT, and UNIX, are incompatible with each other and are, therefore, incapable of sharing data. However, data can be converted with the help of specialized data conversion applications. For example, IBM and HP use software that converts data from mainframe to open system and vice versa. Also, SANs enable server clustering, which makes administration and troubleshooting a comparatively easier and less expensive scenario.

SAN Storage

The storage infrastructure is where confidential and mission-critical data ultimately resides. Therefore, the storage infrastructure has to be fast, capable of storing large volumes (to prevent it from being scattered over various storage devices), easily accessible, manageable, and secure.

SAN storage is consolidated, externalized from the primary network, and can be distributed across the corporate network based on requirements. The various storage devices supported by the SAN are high-capacity and high-performance devices. These include the following:

- JBODs
- Disk storage systems
- Disk arrays
- Tape libraries
- Optical storage libraries

The following section discusses the next component of a storage network—the various SAN interfaces.

SAN Interfaces

In the SAN environment, the shared storage repository is connected to SAN servers through a SAN interface, thus allowing the storage to be externalized from the servers. The most common SAN interfaces are SCSI, High-Performance Parallel Interface (HIPPI), bus and tag, Fibre Channel Arbitrated Loop (FC-AL), Enterprise System Connection (ESCON), and Fibre Connection (FICON). This section describes each of these interfaces.

SCSI is a high-speed parallel interface that is used to connect high-speed SAN storage, such as JBODs, disk arrays, optical storage libraries, and tape libraries, to the SAN. Many vendors are currently using ANSI's SCSI-3 over the Fibre Channel infrastructure to achieve higher speeds, longer device distances, and a greater number of devices that can be connected through the interface.

NOTE   SCSI-3 is a serial version of the earlier interface, which was a parallel interface.

HIPPI is another ANSI standard interface that provides a point-to-point link for transferring data at speeds ranging between 100 Mbps and 200 Mbps over the Fibre Channel.

The bus and tag interface allows SAN servers with the popular Peripheral Component Interconnect (PCI) bus slots to connect directly to the mainframe channel at a data transfer speed of 4.5 MB.

NOTE   A channel is a point-to-point connection between two communicating entities.

The FC-AL is a high-speed (100 Mbps, 200 Mbps, 400 Mbps, and 800 Mbps) fault-tolerant Fibre Channel interface that can connect up to 126 SAN devices and is compatible with the SCSI interface.

The ESCON interface is used to connect IBM's proprietary switches, known as ESCON directors, to other SAN components in half-duplex mode at a comparatively low speed of 17 Mbps.

Finally, FICON is a high-speed (100 Mbps) interface that is used to connect FICON directors to other SAN components in full-duplex mode. FICON directors are IBM's proprietary next-generation Fibre Channel switches that provide additional management functions in addition to higher data transfer rates—100 Mbps—and full-duplex bidirectional communication.

<table>
<tr><td>**NOTE**</td><td>Compared to ESCON directors, FICON directors are about eight times faster. In addition, FICON directors can efficiently support physical connectivity up to 20 kilometers, compared to the mere three kilometers that is supported by ESCON directors.</td></tr>
</table>

SAN Interconnects

SAN interconnection devices, also known as SAN interconnects, are used to connect local and remote storage interfaces to various topologies. They also connect SAN interfaces to the SAN Fabric. The SAN Fabric is the interconnection of switches that is supported by hubs, gateways, and routers. Commonly used SAN interconnects are cables, connectors, adapters, extenders, hubs, bridges and multiplexors, routers, gateways, and switches. Each of these is described in the following sections.

Cables

As in a traditional networking environment, two types of cables are used in the SAN environment—copper and fiber-optic cables. Copper cabling is used for relatively short distances of 30 meters. Fiber-optic cables are used for longer distances that range from 2 to 10 kilometers. There are two types of fiber-optic cables:

- Multi-mode fiber (MMF) cables that are used in connections spanning up to 2 kilometers
- Single-mode fiber (SMF) cables that are used over longer distances spanning up to 70 kilometers

<table>
<tr><td>**NOTE**</td><td>For detailed information on Fibre Channel cabling, see Chapter 5, "Fibre Channel Cabling."</td></tr>
</table>

Connectors

Connectors are used in an environment where both copper and fiber-optic cabling is used. Connectors allow the interconnection of fiber-optic devices with copper devices. Gigabit Interface Converters (GBICs) are small interface modules that are used to connect copper or fiber-optic devices to hubs, switches, and adapters. Media Interface Adapters (MIAs) handle the conversion of copper-based connections into fiber-based connections and vice versa. MIAs can also convert a signal into the appropriate media type. MIAs are connected to most of the systems with the help of Fiber Channel transceiver units known as Gigabit Link Models (GLMs). For detailed information on Fibre Channel connectors, see Chapter 4.

Adapters

Adapters are also commonly referred to as network interface cards (NICs) and Host Bus Adapters (HBAs). Adapters provide a physical interface between the host bus and SAN interfaces. To facilitate proper communication, the adapters support various upper-level protocols (ULPs), such as SCSI, TCP/IP, FICON, and ESCON. Generally, most adapters are shipped with device drivers that control their behavior. Various adapters that are available in the market differ in terms of interoperability with other adapters, protocols supported, and the physical media interface. For detailed information on HBAs, see Chapter 4.

Extenders

Similar to repeaters in a normal network, extenders are used to extend the length of physical media, both copper-based and fiber-optic.

NOTE   Extenders are not as popular as Fibre Channel bridges, routers, and hubs because they do not provide any additional functionality apart from extending the Fibre Channel links. Most SAN designers and builders prefer Fibre Channel hubs that effectively extend the distance and provide additional management facilities.

Hubs

Similar to the hubs used in normal LANs, Fibre Channel hubs act as the central point of connection for various SAN devices. A typical Fibre Channel hub can support up to 126 nodes. Each port on a hub contains a Port Bypass Circuit (PBC), which opens or closes loops automatically to prevent a physical change or a device failure from affecting the functionality of other devices connected to the hub. A category of Fibre Channel hubs known as managed hubs also provides some of the management functionality offered by switches in a LAN environment. For detailed information on hubs, see Chapter 4.

Bridges and Multiplexors

Bridges facilitate communication between Fibre Channel interfaces (such as FICON and ESCON) and SCSI interfaces, which enables communication between the primary LAN and SAN. Bridges also provide connectivity between networks that operate on dissimilar protocols.

Multiplexors are specialized bridges that interleave signals from multiple devices and transmit them simultaneously through a single transmission medium. This helps in the effective utilization of the available network bandwidth.

Routers

Fibre Channel routers, which are also commonly known as storage routers, act much like routers that you use in normal networks. Similar to the normal routers, storage routers are responsible for transferring storage data between networks by using different transmission media and addressing schemes. However, the storage routers use the Fibre Channel Protocol (FCP) to route data instead of routed protocols such as TCP/IP.

Gateways

As in normal networks, a Fibre Channel gateway is used to interconnect dissimilar LANs and distant networks over a wide-area network (WAN). However, a gateway may or may not perform protocol conversion.

Switches

Fibre Channel switches provide the same functionality as network switches. They are used to interconnect a large number of devices. However, the connected nodes do not share bandwidth, as is the case with hubs. Instead of broadcasting a signal to all its ports, a switch allows on-demand connections because it transmits the signal only to that port to which the destination device is connected. As a result, switches help considerably in reducing network traffic. They also help in the effective utilization of network bandwidth and increase the aggregate throughput.

NOTE   Earlier switches were referred to as *directors*. There are two types of directors—ESCON directors and FICON directors. Refer to the section "SAN Interfaces" for more information on ESCON and FICON.

SAN Software

The SAN software component includes the following types of management applications:

- Applications to configure, maintain, and manage the SAN Fabric. For example, IBM's popular management software—Tivoli SANergy—allows simultaneous sharing of the same storage, file systems, and even the same files between multiple computers connected to a SAN. Another popular IBM management product is Tivoli Storage Network Manager, which discovers, displays, allocates, monitors, automates, and manages various components of the SAN Fabric and disk storage resources. BakBone's SmartClient allows network administrators to centrally control the attached media devices. Compaq also has a rich line of SAN management applications, including SANworks Enterprise Network Storage Manager and SANworks Storage Resource Manager.

- Applications to help exploit SANs to the fullest to achieve maximum benefits. These applications include backup and recovery packages, volume managers that enable host-based and remote mirroring, disk striping, data replication, and other network management software. For example, IBM's Tivoli Storage Manager is a comprehensive SAN management software suite that offers SAN-enabled integrated enterprise-wide network backup, archive, and disaster recovery capabilities. Another software suite is BakBone's NetVault Dynamically Shared Drives (DSDs), which is a powerful LAN-free backup software tool.

- File- or data-sharing software, extended file systems, and shared file systems. Generally, these applications use zoning and Logical Unit Number (LUN) masking techniques. Viacom's SV Zone Manager offers centralized and flexible access management to resources in the storage network. In addition, SV Zone Manager allows administrators and network managers to control user access to virtualized storage. Veritas SANPoint is another line of popular software products in this category.

NOTE   Some vendors, such as IBM, consider *services* as one of the basic SAN components. Services include education and support in implementing SAN solutions.

Data Access over SANs

In a network, it is possible that more than one client (local or remote) will request access to the same data simultaneously. The setup of the SAN environment is such that multiple servers belonging to different platforms can access a storage resource at the same time. Data can be accessed from a storage device in the following ways:

- Physical partitioning of the storage disk volumes
- Logical partitioning of the storage disk volumes
- File pooling
- Sharing data

Physical partitioning of storage disk volumes is the simplest method of accessing data from the storage repository. In this method, disk volumes are assigned to each server for their exclusive use. After a disk volume is assigned to a server, it becomes inaccessible to other servers. This method is commonly used in a heterogeneous server environment.

With the logical partitioning of disk volumes, logical disk volumes are defined within the storage repository and assigned to their respective servers. A logical disk can either span across several storage resources or can be located on a single storage device. However, the storage controller must be capable of managing the logical grouping of the volumes and ensuring that one server cannot access another server's logical volume.

NOTE   Generally, storage controllers are supported by the operating system to manage logical partitions. In addition, management packages also facilitate the management of logical groups of volumes.

In file pooling, instead of assigning disk space to a server, a mountable namespace is assigned to it. The size of this namespace can vary according to the size of the data file being accessed. After the server has accessed the files, the disk space is released so that it can be used by other servers that need to access data.

NOTE   The mountable namespace allows file systems to be added or removed from a partition set while the system is still running. Partitions can also be added to a partition set (or removed if the remaining partitions have enough space to contain all the data) while the system is running. The main advantage of mountable namespace is that it allows several mountable file systems to share the same pool of storage space, which enables the easy addition of more hard drives.

With the sharing data method, data can be accessed either in the form of data copy or the real-time sharing of data by multiple servers. Data sharing is accomplished in two ways, as noted in the following:

- **Sharing data copy**—According to this method, a copy of the requested data is assigned to the server. After the entire requested file is copied to the server, either the entire database (or file) is updated at the server-side at regular intervals or only the incremental updates are copied as and when any changes in the source copy occur. When the entire database or file is updated at regular intervals, the method is known as sharing the complete copy. The latter method is known as sharing the incremental copy. Complete copy sharing is frequently used by the backup and restoration applications, and the incremental copy is shared by data warehousing and data mining applications.

- **True data sharing**—According to this method, the same copy of the data is accessed by more than one server simultaneously. This method is considered to be the best because it generates less network traffic and allows the actual consolidation of storage. The servers can access the data in three ways. One-at-a-time access allows the requesting entities to read and update data in a sequential manner. The multiple read access method allows the requesting servers to read the data simultaneously. However, only one server at a time can update the data on the storage device. The multiple read/write access method allows multiple servers to read and update the data simultaneously. This method is practically obsolete because the simultaneous updating of data can cause severe conflicts related to data integrity.

NOTE	The true data sharing method allows more than one simultaneous read and write operation. As a result, there is a possibility of more than one operation overwriting the same data. Therefore, serialization mechanisms are employed with this data access method. These serialization mechanisms prevent the simultaneous writing of the same data and at the same time ensure that the data is written to the physical or logical disk volume in an orderly manner.

Summary

In this chapter, you learned about the evolution of SAN technology. SANs evolved out of the need for fast and secure data access. Until the Internet became a household name, SCSI technology worked fine because data transfers were not bandwidth-intensive. However, the advent of the Internet heralded the era of storage-intensive applications. Managing huge amounts of data became the bane of network administrators. When NAS technology entered the market it stabilized the data-management scenario for some time, but it failed to provide a long-lasting solution. Thus emerged the SAN technology of today. The technology is young, but it is gaining fast industry-wide acceptance. SANs are slowly becoming the darling of network administrators and managers because they are effectively helping them to combat the ever-threatening problems related to storage management.

You had a glimpse of the basic blocks that are used to build a SAN. These include the following:

- Servers
- Storage devices
- Interfaces

- Interconnects
- Fabric
- Software and applications

You'll learn more about these components in subsequent chapters, especially in Chapter 4. Finally, you learned about the various methods that are employed in a SAN to access data. These data-access methods include the following:

- Physical partitioning of the storage disk volumes
- Logical partitioning of the storage disk volumes
- File pooling
- Sharing data

In this chapter, you will learn about the following topics:

- Overview of Fibre Channel technology
- Fibre Channel ports
- Fibre Channel topologies
- Fibre Channel layers
- Classes of service

CHAPTER 3

Fibre Channel Basics

The last decade has witnessed enormous advancement in the performance of computers, which has led to the popularization of bandwidth- and storage-intensive applications. The existing framework has been slow to keep up with the increasing demands related to performance and storage, which has resulted in the framework bogging down with restrictions in the areas of speed, distance, and device connectivity. For example, Small Computer System Interface (SCSI)—one of the popular infrastructures—is limited to 80 Mbps of speed, up to 25 meters of bus length, and a maximum of 32 devices per bus. These restrictions are major bottlenecks for online trading and transactions.

Over the years, Fibre Channel has emerged as an ideal solution for storing, retrieving, and transferring data between servers, storage devices, other network devices, and ultimately users. Despite the high-speed, high-performance, and reliable solution that Fibre Channel offers, it remains relatively inexpensive. Because of these advantages, Fibre Channel has been adopted as the native technology in storage area networks (SANs).

Overview of Fibre Channel Technology

Fibre Channel is an integrated set of technology standards that was developed by the American National Standards Institute (ANSI) to overcome the limitations posed by the SCSI infrastructure. The main aim behind the Fibre Channel technology was the following:

- Facilitate high-speed data transfers between servers, storage devices, and other network devices

- Provide a high-performance, yet inexpensive solution, which does not lead to skyrocketing implementation costs

- Provide a highly mature infrastructure that responds well to future growths and advancement

- Provide a generic solution that supports the heterogeneous environments seamlessly

- Reuse existing protocols and infrastructures

In a networking environment, processors can communicate with other processors and peripheral devices by using two technologies—network and channel. Fibre Channel was designed to combine the benefits of these two technologies. A *channel* is a direct or switched point-to-point communication between two devices. As a result, channel communication is hardware-intensive, fast, and produces low overhead. On the other hand, the *network* is a multi-point communication, which is highly dependent on software implementations called *protocols*. Because of multi-point connections, which are used predominantly in a network, and high dependency on protocols, network communication is slower than channel communication. Network communication also produces high overheard. However, networks can support extensive communication between various devices, as compared to channels that operate with a limited number of devices.

As a channel technology, Fibre Channel uses Fabric—a high-performance switched interconnection scheme—to connect network devices. Fabric provides a point-to-point connection between two communicating devices. The point-to-point connection helps the communicating devices to exploit the full bandwidth of the Fibre Channel connection until the transaction is over.

NOTE   Despite the implementation of acknowledgments and flow control, communication overhead is kept to a minimum by the use of *time-division multiplexing (TDM)*. TDM is a multiplexing technique that allows multiple signals from different users to be combined over a single transmission medium—link or channel—which significantly reduces communication overhead and delays.

Fibre Channel offers the benefits of networking technology by allowing any device to communicate with any other host on the network. At the same time, it avoids the pitfalls of networking technology. To enable high-speed communication, data is directly transferred from the buffer of the source device to the buffer of the destination device without the interference of supported protocols. The role of protocols in Fibre Channel technology is to process data before and after the data has been transferred to the buffers. This reduces the overhead that is generated when protocols are actively involved in data transfers.

Fibre Channel supports point-to-point, network, and peripheral interfaces through the same port, and it also allows the simultaneous transmission of data related to different protocols over a single link. In addition, Fibre Channel provides strong flow and error control mechanisms.

Advantages of the Fibre Channel Technology

Until recently, SCSI has been the most popular interface used for storage systems. It has proved to be a long-standing, relatively simple, robust, and cost-effective solution.

However, Fibre Channel technology still has a definite edge over SCSI technology. Table 3-1 explains the advantages of Fibre Channel over SCSI.

Table 3-1   *Advantages of Fibre Channel over SCSI*

SCSI	Fibre Channel
The maximum data transfer rate supported by SCSI is 80 Mbps.	The data transfer rates offered by Fibre Channel are 133 Mbps, 266 Mbps, 530 Mbps, 1 Gbps, and 2 Gbps. Data rates of 4 Gbps will soon be available.
The maximum number of devices that SCSI can support simultaneously is 32. However, SCSI can support only 15 storage devices at a time.	The maximum number of storage devices that can be connected to the Fibre Channel interface ranges from 126 to 2^{24} (approximately 16 million).
The maximum length of a SCSI bus permitted between storage devices and servers is 25 meters.	The maximum distance permitted between a server and a storage device in case of copper cabling is 30 meters, and ranges from 500 meters to 10 kms in the case of optical fiber links. However Cisco devices, such as Catalyst 5000 switching modules can support Fibre Channel connectivity up to 70 kms (43.5 miles), thus overcoming the current distance constraints of 10 kms.
Fault tolerance for SCSI cables and connections is low, which leads to high downtime and reduced data availability.	Fault tolerance is high because Fibre Channel (with switches) provides more connection points and no termination of transmission media (links). More connection points ensure less chance for a single connection to bring down the SAN. Therefore, network downtime is low, which in turn leads to high data availability.
Administrative costs are high because of high downtime and reduced data availability.	Administrative costs are low because of reduced network downtime, high fault tolerance, and increased data availability. Lowered administrative costs result in a significant reduction in total cost of ownership (TCO) of a network.

In addition to all the advantages mentioned in Table 3-1, Fibre Channel technology also offers high scalability and the potential of future growth. For example, it can support the existing file and network protocols and the new protocols specially designed for SANs. Fibre Channel is also gearing up to support laser technology.

Fibre Channel Ports

Located on a network device (or node), a *port* is a point of connection between a network device and the Fibre Channel cabling (link). The communication between two entities over

Fibre Channel occurs through their respective ports. Fibre Channel supports five types of ports, which are categorized on the basis of their use. The various Fibre Channel ports are the following:

- **Node ports (N_Port)**—These ports are a part of Fibre Channel nodes and are used to connect Fibre Channel nodes to the Fabric (an interconnection of Fibre Channel switches). These ports can be attached only to other N_Ports and Fabric ports (F_Ports).

- **Loop ports (L_Port)**—Loop ports are basic ports used in the Fibre Channel-Arbitration Loop (FC-AL) topology and are a part of FC-AL nodes. These ports can be of two types—NL_Ports or FL_Ports. NL_Ports are a part of the Fibre Channel nodes and are used to connect a node to the FC-AL topology. These ports can be attached only to other NL_Ports and FL_Ports. FL_Ports are a part of the Fibre Channel switched Fabric and are used to connect the FC-AL loop to the Fibre Channel Fabric. Similar to F_Ports, these ports also act as the middlemen between the communicating ports. They can be attached only to other NL_Ports.

> **NOTE**   For more information on FC-AL, refer to the next section "Fibre Channel Topologies." The FC-AL topology is discussed in further detail in Chapter 6, "SAN Topologies."

- **Fabric ports (F_Port)**—These basic ports are a part of the Fibre Channel switched Fabric. These can act as neither the source nor destination ports during communication. They simply act as middlemen by facilitating communication between two entities. These ports can be attached only to other N_Ports.

- **Expansion ports (E_Port)**—These ports are a part of the Fibre Channel switched Fabric and are used to connect Fibre Channel switches to other Fibre Channel switches and routers. Similar to NL_Ports and FL_Ports, expansion ports also act as middlemen and facilitate communication between switches or routers involved in communication. They can be attached only to other E_Ports.

> **NOTE**   Some vendors also define another category of Fibre Channel ports—the Group ports (G_Ports). A G_Port can act as an E_Port and an F_Port. G_Ports with looping capabilities are known as GL_Ports.

Figure 3-1 depicts the various Fibre Channel ports and their connections.

In Figure 3-1, Server 1, Server 2, and the disk array are connected to Switch 1 through N_Ports because they are normal Fibre Channel nodes that are not a part of any Fibre

Channel loop. Server 3, Just a Bunch of Disks (JBOD), and the workstation shown in Figure 3-1 belong to a FC-AL topology. Therefore, they are connected to the Fabric Hub through NL_Ports. The loop Hub in turn is attached to Switch 1 through an FL_Port.

Figure 3-1   *Fibre Channel Ports and Their Connections*

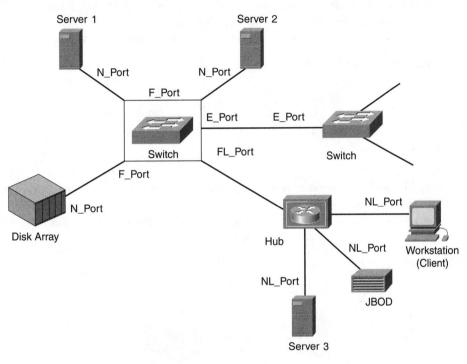

Fibre Channel Topologies

As discussed earlier, Fibre Channel is strongly based on network and channel technologies. Network technology is highly dependent on topology (that is, the physical layout of network devices). However, major network topologies, such as Ethernet, Token Ring, and FDDI are incompatible with each other because of the differences in their media access methods, frame length, clock speed, and so on. In contrast, the three topologies offered by Fibre Channel are highly flexible and compatible with each other. These topologies include *point-to-point*, *FC-AL*, and *switched Fabric*. Each of these is discussed in the following sections.

NOTE   Point-to-point, FC-AL, and switched Fabric are also discussed in Chapter 6. The purpose of discussing them here is to provide an overview.

Point-to-Point Topology

In the point-to-point topology, two Fibre Channel nodes are directly connected to each other through N_Ports. The *transmit* fiber of one port must be connected to the *receive* fiber of the other port. Similarly, the receive fiber of the first port must be connected to the transmit fiber of the other port. Because the connection between two nodes is direct, there is no media sharing. This allows the two connected nodes to use the complete bandwidth of the link. Figure 3-2 shows the typical point-to-point topology setup.

Figure 3-2 *The Point-to-Point Topology Setup*

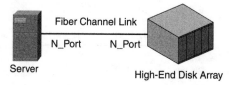

In this topology, a network node can also be connected to more than one node at the same time, yet maintain a point-to-point connection with the two. As evident in Figure 3-3, each device is connected to node A in a point-to-point connection. However, this is possible only if the node has more than one N_Port.

Figure 3-3 *Point-to-Point Connection with More Than One Node*

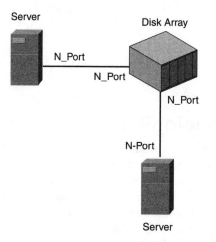

Point-to-Point topology is the fastest, simplest, and easiest to implement. It is also easy to administer. The possible implementations of this topology include the following:

- Connection of a server to a high-performance device, such as a disk array, tape library, or optical library.
- Connection of two high-performance devices, such as disk array to disk array, disk array to tape library, tape library to optical library, and so on.

Having looked at the point-to-point Fibre Channel topology, now consider the FC-AL topology.

FC-AL Topology

In the FC-AL topology, up to 126 nodes can be connected to form a complete loop. Figure 3-4 depicts the setup of nodes in an FC-AL topology.

NOTE   Although the arbitrated loop topology can support up to 126 nodes at a time, it is not recommended. This is because the link that forms the loop is a 100 MB shared link. The larger the number of nodes attached to the loop, the lower the performance of the loop.

Figure 3-4   *The FC-AL Topology Setup*

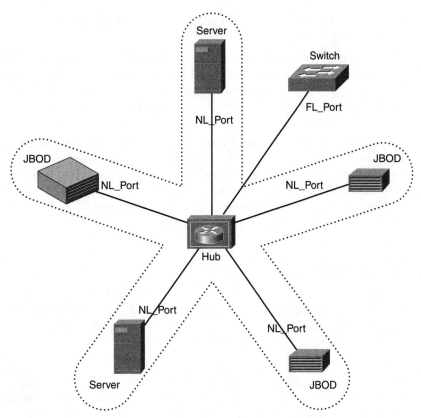

To transfer data, all nodes that are a part of the loop must arbitrate to gain control of the loop. After a node gains control of the loop, it establishes a virtual point-to-point connection with the intended recipient and starts transferring data. During the transmission, the entire bandwidth is available to the two communicating ports. When the transmission is complete, the connection is terminated and the rest of the loop nodes can arbitrate for control of the loop.

The FC-AL topology offers several advantages that make it a preferred topology. These advantages are as follows:

- FC-AL is a cost-effective solution that allows up to 126 nodes to be connected to a single link.

- The virtual point-to-point connection enables high-speed transmissions and full use of the available bandwidth.

- It is a scalable topology that allows the interconnection of many loops through switches.

- Addition or deletion of nodes from the loop by the implementation of hubs and bypass ports is dynamic.

- It is capable of discovering all information about the attached nodes without the interference of an administrator. Also, loop ports (NL_ports) have an embedded logic that allows a port to be excluded from the loop without disturbing normal loop operations. This capability of self-discovery and self-exclusion reduces administrative overhead.

FC-AL topology is generally implemented when high bandwidth is required for data transmissions. Therefore, it is most commonly used for the interconnection of storage devices. However, a serious disadvantage of this topology is that the larger the number of nodes attached to a loop, the lower the performance of the loop. The maximum number of nodes that the FC-AL topology can support is 126. However, as noted earlier, a Fibre Channel loop with 126 nodes is not recommended.

Switched Fabric Topology

In this topology, Fabric—a set of one or more interconnected switches—is used to interconnect nodes to form a virtual mesh. As a result, each node can access all the other nodes that are connected to the Fabric. This topology can support up to 2^{24} nodes. Figure 3-5 shows the switched Fabric topology setup.

The configuration of the Fabric can be either *cascaded* or *non-cascaded*. In the case of switched, non-cascaded Fabric, the switches are not interconnected. However, every node is connected to the switches. Although the performance of the Fabric is degraded when a switch fails, the nodes can still access each other. Figure 3-6 depicts the switched, non-cascaded Fabric configuration.

In the switched, cascaded Fabric configuration, all the switches are interconnected with each other to form a mesh. The configuration resembles a large logical switch. By being connected to one switch, a node can access any other node that is connected to one of the switches that belongs to the Fabric. Figure 3-7 depicts the switched, cascaded Fabric configuration.

Figure 3-5   *Switched Fabric Topology Setup*

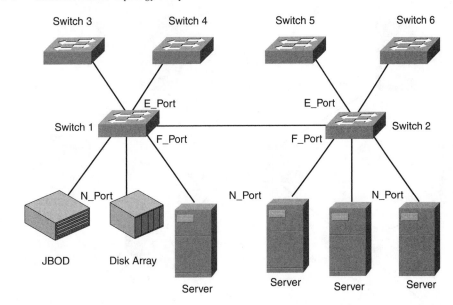

Figure 3-6   *Switched Non-Cascaded Fabric*

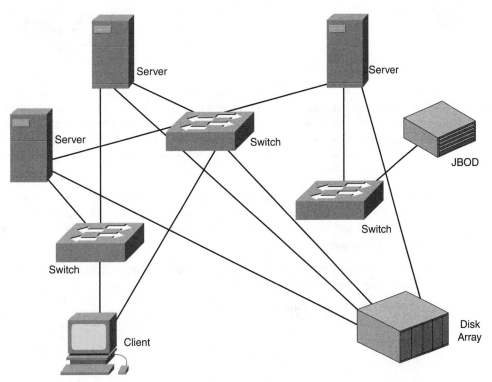

Figure 3-7   *Switched Cascaded Fabric*

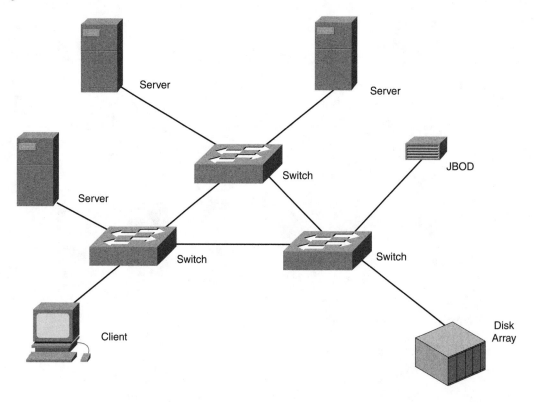

NOTE	When multiple switches are interconnected to form a Fabric, the information related to the configuration of each switch must be copied to all the other switches of the Fabric so that the rest of the switches are aware of the status of the given switch in the Fabric.

The biggest advantage of the switched Fabric topology is that it allows for several communications to occur simultaneously. However, the media is not shared with other local-area network (LAN)-side network traffic. The other advantages of this topology include the following:

- Availability of high bandwidth for each communication because media is not shared with other LAN-side network traffic

- Support to a large number of nodes (2^{24})

- Increased fault tolerance due to the implementation of virtual mesh, which prevents other nodes and communications from being affected when a node or link fails

- Improved scalability because devices (nodes) can be hot-swapped without affecting other nodes, ports, or ongoing communications

Now that you have looked at the three Fibre Channel topologies, consider the five layers that constitute the Fibre Channel standard.

Fibre Channel Layers

Understanding the workings of a protocol is easier when it's broken down into layers. The International Standards Organization's (ISO's) seven-layer Open System Interconnect (OSI) model is one such example. Similarly, the Fibre Channel standard has been structured as a stack of five layers. These layers define the physical media, transmission rates, flow control, encoding-decoding method, framing scheme, common services, and upper-layer applications. However, similar to the other reference models, such as the Transmission Control Protocol/Internet Protocol (TCP/IP) model, Fibre Channel layers do not directly map to the OSI layers.

As shown in Figure 3-8, the five Fibre Channel layers—*FC-0*, *FC-1*, *FC-2*, *FC-3*, and *FC-4*—are generally organized into two functional levels. These two functional levels are the *Physical and signaling level* and the *Upper level*.

Figure 3-8   *Fibre Channel Layers and Functional Levels*

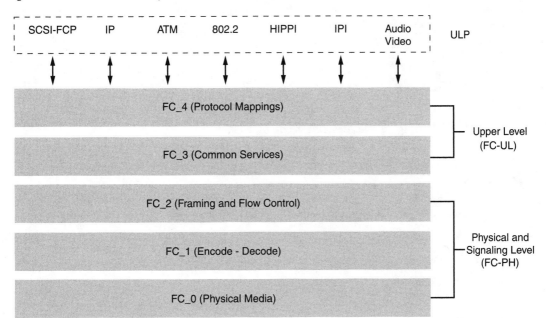

The Physical and signaling level (FC-PH) is part of the functional level. It is also referred to as the *Port level*. It includes the three lowest layers from FC–0 through FC–2. FC-PH is implemented at the port level and plays a major role in facilitating communication between two network nodes. The layers of the FC-PH are discussed in the next section of this chapter.

The Upper level (FC-UL) functional level is also referred to as the *Node level* because it is implemented at a node. However, it does not control the functioning of the node ports that are controlled by the FC-PH level. FC-UL includes layers FC-3 and FC-4, which play an important role in providing services and mapping upper-level protocols and applications. These layers are also discussed in more detail in the following sections.

NOTE   Applications, device drivers, and operating systems are considered a part of a third level known as *Upper Level Protocols (ULPs)* by some Fibre Channel vendors, such as Hewlett-Packard. This level is placed above FC-4 and facilitates communication among high-end software, applications, and the FC-4 layer.

Figure 3-9 shows the physical implementation of the five Fibre Channel layers.

Figure 3-9   *Physical Implementation of Fibre Channel Layers*

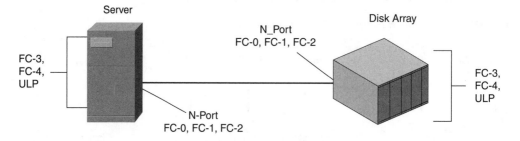

The following sections describe each of the layers.

FC-0 Layer

Also known as the physical layer, FC-0 is the lowest layer and is responsible for the physical aspects of communication, such as the following:

- Cabling (or links), which can be copper-based or optical fiber
- Optical and electrical parameters that control the data rates
- Connectors

This layer was designed to accommodate the maximum number of physical requirements, such as connectors, electrical parameters, and data rates, that are posed by various protocols over a wide range of transmission media. This layer also offers high flexibility in the use of physical media. For example, copper cabling can be used for short-distance communications, and optical fiber cabling can be used for signals that traverse longer distances. This flexibility allows network designers and administrators to go for specialized configurations according to the requirements of the company, which makes the network cost-effective.

Open Fibre Control

Although copper links are also used, Fibre Channel technology predominantly uses optical fiber links because they are fast, extend to a few kilometers, and the signals are not attenuated despite long distances. However, optical fiber links use laser technology to transmit data. When a disconnect or break occurs in the optical cable, leakage of lasers can pose a serious health hazard. This holds true especially in the case of optical fibers that use high-intensity lasers.

The FC-0 layer implements Open Fibre Control (OFC) as a safety measure to prevent humans from being exposed to high-intensity laser radiation. According to this system, when the open fiber situation occurs in a break in the link, the receiver fiber of the recipient port detects the break with the help of a built-in logic. On detecting a break, the receiver fiber starts pulsing its lasers within a range that meets the safety requirements. The receiver fiber of the port on the other end of communication, on receiving low-cycle pulses, forces its transmitter fiber to reduce the pulse-cycle within a range that meets safety norms. As a result, despite the break in the link, the health hazard is reduced to a minimum. After the link has been repaired, both ends can resume normal transmission after a double handshaking procedure.

FC-1 Layer

Also known as the *transmission protocol layer*, the FC-1 layer is responsible for defining the following:

- Character conversion and coding rules
- Error detection
- Byte synchronization and word alignment
- Link maintenance

Each of these is discussed in the following sections.

Character Conversion and Coding Rules

Fibre Channel uses the *8B/10B encoding method* to encode/decode information. This encoding method, which was developed by IBM, is considered one of the best methods to not only encode information, but also to effectively control the errors that occur during transmissions. In fact, the system Bit Error Rate (BER) offered by this method is less than 10^{12}. This implies that for every 10^{12} bits being transmitted, only one bit might be erroneous.

As per the 8B/10B-coding rule, each byte (8 bits) is encoded into 10-bit *transmission characters*. The unencoded byte is represented by eight bits—A, B, C, D, E, F, G, and H, and one control variable, which is referred to as Z. After the FC-1 layer encodes these bits by using the 8B/10B method, these bits are converted into a, b, c, d, e, f, g, h, i, and j, which constitute the 10-bit transmission character. The format of the newly formed transmission character is Zxx.y. The following breaks down the format:

- Z is the control variable of the unencoded information. Z can have one of two valid values—D and K. D represents Data-type (or D-type) and indicates that the following information consists of data characters. K represents K-type and indicates that the following information consists of special characters, which are used to control the transaction.

NOTE   The 8B/10B encoding method uses 12 special characters (K-types). However, only one special character known as *K28.5* is used currently. This is because it has a positive disparity when depicted as 0011111010 and a negative disparity as 1100000101. In both cases, two bits of the same type (1 or 0) are followed by five bits of the opposite type. As a result, the K28.5 command character can be easily distinguished from data characters.

- xx represents the decimal value of the binary number obtained from the lower five bits—E, D, C, B, and A—of the unencoded information.
- "." represents ASCII ".".
- y represents the decimal value of the binary number obtained from the upper (left-most) three bits—F, G, H—of the unencoded information.

For example, consider the steps for encoding hexadecimal 85 as it would be sent as data through the Fibre Channel:

1 First, the binary representation of 85 is 1000 0101.

2 Next, because A, B, C, D, and E form xx, the value of xx here is 00101. Similarly, the value of y is 100.

3 According to the 8B/10B encoding method, the encoded information must resemble the EDCBA HGF (xx.y) format. Therefore, the number is converted to 00101 100.

4 The complete binary value of xx is 00000101, which when converted into decimal representation ($0+0+0+0+0+2^2+0+1$) is equal to 5. Similarly, the decimal value of y is 4.

5 Therefore, the unencoded hexadecimal 85 is equal to D5.4 in the 8B/10B encoding method.

Figure 3-10 shows the entire process of conversion.

Figure 3-10 *Converting Hexadecimal 85 into 8B/10B Code*

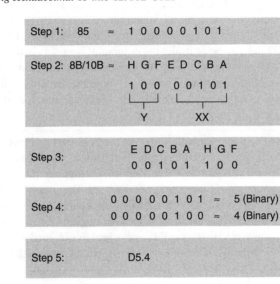

When a 10-bit transmission character is received, the value of Z is examined first. Transmission words starting with D (Dxx.y) are decoded into one of the 256 8-bit combinations. On the other hand, transmission characters starting with K (Kxx.y) are used for tasks related to protocol management. If the data stream starts neither with D nor K, it is considered a code violation error and is reported by the FC-1 layer. The upper layers take appropriate action.

A set of four transmission characters makes a *transmission word*. The total length of a transmission word is 40 bits. Depending on the transmission characters contained, a transmission word can be of two types—*data* and *ordered set*:

- **Data**—All the four transmission characters contained by the data transmission word are 8B/10B encoded D-types that contain data.

- **Ordered set**—The first transmission character is a K-type that contains special characters. The rest of the three transmission characters of the transmission word are D-types.

You will now learn how the Fibre Channel standard detects errors that occur during transmissions.

Error Detection

Fibre Channel detects errors by using the following three checks:

- **Code violation**—When the recipient port receives a transmission character that is neither D-type nor K-type, it is considered a code violation error and is reported to the upper layers.

- **Disparity violation**—Every 8B/10B-transmission character is associated with a *Running Disparity* (*RD*) parameter, which can be either positive, negative, or neutral. If the transmission character has more binary 1s than 0s, the RD is negative (RD-). If the number of binary 0s is greater than the number of 1s, the RD is considered positive (RD+). RD can also be neutral if the number of binary 1s in the transmission character is equal to the number of binary 0s. During communication, if the RDs at both ends do not match, the sender node is notified about the disparity violation error. The upper layer protocols at both ends take the appropriate action to deal with the situation.

NOTE   The disparity violation error method used by Fibre Channel is more effective than the parity check method. This is because parity checks can detect only an odd number of bit errors. An even number of bit errors is not detected. The idea behind the concept is that if the 8B/10B-transmission contains all 1s, the RD is neutral (four positive 1s and four negative 1s). If two of the 1s are converted to 0s, a valid parity check is obtained. However, the RD is either positive or negative, depending on which bits are flipped.

- **Cyclic Redundancy Check (CRC)**—Fibre Channel also uses CRC algorithms to verify the correct reception of data during a transmission. The CRC concept used in Fibre Channel technology is similar to the CRC concept used in network technology.

Next, you will learn how the FC-1 layer provides for byte synchronization and data alignment.

Byte Synchronization and Data Alignment

For successful data transfer, serial transmissions are highly dependent on the accuracy of clock information. The FC-1 layer integrates clock information into data streams to synchronize the sender and receiver ports at all times. It also ensures clock recovery if byte synchronization is lost.

The FC-1 layer ensures data alignment by using the K28.5 special character. After the receiver-end detects this character in the data stream, it can distinguish the following data characters by counting 10 bits each.

The ordered set transmission words, also known as *frame delimiters*, help align the data correctly. Because the control information is embedded in the data stream in the form of Start of Frame (SOF) and End of Frame (EOF), it helps the recipient node in determining the word boundaries.

Link Maintenance

The receiver and the sender nodes might have different electrical requirements. If so, the exchange of data is not possible. The FC-1 layer ensures that the transmission characters are DC-balanced so that data can be exchanged successfully.

NOTE   DC stands for Direct Current. DC electricity is the unidirectional flow of electrons from the negative (-) terminal to the positive (+) terminal of a photovoltaic cell, battery, or generator through a conducting material such as a metal wire. The electricity goes in a complete circuit from the source and back again. This combination of the source of power and wires, light bulbs, and motors is referred to as an *electrical circuit*. Virtually all electronic devices including computers function on DC.

Ordered sets, which are transmission words starting with special characters, play an important role in link maintenance. When the Fibre Channel link remains inactive during a transmission (that is, nothing is sent over the link for a specified time period), the connection is terminated automatically. Transmission words called *primitive idles* prevent the transmission from being terminated prematurely by filling in the pauses during transmission.

Also, ordered sets called *primitive sequences* are responsible for notifying the receiver about a link failure. This helps the upper layers to start the appropriate actions, such as link-failure notifications to the end-user or retransmission requests.

FC-2 Layer

Also known as the *framing and signaling protocol layer*, the FC-2 layer is responsible for the following functions:

* Segmentation and re-assembly of data into frames
* Determination of the framing rules
* Control of the sequence in which data is transferred
* Exchange management

- Flow control
- Provision of various service classes to ensure efficient transmissions

This layer is self-configuring and supports all three Fibre Channel topologies. On the basis of physical topology, this layer is responsible for the successful and reliable transmission of data over Fibre Channel without collision or data loss. It specifies the data transport mechanism, which is independent of the upper layers.

The FC-2 layer transfers are controlled by protocols. This Fibre Channel layer uses its own set of protocols to manage data transfers. These protocols include the following:

- **Primitive sequence protocol**—This protocol starts the transfer of primitive sequences in case of a link failure.

NOTE   For more information on primitive sequences, refer to the next section "Ordered Sets."

- **N_Port Login protocol**—This protocol helps the N_Ports of the communicating ends in establishing the identity of each and agreeing upon mutually supported service parameters, such as Constant Bit Rate (CBR), traffic, and Quality of Service (QoS).
- **Fabric Login protocol**—This protocol helps the Fabric identify an N_Port, collect information about it, and negotiate mutually supported service parameters when an N_Port logs on to the Fabric to communicate with another port.
- **Data transfer protocol**—This protocol, along with the FC-1 layer, helps both communicating ends to establish a mutually supported data transfer method and flow control.
- **N_Port Logout protocol**—This protocol terminates a connection and frees the resources between the two ports that were involved in communication.

The FC-2 layer can transport data in any of the following forms:

- Ordered set
- Frame
- Sequence
- Exchange

Each of these forms is discussed in the following sections.

Ordered Sets

Ordered sets are transmission words that always begin with a special character. In an ordered set, the first transmission character is always K28.5 (because this is the only special character being used currently). The rest of the three transmission characters contain encoded data. In addition to allowing control functions to be embedded in data streams, ordered sets also help the recipient nodes in determining and aligning word boundaries. Thus, ordered sets play a major role in word alignment and byte synchronization.

FC-2 defines three types of ordered sets as follows:

- **Frame delimiter**—A frame delimiter immediately precedes or follows the contents of a frame. There are two types of frame delimiters— SOF and EOF. The SOF frame delimiter always precedes the frame, and the EOF always follows the frame.

- **Primitive signal**—A primitive signal precedes the SOF frame delimiter and has special meaning. There are two types of primitive signals:

  - **Receiver Ready (R_RDY)**—This signal indicates that the receiver buffer at the recipient's end is ready to receive frames.

  - **Idle**—This signal indicates that a port is operational but idle. The idle signals (or idle primitives, as they are popularly known) consist of a set of transmission words that are sent by the sender node to fill in the pauses between transmissions. This primitive signal prevents the loop from being terminated prematurely.

- **Primitive sequence**—A primitive sequence consists of three identical ordered sets that are transmitted repetitively to notify a link failure. On receiving a primitive sequence, the receiver port either sends a primitive sequence in response or starts transmitting idle primitives. Depending on the error that led to the link failure, there are four types of primitive signals:

  - **Offline State (OLS)**—The primitive indicates that the port transmitting a sequence is either initializing the link, receiving a Not Operational State (NOS) primitive, or entering the offline state.

  - **Not Operational State (NOS)**—The primitive indicates that the port transmitting a sequence has either detected a link failure or is offline and waiting for the OLS primitive from the other end.

  - **Link Reset (LR)**—The primitive sequence transmitted by a port indicates an attempt to start the Link Reset protocol or to recover from a link timeout.

  - **Link Reset Response (LRR)**—The primitive indicates the response of a port to the Link Reset primitive.

Frames

At the sender-end, the FC-2 layer is responsible for breaking down information into frames of a stipulated size that can be successfully transmitted over Fibre Channel links. Frames are basic units of transmission over Fibre Channel. The Fabric, however, is responsible for routing the received frames to the intended destination port. At the receiver-end, again, the FC-2 layer is responsible for re-assembling frames into the original information transmitted by the sender.

Depending on the data being carried, frames are categorized as the following:

- **Data frames**—From 0 to 2112 bytes in length, these frames carry data. They can also be used as Link_Data frames that carry information about the link and Device_Data frames that carry information about the transmitting device.

- **Link control frames**—These frames carry the control information related to a link. They can carry either acknowledgment (ACK) of successful data delivery or a Busy or Reject link response, which indicates a failure in the data transmission operation. Because these frames contain no data, the length of the Payload field of these frames is zero.

The maximum length of a frame can be 2148 transmission characters (or 537 transmission words). The frame contains data (also known as Payload), the address of the source and destination ports, and link control information. A frame can be followed by a minimum of six idle primitives to fill in transmission pauses. Figure 3-11 shows the FC-2 layer frame format.

Figure 3-11 *FC-2 Layer Frame Format*

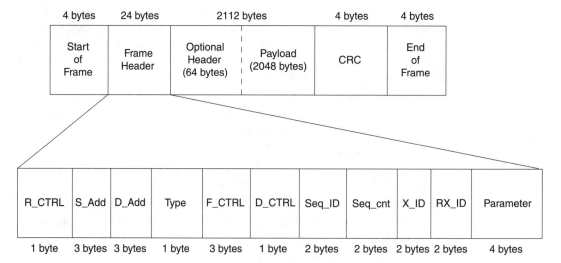

The fields in a FC-2 layer frame include the following:

- **SOF**—The length of this field is four bytes. It indicates the beginning of a frame.

- **Frame header**—The length of this field is 24 bytes. This field controls information regarding the link and the transmission. It also carries information to detect missing or out-of-order frames. A frame header consists of the following fields:

    — **Routing Control (R_CTRL)**—This field contains information regarding the frame type and the type of information being carried in the Payload field. The length of this field is one byte.

— **Source address (S_Add)**—This field contains the address of the source port that started the communication. The length of this field is three bytes.

— **Destination address (D_Add)**—This field contains the address of the destination port. The length of this field is three bytes.

NOTE   Port addresses can be either well-known port addresses or address aliases. A port's number can vary from 0 to 65535. Assigned by the Internet Assigned Numbers Authority (IANA), port numbers below 1024 are referred to as well-known port numbers because these port numbers are assigned to well-known services, such as File Transfer Protocol (FTP), Telnet, SMTP, and so on. For example, FTP is associated with port number 21, Telnet with port number 23, and SMTP with 25. When more than one IP address is assigned to a single port, it is commonly referred to as an address alias.

— **Type**—This field contains information about the protocol that is associated with information carried in the Payload field. The length of the field is one byte.

— **Frame Control (F_CTRL)**—This field contains information that identifies a transfer sequence. The transfer sequence can be either the beginning of the sequence, the middle of the sequence, the end of the sequence, or the end of the connection. The length of this field is three bytes.

— **Data Field Control (D_CTRL)**—This field contains the additional header information, if any. This field is optional. The length of this field is three bytes.

— **Sequence Identifier (Seq_ID)**—Data is transferred from one port to another as a set of related unidirectional frames, which are known as a sequence. The Seq_ID field contains a unique number that identifies a sequence within the stream of data traveling between two ports. The length of this field is one byte.

NOTE   Refer to the next section "Sequence" for more information on sequences.

— **Sequence Count (Seq_Cnt)**—This field contains a unique frame number that identifies the position of the frame in a given sequence. The length of this field is three bytes.

— **Exchange Identifier (X_ID)**—This field contains a unique number that identifies an exchange. The length of this field is one byte.

— **Response Exchange Identifier (RX_ID)**—This field contains a unique number that identifies a response to an exchange. The length of this field is one byte.

— **Parameter**—This field contains information that varies with the frame type (D-type or K-type). Typically, this field is used as an offset of the Payload field. The length of this field is four bytes.

- **Payload**—The length of this field is variable. The maximum length of the field is 2112 bytes. This field contains the data that is being exchanged between the two communicating ends.

- **Cyclic Redundancy Check (CRC)**—The length of this field is four bytes. This field contains an algorithm to detect transmission errors.

- **End of Frame (EOF)**—The length of this field is four bytes. This field indicates the end of the current frame.

Although frames form the basic unit of data exchange, sets of frames are sent together instead of as individual frames during a transmission. Next, consider these sets of data-exchange units in Fibre Channel media.

Sequence

A *sequence* is a set of one or more frames that are transmitted in one direction during a transmission. The Seq_Cnt field of a frame indicates that each frame that belongs to a sequence must be unique. The value of Seq_Cnt helps the upper layers in identifying the frame that was corrupted or lost during transmission. The upper layers can then start the appropriate actions that can include retransmission of the lost frame(s) and notification to the users about the retransmission.

Exchange

An *exchange* is a set of one or more non-concurrent sequences that belong to a single transmission or set. The exchange can be unidirectional or bidirectional.

NOTE   A good analogy of a sequence is a SAN server requesting a file from a SAN device. The operation of sending and receiving the requested file between the SAN server and the SAN device represents an exchange.

FC-3 Layer

Also known as the *common services layer*, FC-3 is a single point of the Fibre Channel stack through which all traffic flows. As you know, a Fibre Channel node can support more than one port that might be involved in different transactions simultaneously. FC-0, FC-1, FC-2, and FC-4 might be implemented separately for each port. However, there is only one FC-3 layer implementation that all the ports of a Fibre Channel node share. In other words, the FC-3 layer acts as a middleman between the various ports of a Fibre Channel node. The FC-3 layer is responsible for defining services that are common to all ports on a Fibre Channel node, no matter what protocols they support. It also provides common services to multiple ports on a Fabric.

NOTE   To provide services that are common to all ports, the FC-3 layer maintains a set of tables that contain complete information about the ports that are currently active.

The services or functions offered by the FC-3 layer are the following:

- **Multicasting**—This service allows a message to be sent to multiple destination ports simultaneously. The message can be broadcast to either all the ports on a node, a set of ports, a set of nodes, or to the entire Fabric.

- **Hunt groups**—This service allows all or a set of ports of a Fibre Channel node to be assigned an alias identifier. The group of ports that share a common alias identifier is known as a *hunt group*. During a transmission, if the originator transmitter port is busy, the information can be forwarded to any of the ports that belong to the hunt group. This service makes the transmission faster and more efficient by reducing the latency that is generated while waiting for the originator port to be free.

- **Striping**—This service allows the use of multiple ports of a node and multiple links to send a single information unit parallel-like. The simultaneous use of multiple ports and links to transmit information increases the speed of transmission many fold. At the same time, striping helps in exploiting the maximum available bandwidth.

After having looked at FC-3, now consider the last layer of the Fibre Channel standard: FC-4.

FC-4 Layer

Also known as the *upper layer protocol mapping layer*, FC-4 is the highest layer of the stack. The responsibilities of this layer include the following:

- Definition of the interfaces that allow applications, device drivers, and operating systems to function seamlessly over the Fibre Channel

- Mapping of upper-level protocols with the lower layers (FC-2 and FC-3) to improve the interoperability between applications

This layer also allows the Fibre Channel to transmit channel data and network data with equal ease. Sending Intelligent Peripheral Interface (IPI) commands to a processor is an example of transportation of channel information. Exchanging TCP/IP packets between network devices (nodes) is an example of transportation of network information. Not only does the FC-4 layer allow for channel transportation of information, but it also enables the concurrent transportation of network and channel protocols over the same physical interface.

The channel protocols supported by the FC-4 layer are the following:

- **Small Computer System Interface (SCSI)**—An ANSI standard parallel interface that provides high-speed connectivity to peripheral devices, such as printers and CD-ROMs.

- **High Performance Parallel Interface (HIPPI)**—HIPPI is a high-performance point-to-point computing interface used for the transmission of huge amounts of data over relatively short-distances. It enables the transmission and reception of data simultaneously at 200 to 1600 Mbps at a distance of 25 meters.

- **Intelligent Peripheral Interface (IPI)**—Intelligent Peripheral Interface (IPI) is an ANSI standard for controlling peripheral devices by a host computer. IPI is a high-bandwidth interface between the host computer and its peripheral devices (hard drives, tape drives, optical libraries, and so on) that supports transactions ranging from 3 to 25 Mbps. IPI-3 is the latest version of IPI, which also provides RAID support.

- **Fibre Channel Link Encapsulation (Fibre Channel-LE)**—Also referred to as ANSI X3.254, this specification maps Fibre Channel HIPPI-FP.

- **Single Byte Command Code Set (SBCCS)**—The SBCCS interface is used to implement block multiplex interfaces and ESCON directors.

The network protocols supported by the FC-4 layer are the following:

- **Internet Protocol (IP)**—IP is one of the best-known network protocols today. It is used to interconnect disparate networks over the Internet. The IP protocol facilitates transmission of data blocks from source to destination computers (or hosts) that are identified by unique IP addresses. If the data to be transmitted is large, IP fragments the data into smaller blocks known as *datagrams* at the sender-end and reassembles them into their original size at the receiver-end.

- **ATM Adaptation Layer-5 (AAL-5)**—The five ATM adaptation layers (AALs) specify how data is fragmented into cells and reassembled to their original format. AAL-5 is the most commonly implemented ATM level that focuses on high-speed, reliable, and efficient data transfers with optimum throughput.

- **IEEE 802.5**—Based on the Token Ring specifications developed by IBM in the 1970s, the IEEE 802.5 standard specifies the operation of single- and multi-ring networks. All the nodes in the network are connected to form a logical ring and use the token-passing scheme for data transfers.

Classes of Service

Fibre Channel offers six communication strategies to ensure successful, efficient, and fast delivery of different types of traffic. These strategies are commonly known as *classes of service*. The six classes of service play a major role in communication, be it between two N_Ports or between an N_Port and the Fabric. For every port-to-port and port-to-Fabric communication, at least one class of service must be supported by the communicating entities and the corresponding Login protocols (N_Port Login or Fabric Login protocol).

The six classes of service are *Class 1*, *Class 2*, *Class 3*, *Class 4*, *Class 5*, and *Class 6*. Each class of service is related to different aspects of communication, such as the following:

- Connection establishment
- Allocation of bandwidth to the connection
- Delivery of frames between the two communicating ends
- Acknowledgment (negative and positive) of a delivery, if required
- Flow control mechanism

The following sections describe the various classes of service.

Class 1

Class 1 service provides acknowledged, reliable, connection-oriented transactions. The main features of this service class include the following:

- Dedicated circuit-switched connection through the Fabric between two communicating entities
- Maximum-bandwidth and high-throughput transactions
- Guaranteed delivery of frames in the same order as they were transmitted

---

NOTE   The guaranteed delivery feature of Class 1 ensures that all successful deliveries are acknowledged positively. For all the unsuccessful deliveries, a negative acknowledgment is sent to the sender. A negative acknowledgment notifies the sender to re-send the lost or corrupted data frames.

Because of these features, this class of service makes data deliveries reliable without the overhead that is generated by network protocols. This class of service is ideal for bandwidth-intensive applications that require the data to be transferred quickly and continuously, such as backup, restore, and various multimedia applications.

Other advanced features offered by this class of service are the following:

- **Camp on**—When a Fabric switch receives a connection request for a busy port, the switch queues the port for connection instead of sending the busy signal to the requesting N_Port. After the destination port becomes available, the connection is established between the two ports. This switch service is known as *camp on*, and it speeds up connections considerably because the requesting port does not need to attempt reconnection.

- **Intermix**—If a connection has been established, but Class 1 frames are not being transmitted currently, intermix service allows the transmission of Class 2 and Class 3 frames. This service, therefore, helps prevent the bandwidth from being wasted. However, the communicating N_Ports and the Fabric must support the intermix service to allow the concurrent transmission of Class 2 and Class 3 frames.

- **Dedicated simplex**—The dedicated simplex service allows a Fibre Channel node to simultaneously transmit data to one node and receive data from another, when necessary. In other words, this service breaks bidirectional Class 1 connections into two unidirectional connections. This service helps in eliminating latency that arises when one port waits for the destination port to be free.

- **Stacked connect**—When a Fabric switch receives sequential connection requests from one port, it queues all the requests until the connections can be established. This service reduces the overhead caused by re-requests.

Class 1 connections use flow control to manage data flow between Fibre Channel nodes and devices. Now you will consider what type of flow control is applicable in Class 1 connections.

Class 1 Flow Control

Because Class 1 connections are dedicated, a transmission is not affected by other connections. Therefore, the frames need not be buffered by the Fabric while the frames are routed to the destination port. This eliminates the need of buffer-to-buffer flow control. Only end-to-end flow control is required for Class 1 connections.

In end-to-end flow control, if the packets arrive with a delay or are lost during the transaction, only the sender and receiver node are involved in packet recovery. Therefore, end-to-end flow control is also referred to as source-to-destination flow control.

Class 2

Class 2 provides an acknowledged, multiplexed, and connectionless service. The main features of Class 2 service are the following:

- Nondedicated connections, due to which the bandwidth is shared with other transactions

---

NOTE	Transmission speeds can vary, depending on the media that make up the Fibre Channel link.

- Multiplexed connections that allow a port to communicate with more than one port simultaneously
- Guaranteed delivery of frames with acknowledgments
- Out-of-order delivery of frames because a single transmission link is shared between many simultaneous transactions

Because of these features, Class 2 service is ideal for traffic, where timeliness and order of delivery are not critical. Class 2 service is commonly used for transferring IP packets and FTP data.

Class 2 Flow Control

Because Class 2 provides a connectionless service, frames are switched independently. Also, the same link is shared between different connections. As a result, frames need to be buffered by the Fabric as they are routed to their respective destinations. Therefore, both buffer-to-buffer and end-to-end flow control mechanisms are used in Class 2 transactions.

Class 2 also uses credit-based flow control, which prevents frames from being discarded if the intended destination port is busy. If the destination port is busy, the Busy signal is sent to the requesting port to prevent the connection-originator port from sending further frames. This also helps in avoiding link and port congestion situations, which are common occurrences in connectionless networks.

Class 3

Class 3 service provides an unacknowledged connectionless service. The main features of this class of service are the following:

- Non-dedicated connections, where the bandwidth is shared with other transactions
- Non-guaranteed data delivery, where neither a successful nor an unsuccessful delivery of frames is confirmed
- Out-of-order delivery of frames because a single transmission link is shared between many simultaneous transactions

Because of these features, Class 3 service is also referred to as *datagram service*. Class 3 service is used when timeliness and the order of frames delivery is not important. Situations related to the loss or corruption of frames during transmissions are handled by upper-level protocols and applications.

Class 3 service is generally used to transfer SCSI data and for network broadcasts and multicasts (sending data to a set of nodes or ports). Storage devices in the FC-AL topology also use this class of service to transfer data. This is because the loop establishes a dedicated connection between the two communicating ends. As a result, the normally slow FC-AL transactions become faster because deliveries need not be acknowledged.

Class 3 Flow Control

Any situation related to the loss or corruption of frames during transactions is handled by the upper-level protocols and applications. As a result, Class 3 service only uses buffer-to-buffer flow control, while frames are being routed to the destination port.

Class 4

Class 4, which is similar to Class 2, provides acknowledged, multicast, and connection-oriented service. The main difference between the two service classes is that in Class 2, bandwidth is shared between simultaneous transactions. In Class 4, although bandwidth is shared, each transaction is allocated a fraction of the available bandwidth, which cannot be shared with the other transactions that are happening at the same time. The main features of Class 4 service include the following:

- Dedicated connection, which is allocated a part of the total bandwidth. This Class 4 connection is referred to as a virtual circuit (VC). A VC in turn consists of two unidirectional VCs that operate in opposite directions.

- Shared bandwidth because multiple Class 4 connections can be established simultaneously. Therefore, bandwidth is shared between many Class 4 VCs.

- Multicast connections that allow a port to communicate with more than one port simultaneously.

- Guaranteed delivery of frames, which is achieved with the help of acknowledgments.

- In-order delivery of frames because of the dedicated nature of Class 4 VCs.

Because of these features, Class 4 service is highly suitable for time-critical, real-time applications, such as voice and video. Timeliness, continuity, and the order of frame delivery are critical for these applications. Also, this class of service provides a predictable QoS, which is negotiated between the two ends during the establishment of the VC. Class 4 data transfers are generally high quality.

Class 4 Flow Control

Because this class provides acknowledged and dedicated service along with reserved bandwidth to a connection, the frames on their way to the destination port need not be buffered by the Fabric. Therefore, Class 4 uses end-to-end flow control.

Class 5

Class 5 service is reserved for future operations and is still under development. This class is meant for isochronous (parallel) transactions by multiple ports. Audio and video broadcasts are being sighted as the future use of this class of service.

Class 6

Class 6 provides acknowledged, connection-oriented, and reliable transactions. It is similar to Class 1 service except that it is unidirectional. Class 6 also provides a multicast facility by allowing one port to transfer the same data to more than one port simultaneously. This class is ideal for video broadcasts (which are unidirectional) and other real-time applications that need to transfer large quantities of data. This class uses end-to-end flow control.

Table 3-2 summarizes the six classes of service. Of these six classes, Class 1 and Class 6 are best suited for time-critical data transactions over Fibre Channel links. Class 2 offers multiplexing, whereas Class 3 and Class 6 support multicasting. Class 4 provides fractional bandwidth for each ongoing transaction, thus allowing dedicated connections despite media sharing. Class 5 service remains yet undeveloped.

Table 3-2   *The Six Service Classes at a Glance*

Feature	Class 1	Class 2	Class 3	Class 4	Class 5	Class 6
Connection	Dedicated Bidirectional	Non-dedicated	Non-dedicated	Dedicated Bidirectional	NA	Dedicated Bidirectional
Bandwidth	Full	Shared	Shared	Full use of the allocated fractional bandwidth	NA	Full
Data delivery	Guaranteed	Guaranteed	Non-Guaranteed	Guaranteed	NA	Guaranteed
In-order frame delivery	Yes	No	No	Yes	NA	Yes
Flow control	End-to-end	Buffer-to-buffer End-to-end Credit-based	Buffer-to-buffer	End-to-end	NA	End-to-end
Multicast/ Multiplex	No	Multiplex	Multicast	No	NA	Multicast

Summary

In this chapter you learned about Fibre Channel technology. Fibre Channel technology is the backbone of SANs. They have many advantages to offer, which keeps Fibre Channel abreast of SCSI and other contemporary technologies. High-speed, high-performance, reliability of transmissions, and adaptability to future growth are some of the major benefits of Fibre Channel technology.

Fibre Channel devices support five types of ports that enable communication between two nodes. These include N_Ports, L_Ports, F_Ports, and E_Ports.

Fibre Channel supports three topologies. The point-to-point topology is the simplest of the three and consists of two Fibre Channel devices that are directly connected to each other. FC-AL is another popular ring-like topology that allows the connection of 126 nodes to a single link to form a complete loop. However, media sharing performance-related issues usually crop up in this topology. Switched Fabric is the third Fibre Channel topology that is based on the interconnection of switches. It is the most resilient topology of the three. You'll learn more about these three topologies in Chapter 6.

Similar to any other networking model, the Fibre Channel standard is logically broken up into five layers (FC-0 to FC-4). Finally, Fibre Channel offers six service classes—from Class 1 through Class 6—to ensure the successful, efficient, and fast delivery of different types of traffic.

In this chapter, you will learn about the following Fibre Channel products:

- Host Bus Adapters
- Connectors
- Hubs
- Switches
- Bridges
- Routers
- Storage devices

CHAPTER 4

Fibre Channel Products

With the growing popularity of storage area networks (SANs), Fibre Channel technology has emerged to the forefront as an effective means of solving storage-related problems that have plagued corporate networks all over the world. A wealth of Fibre Channel products are available, including Host Bus Adapters (HBAs), connectors, switches, hubs, gateways, and Fibre Channel-to-Small Computer System Interface (SCSI) bridges. Along with optical cables, Fibre Channel products enable network administrators and designers to develop solutions to storage problems related to performance, distance, backups and restoration, bandwidth, and security. For example, Fibre Channel switches play an important role in enhancing the performance of database servers by switching data queries and their results much faster. Similarly, switched Fibre Channel hubs provide high-speed access to disk arrays, tape libraries, and Just a Bunch of Disks (JBODs).

To build a successful SAN that fulfills all or most of the requirements of a corporation, you must choose each device of a SAN with care and understanding. Understanding the purpose and the capabilities of each Fibre Channel device will help you make effective choices while designing a SAN.

With the infiltration of SAN and Fibre Channel technology in corporate storage solutions, many vendors have jumped into the field of Fibre Channel devices. You need not restrict yourself to the Fibre Channel products offered by one single vendor. As a SAN designer, an intelligent mix and match of compatible products will help you to implement a cost-effective and high-performance storage solution.

HBAs

Similar to network interface cards (NICs) that are used in traditional Ethernets, *HBAs* provide the physical interface between the input/output (I/O) host bus of Fibre Channel devices (such as servers and storage devices) and the underlying Fibre Channel network. In other words, HBAs connect Fibre Channel devices to Fibre Channel links.

NOTE   Popularly used I/O host buses include IBM's PCI-MCA, HP's HSC, and Sun's SBus. The term PCI-MCA is a combination of two terms—PCI (Peripheral Component Interconnect) and MCA (Micro Channel Architecture). PCI-MCA is a 32-bit, high-speed interface between the processor of a computer and the attached peripheral devices and expansion cards. HP's High Speed Connect (HSC) is a high-speed proprietary interface that functions much like PCI. SBus is a 32-bit bus used in Sun's SPARC workstations. SBus facilitates the transactions between the processor and the attached peripheral devices. SBus can also help the processor in identifying the corresponding device drivers of the attached devices.

In addition to acting as the physical interface between the host bus and the underlying Fibre Channel link, other functions of HBAs include the following:

- Initialization of Fibre Channel nodes and ports onto the underlying arbitrated loop or Fabric. Similar to NICs, HBAs also provide a hard-coded, 64-bit Node_Name or World-Wide Name (WWN) address and Port_Name or World-Wide Port Name (WWPN) address to the device and its ports. These addresses help the Fabric in identifying a node or a port before the node or port has been initialized by the loop or has attempted a Fabric logon.

NOTE   For more information on WWN and WWPN, see Chapter 6, "SAN Topologies."

- Support to various upper-level protocols (ULPs), such as TCP/IP, SCSI, and so on.
- Interpretation of incoming data streams by performing context switching. When context switching is done at the HBA level, a significant amount of switching overhead is reduced.

NOTE   Context switching is the capability of an HBA to issue and process multiple commands to various SAN storage devices simultaneously to maximize efficiency when accessing data. The entire concept is similar to multitasking. However, the basic difference between multitasking and context switching is that in multitasking, inactive programs continue to run in the background. In contrast, in context switching, any inactive program is suspended until it becomes active again.

- 8B/10B encoding of data

| NOTE | For detailed information on 8B/10B coding, refer to Chapter 3, "Fibre Channel Basics." |

HBAs can differ on the basis of many criteria. These criteria include the following:

- **Physical links supported**—Fibre Channel physical links include copper links, single-mode fiber-optic links, or multi-mode fiber-optic links.

- **Protocols supported**—Commonly implemented Fibre Channel protocols include SCSI, IP, FCP-SCSI, IPI-3, and SB-2.

| NOTE | IPI is a high-bandwidth interface between the host computer and its peripheral devices (hard drives, tape drives, optical libraries, and so on) that supports transactions ranging from 3 to 25 Mbps. IPI-3 is the latest version of IPI. Based on the Single Byte Command Code Set (SBCCS), Single Byte-2 (SB-2) is a signaling protocol that provides high-bandwidth and high-performance communication between the processor and I/O devices. In addition, SB-2 also facilitates long-distance data exchanges. |

- **Operating systems supported**—UNIX, Windows NT, AIX, and Macintosh are some of the operating systems that are commonly used in storage environment.

- **Topologies supported**—Point-to-point, Fibre Channel-Arbitrated Loop (FC-AL), and switched Fabric are the three Fibre Channel topologies.

- **Number of connections supported**—Connections can be single node to Fibre Channel link connections, multiple connections, or multiple switched connections.

| NOTE | For detailed information on the three topologies mentioned in the preceding list, see Chapter 6. |

With an increase in the number of vendors manufacturing Fibre Channel products, SANs are growing heterogeneous in nature. This implies that SANs are using more and more varied hardware and software platforms. Therefore, of the many HBAs that are available today, it is very important to choose HBAs that can support a wide variety of platforms.

Several vendors offer a variety of HBAs. IBM, JNI Corp., Qlogic, and HP are some of the more popular HBA vendors. The price of an HBA can range from $500 to $1500 per adapter. Figure 4-1 shows an HBA.

Figure 4-1   *HBA*

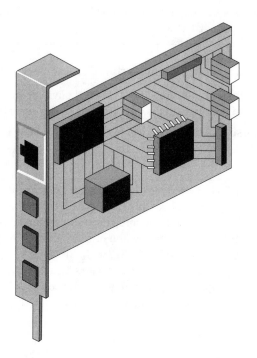

Fibre Channel Connectors

Data transfer rates over the Fibre Channel infrastructure are measured in gigabits. As a result, the data transported over Fibre Channel links is sometimes referred to as *gigabit transport*. Fibre Channel connectors play an important role in facilitating the gigabit transport between two communicating ends. The connectors provide an interface that converts any type of communication transport into gigabit transport.

Four types of Fibre Channel connectors are used to interconnect Fibre Channel devices:

- Gigabit Interface Converters (GBICs)
- Gigabit Link Modules (GLMs)
- Transceivers
- Media Interface Adapters (MIAs)

The following sections discuss each of these connectors.

GBICs

Fibre Channel devices use electronic signals known as *differential serial data signals*. These signals are encoded according to the 8B/10B encoding method. However, the link between two communicating devices is either copper-based or fiber-optic. Copper and fiber-optic links are not capable of transmitting differential serial data signals. Using GBICs solves this problem.

GBICs are hot-pluggable and easily replaceable interface modules that are responsible for converting differential serial data signals into corresponding optical or copper signals that can be transported to the destination. At the sender end, a GBIC takes differential serial data signals as input and converts them according to the Fibre Channel link on which the data is transmitted in the form of signals. At the recipient end, the GBIC receives the optical or copper signal and delivers it to the device as differential serial data signals.

On optical links, GBICs support two modes of optical operations depending on the wavelength of the laser being used. The two optical modes of a GBIC are *ShortWave (SW)* mode and *LongWave (LW)* mode.

ShortWave GBICs provide connectivity for comparatively short distances—up to 500 meters. The 50-micron fiber-optic cables offer SW mode at a distance of 2 to 500 meters. The 62.5-micron fiber-optic cables offer the SW mode at a distance of 2 to 175 meters. The 9-micron fiber-optic cables do not support the SW mode.

NOTE   For more information on SW and LW Fibre Channel connections, see Chapter 5, "Fibre Channel Cabling."

As the name suggests, GBICs that function in LW mode offer long connectivity distances of up to 10 kilometers. The 9-micron fiber-optic cables offer LW mode up to a distance of 10 kilometers. Both 50-micron and 62.5-micron fiber-optic cables offer the LW mode up to a distance of 550 meters.

GBICs are external pull-push type connectors that need to be attached to the HBA as shown in Figure 4-2. GBICs plug into the Fibre Channel device. Fibre Channel cables, or links, are then attached to the GBIC. They are commonly used with HBAs, switches, and gateways and support transfer rates of 1063 Mbps and above. Prices of GBICs range from $250 to $3000.

NOTE   Apart from Fibre Channel networks (such as SANs), GBICs can also be used in Gigabit Ethernets.

Figure 4-2   *GBIC*

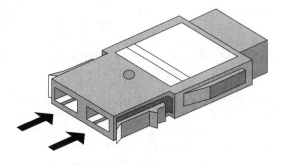

Fibre Channel Link

GLMs

Also referred to as Gigabaud Link Modules, GLMs are the low-cost predecessor of GBICs. GLMs facilitate full-duplex communication between Fibre Channel devices. They convert differential serial data signals to optical or copper signals so that the signals can be transmitted over the Fibre Channel link. At the recipient end, GLMs reconvert the optical or copper signals to differential serial data signals that the recipient can understand and process.

Although the GLMs function similarly to the GBICs, there are differences between the two. Table 4-1 enumerates the differences between GLMs and GBICs.

Table 4-1   *The Differences Between GBICs and GLMs*

GBICs	GLMs
GBICs offer transfer rates of 1063 Mbps and above.	GLMs offer transfer rates of 266 Mbps and 1063 Mbps.
GBICs are hot-pluggable. This means that the GBICs can be attached to or removed from the Fibre Channel device while the device is still operational.	GLMs are not hot-pluggable. The Fibre Channel device needs to be shut down before GLMs can be attached, replaced, or repaired.
GBICs are easy to configure and use.	GLMs are difficult to configure and use.
GBICs are more expensive than GLMs.	GLMs are comparatively cheaper than GBICs.

Similar to GBICs, GLMs also use two types of lasers for transportation of data over fiber-optic links. These include the following:

- SW
- LW

You can attach GLMs to the Fibre Channel devices as external connectors, or you can build GLMs into the HBA. Figure 4-3 shows an external GLM. Figure 4-4 shows a GLM that is a part of the HBA. The price of GLMs ranges from $900 to $2500.

Figure 4-3   *External GLM*

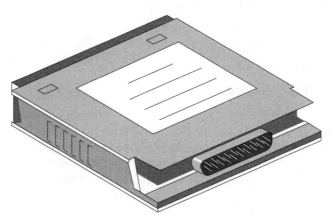

Figure 4-4   *GLM as a Part of the HBA*

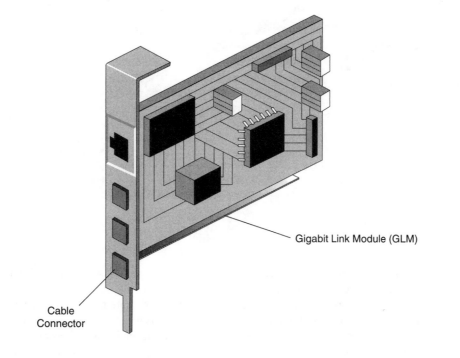

Gigabit Link Module (GLM)

Cable
Connector

Transceivers

Transceivers are hot-pluggable Fibre Channel connectors that are generally used in switch implementations. They facilitate high-speed, bidirectional, point-to-point communication between Fibre Channel devices. Transceivers support communication speeds of 2 Gbps and above (3.25 Gbps to 10 Gbps). Some transceivers can also provide transaction speeds up to 10 Gbps.

Commonly used Fibre Channel transceivers include the following:

- 1×9 transceivers
- Small Form Factor (SFF) transceivers
- 1×28 transceivers

1×9 optical transceivers are the most commonly used transceivers. Transceivers are preferred over GBICs because they are roughly two times faster and are much easier to maintain than GBICs. However, transceivers are also more expensive than GBICs and GLMs. The price of transceivers ranges from $350 to $2000.

Figure 4-5 shows a 1×9 transceiver.

Figure 4-5   *1×9 Transceiver*

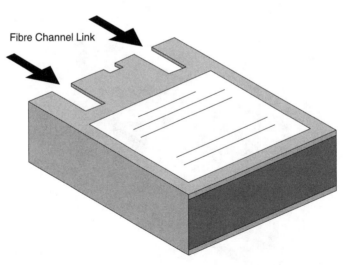

SFF transceivers are small, laser-based optical connectors that are the same size as RJ-45 connectors. These transceivers offer high data transfer rates (1063 Mbps) and are well suited for networking applications that require a high-speed serial interface. Being small in size, SFF transceivers are highly recommended for environments where devices are squeezed in less space. The performance of SFF connectors is directly related to the precision of fiber alignment. Therefore, take special care while connecting these transceivers to Fibre Channel devices. The price of SFF transceivers ranges from $450 to $3000.

Figure 4-6 depicts an SFF transceiver.

Figure 4-6   *SFF Transceiver*

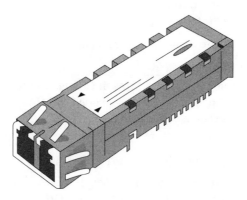

1 × 28 transceivers are high-speed optical transceivers that can support data transfer rates up to 1.25 Gbps. In addition to facilitating connections between Fibre Channel devices and links, 1 × 28 transceivers are also capable of providing link status information and diagnosing link problems. This helps the Fibre Channel device that they are connected to promptly diagnose transmission- and link-related problems.

Figure 4-7 depicts a 1 × 28 transceiver.

Figure 4-7   *1 × 28 Transceiver*

NOTE   Some vendors, such as Vixel, 3Com, and Finisar, categorize GBICs as transceivers.

MIAs

MIAs, a cost-effective category of Fibre Channel connectors, are responsible for the conversion of DB9-based copper signals into corresponding optical signals and vice versa. MIAs are useful in the following situations:

- Extending a Fibre Channel copper link distance beyond the stipulated 30 meters.

NOTE	Currently, optical MIAs are available only for SW lasers. Therefore, the cables supported by MIAs can stretch up to a maximum of 500 meters.

- Connecting the copper interface to a Fibre Channel hub or switch.

MIA prices range from $50 to $1500. Although MIAs are cost-effective compared to other Fibre Channel connectors, they are not considered to be good Fibre Channel solutions for the following reasons:

- MIAs are not hot-pluggable. Therefore, the Fibre Channel to which they are connected must be powered down before they can be removed or replaced.
- MIAs are difficult to manage.
- MIAs do not provide support to the High Speed Serial Data Connectors (HSSDC) copper interface, which is often used in Fibre Channel networks.
- MIAs are dependent on DB-9 connectors for power supply. However, not all DB-9 connectors are capable of supplying power to MIAs.

Figure 4-8 shows a Fibre Channel MIA.

Figure 4-8   *A Fibre Channel MIA*

The next section discusses Fibre Channel hubs in detail.

Hubs

The FC-AL topology allows cost-effective connection of up to 126 devices without the need of an underlying Fabric. However, a daisy chain of devices connected to form a loop makes it difficult to troubleshoot the network. Adding or removing devices from the loop is a highly time-consuming exercise. Also, any cable break or power loss can lead to the temporary shut down of the entire loop and all the nodes attached to the loop until the problem is remedied.

Fibre Channel hubs are used to effectively solve the problems that occur in the FC-AL topology. Analogous to the hubs used in traditional local-area networks (LANs), Fibre Channel hubs form the focal point of the FC-AL topology, as shown in Figure 4-9. As a result, network administrators can centrally monitor and manage the loop. The *Port Bypass Circuitry (PBC)* used in hubs allows devices to be dynamically added or removed from the loop while the loop is still functional. If a device is added or removed from the loop, these hubs can automatically reconfigure the loop.

NOTE   A daisy chain is a serial connection of network devices to a single cable.

Figure 4-9   *Hub—The Focal Point of the Loop*

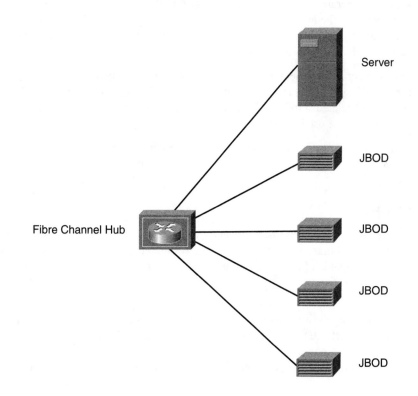

Fibre Channel hubs are of the following three types:

- Unmanaged hubs
- Managed hubs
- Switched hubs

The following sections describe each type of hub.

Unmanaged Hubs

Unmanaged hubs are not shipped with built-in software to manage them, thus the name unmanaged hubs. These hubs are used for extending loop distances. A typical unmanaged hub provides eight ports. Some unmanaged hubs also support 12 and 16 ports. Of the available hub ports, one port is used to connect to another hub. The rest of the ports can support loop nodes.

Each loop node is attached to the hub through a GBIC, which plugs into the hub port. When an attached node communicates with another through the hub, the hub port receives the signal, regenerates it, and forwards the signal to the next port. If any part of the loop node is inoperative, the hub detects the missing node with the help of port bypass circuits and automatically excludes the node from the loop. Similarly, any node that is attached to the hub through a GBIC is automatically included in the loop.

Unlike other interconnect devices, such as switches and HBAs, unmanaged hubs used in arbitrated loops are not assigned Fibre Channel addresses. As a result, they cannot take part in protocol-related activities. This makes them merely passive members of the storage network that are used to extend the loop.

Various vendors offer a wide range of unmanaged hubs. These vendors include Vixel, IBM, HP, 3COM, and Veritas. The prices of these hubs can range from $1500 to $8000.

Managed Hubs

Unlike unmanaged hubs, managed hubs are SNMP-controllable and are shipped with integrated hub-management software. As a result, they are highly manageable and to some extent are capable of participating in the activities that are controlled by the protocols.

NOTE   SNMP is an application layer protocol that facilitates the exchange of management information between network devices. SNMP consists of three components—SNMP manager, agent, and Management Information Base (MIB). The SNMP manager resides on a central management console and retrieves and collates the management information provided by the various SNMP agents. An SNMP agent resides on devices, such as managed hubs, switches, bridges, and routers. The SNMP agent is responsible for storing the local information in a MIB, which in turn is retrieved by the SNMP manager.

Managed hubs are also better at fault isolation. This is because they can isolate Loop Initialization Primitives (LIPs) from general application-related traffic, such as backup and video data that is extremely sensitive to delays. Managed hubs thus help in increasing overall loop stability. Some other functions of managed hubs include the following:

- Server clustering and storage consolidation

> **NOTE** A server cluster is a group of independent servers interconnected to form a single computing resource.

- Backups and restorations that do not disturb the normal operations of the attached LAN
- LAN-free streaming of audio/video applications
- Remote device monitoring
- Remote disk mirroring

NOTE Similar to most of the Fibre Channel devices, managed hubs are Field Replaceable Units (FRUs) that must be handled by trained professionals, such as network administrators.

Many SAN vendors, such as IBM, Vixel, HP, Brocade, and Gadzoox, offer a wide range of managed Fibre Channel hubs. Most of these hubs share some common features, including the following:

- **Dedicated port speed**—All the individual ports offer 100 Mbps data transfer rates. This data transfer rate is dedicated to the given port and is not affected by simultaneous transactions being carried out by other hub ports.
- **Hot-pluggable ports**—Managed hubs typically provide 8 to 12 hot-pluggable ports. These ports allow dynamic attachment or detachment of nodes (servers, storage devices, and clients) to the loop without the need of shutting down the loop. The nodes are attached to a hub port through a GBIC.
- **Zoning**—Most managed hubs allow dynamic zoning of nodes or ports, thus ensuring increased loop security.

- **Management interface**—Most of the managed hub vendors, such as IBM and Vixel, offer a graphical user interface (GUI) for management and configuration purposes. Other vendors provide an easy-to-use command-line interface (CLI).

- **Diagnostic capabilities**—Managed hubs offer comprehensive online diagnostic capabilities along with Power-On Self Test (POST). POST is run at the time the hub is powered on and helps the hub gather information about the status of all the attached nodes and environmental components such as fans.

  Online diagnostics constantly monitor the status of attached nodes and environmental components. On detecting a failed node or a non-critical component, the corresponding port is excluded from the loop with the help of port bypass circuitry. If a critical component of the hub fails, an appropriate warning is issued to all ports before shutdown.

Switched hubs belong to the third category of Fibre Channel hubs. You will now learn about this category of Fibre Channel hubs.

Switched Hubs

Switched hubs are the third and most recent category of Fibre Channel hubs. Unlike the previous categories of Fibre Channel hubs, switched hubs actively participate in protocol-related activities, such as discovery, identification, and management of other devices on the storage network, event logging, and diagnostics. Similar to managed hubs, each individual port of a switched hub is allocated a dedicated bandwidth of 100 Mbps and higher. Switched hubs function well with switches and they actively improve the speed of transactions by performing some of the tasks of switches. Also, they are extremely scalable and adaptable to future growth.

Switches

Fibre Channel switches are one of the most powerful components of a SAN. They are responsible for the efficient and high-speed switching of frames over a storage network. These switches are the basis of the switched Fabric topology, where the switches are interconnected to form the Fabric. The Fabric, in turn, can support numerous point-to-point connections, individual nodes, and arbitrated loops.

Unlike Fibre Channel hubs that are generally used to implement the arbitrated loop topology and extend the effective distance of a loop, Fibre Channel switches offer enhanced and more complex functionality. As a part of the Fabric, Fibre Channel switches are responsible for the following:

- Providing a dedicated bandwidth of 100 Mbps and higher per port. This means that all switch ports can engage in separate transactions simultaneously without affecting other transactions.

- Providing high-speed switching of frames from source to destination ports.

- Providing frame flow control during communication. Switches use services such as buffer-to-buffer credit for this purpose. Buffer-to-buffer credit, also known as BB_Credit, determines the maximum number of buffers available per port if buffer flow control is in use.

- Providing Fabric services, such as Fabric login, Simple Name Server (SNS), State Change Notification (SCN), and Registered State Change Notification (RSCN).

NOTE   See Chapter 6 for more information about Fabric services.

A typical Fibre Channel switch offers 8 to 16 ports. Therefore, a single switch can successfully support a small-scale SAN. A small-scale SAN can consist of a few hubs, application servers, database servers, and high-performance storage devices. A small-scale SAN can also be extended effectively by cascading two or more switches. However, the larger the number of cascaded switches, the greater the possibility that the cascaded links can end up as bottlenecks in switch-to-switch transactions. In this case, redundant links might prove to be an effective solution as they provide an alternate path between Fabric switches.

Types of Switches

Fibre Channel switches are generally classified into three categories—*loop switches*, *Fabric switches*, and *directors*. Loop switches are the most cost-effective category of switches that are used to connect an FC-AL to the Fabric. They support full-duplex data transfers and are ideal for low-bandwidth devices. Mostly, they are implemented for connecting legacy loop devices to the Fabric and tape consolidation. Typically, most loop switches support eight ports.

Fabric switches offer a high-speed category of switches that form the Fibre Channel Fabric. They support full-duplex data transfers that are not affected by simultaneous communications. They can efficiently support small SANs and act as the consolidation point of larger SANs. Fabric switches are generally implemented in SANs where storage devices are distributed geographically, such as storage wide-area networks (SWANs). A typical Fabric switch offers 16 to 32 ports.

Directors are a high-bandwidth, high-availability (99.999%), and high-performance category of switches that offer fully redundant, hot-pluggable components that can include processors and various switching elements. As a result, these switches are considered to be the most reliable. Their downtime is estimated to be about five minutes or less in a year. This makes them the most expensive category of switches. Directors are implemented in mission-critical and performance-intensive applications where downtime must be as low as possible. They are also used to implement the backbone for enterprise SANs. Directors offer 32 or more ports.

The price of switches can range from about $7500 to $45,000, depending on the functionality provided by the switch. Many vendors offer Fabric switches. IBM, Vixel, Compaq, HP, Gadzoox, Brocade Communications, Inc., Hitachi, and McData are some of the most well-known vendors in the field of Fibre Channel switches.

Cisco Systems, Inc., offers the Catalyst 6000 and Catalyst 4000 family of switches for storage networking solutions. These switches are described in the following sections.

Catalyst 6000 Family Switches

The Catalyst 6000 family of switches is actually a set of Catalyst 6500 and Catalyst 6000 series of switches. These switches were designed to offer the following features that are extremely important in gigabit Fibre Channel networks:

- Extensive intelligent network services
- Exceptional scalability
- Optimal price and performance
- High availability
- Support to a wide range of interfaces that are used in Fibre Channel networks

Figure 4-10 shows a Catalyst 6000 family switch.

Figure 4-10 *Catalyst 6000 Family Switch*

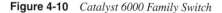

The functionality of members of this family include the following:

- **High performance**—The Catalyst 6513 switch from the Catalyst 6500 series offers switching speeds up to 210 million packets per second. The switch also offers 1152 10/100 and 388 gigabit ports per 7-inch rack.

- **Switch Fabric Module 2**—The Catalyst 6500 family offers scalable switching bandwidth up to 256 Gbps, while ensuring the highest level of availability.

- **Content Switching Module (CSM)**—The Catalyst 6000 and 6500 families offer CSM that helps in tracking network sessions and server load conditions in real-time. CSM also directs each session to the appropriate server.

- **Optical Services Modules (OSM)**—The Catalyst 6500 series switches offer optical WAN interfaces, deep packet buffers, and PXF IP Services Processors for high-speed IP service applications.

- **Supervisor Engine 2**—The Catalyst 6000 and 6500 families offer a CEF-based architecture, which helps in increasing the overall system performance to 100+ Mbps.

- **Cisco Express Forwarding (CEF)**—The Catalyst 6500 family offers CEF, which in collaboration with Supervisor Engine 2 and Gigabit Ethernet Modules delivers next generation solutions for dynamic service provider and enterprise networks.

- **Gigabit Ethernet Switching Module**—The Catalyst 6500 family offers Gigabit Ethernet Switching Modules that are ideal for gigabit backbones, server farms, and high-density wiring closets.

- **Intrusion Detection System (IDS)**—The Catalyst 6000 family switches integrate switching and security functionality to provide comprehensive attack detection against unauthorized and malicious access.

- **Quality of service (QoS)**—The Catalyst 6000 and 6500 families offer high QoS, high-availability, and security.

NOTE   For more information on Catalyst 6000 series switches, refer to the site www.cisco.com/warp/public/cc/pd/si/casi/ca6000.

Catalyst 4000 Family Switches

The Catalyst 4000 family of switches offers modular switches (Catalyst 4003 and Catalyst 4006) that are an integral part of Cisco's Architecture for Voice, Video, and Integrated Data (AVVID) solutions. AVVID offers scalable and manageable solutions for both SAN- and NAS-based networks.

The main features of the Catalyst 4000 family switches include the following:

- IP access to storage
- Support to multimedia traffic, such as IP telephony, unified messaging, and Virtual Private Networks (VPNs)
- Scalability and future growth

NOTE   For more information on Catalyst 4000 series switches, refer to the site www.cisco.com/warp/public/cc/pd/si/casi/ca4000.

Figure 4-11 shows a Catalyst 4000 family switch.

Figure 4-11   *Catalyst 4000 Family Switch*

Fibre Channel Switches Versus Hubs

While designing and implementing a storage network, one source of confusion is when to use hubs and when to implement switches. There are relevant considerations when deciding between hubs and switches including shared bandwidth, network population, services, security, and future growth. The following sections discuss these considerations.

Shared Bandwidth

Except for switched hubs, the bandwidth offered by managed and unmanaged hubs is shared. This means that if a 10-port hub offers 100 Mbps bandwidth, each individual hub port gets a bandwidth of only 10 Mbps. On the other hand, a 10-port 100 Mbps switch provides 100 Mbps bandwidth to each individual switch port.

Some applications, such as sustained full-motion video streams and streaming tape backups, are extremely sensitive to delays. As a result, hubs are not the right choice in storage environments where audio and video data is exchanged or tape backup data is streamed predominantly.

Network Population

The total number of nodes supported by the storage network also affects the choice of a hub or switch. If the number of nodes is smaller (5 to 40 nodes), hubs seem to be an ideal solution. However, for a large number of nodes (more than 100), switches are the best solution because the larger the network population, the greater the need of switching frames from source to destination. For networks that consist of 50–100 nodes, a mix of hubs and switches offers an optimal solution.

Services

In a large storage network populated with a large number of devices, discovering the required nodes or ports can be a tedious and complex task. Moreover, if a node goes down, other nodes might not know about the change in its status and try to contact it. This can result in long request queues for the failed node. Services, such as Fabric login, SCN, and RSCN, are very helpful in the quick and efficient discovery of the required disk, port, or node and their corresponding status. These services, however, are not obligatory, and nodes need to register themselves for notifications regarding changes in topology and individual device status.

The SCN service allows an N_Port to send a change notification to another N_Port that has registered its interest in any change of the given node or port. Therefore, only the port that was notified about the change would know about the change in status. The other members of the Fabric do not know about the change. RSCN offers a better solution to this problem. All the registered nodes are informed about the change simultaneously, thus allowing more than one node or port to know about the change. This helps in the fast discovery of the destination node or port.

Security

If security is a requirement in your storage network, it is advisable to use switches. This is because most of the hubs do not allow zoning, which is a common feature of Fibre Channel switches. Zoning prevents access to nodes or ports that do not belong to the same zone, thereby reducing the risk of unauthorized, malicious attacks to confidential corporate data.

Dynamic zoning also proves to be very helpful in networks where nodes (such as portable computers) are often physically relocated. Instead of moving hubs around and physically rewiring the entire setup, dynamic zoning allows the relocation of nodes without the need of physical rewiring. At the same time, the security setup is not affected.

Future Growth Potential

In a situation where the number of nodes in a storage network is small but is estimated to increase in the near future, switches prove to be an intelligent choice. Switches are highly scalable and have a higher potential for future growth. In contrast, scalability of hubs is limited because of shared bandwidth and security restrictions.

Bridges

Fibre Channel bridges allow the integration of legacy SCSI devices in a Fibre Channel network. By allowing the inclusion of expensive SCSI devices such as legacy SCSI disks and drives, SCSI tape subsystems, and optical CD and DVD devices in Fibre Channel storage networks, Fibre Channel bridges help in reducing the total cost of implementation of SANs. The biggest advantage of Fibre Channel bridges is the LAN-free backup and archiving that reduces traffic overhead from LANs by an average of 400–500%.

Fibre Channel bridges provide the capability for Fibre Channel and SCSI interfaces to support both SCSI and Fibre Channel devices seamlessly. Therefore, they are often referred to as FC-SCSI routers.

Various vendors offer Fibre Channel bridges. IBM, Gadzoox, HP, and Vixel are prominent Fibre Channel bridge vendors. The price of bridges can range from $7000 to $10,000.

Routers

Fibre Channel routers enable the integration of IP-based hosts with Fibre Channel nodes. Thus, the use of Fibre Channel routers increases the reach of SANs by allowing access to remote storage devices over IP WANs through ATM, ISDN, and T1/T3 lines. Many vendors also offer routers that provide Fibre Channel to SCSI interconnectivity. In addition, the use of intelligent routers allows the implementation of firewalls that can play a very important role in preventing unauthorized access.

Depending on the functionality provided, the cost of a Fibre Channel router can range anywhere from $7000 to $35,000. Many vendors offer a wide variety of Fibre Channel routers. These vendors include Cisco, IBM, HP, Gadzoox, and Brocade Communication, Inc. As in the field of network routers, Cisco is considered the leader in Fibre Channel routers. The following sections describe Cisco routers.

Cisco SN 5420 Storage Router

The Cisco SN 5420 storage routers allow access to storage devices anywhere on an IP network. The routers offer the complete robustness of the TCP/IP protocol suite including security, manageability, availability, and QoS. The Cisco SN 5420 storage routers also enable SCSI over IP (iSCSI) access.

The main features of these routers include the following:

- Seamless integration of legacy devices with IP applications.
- Seamless interoperability with existing LANs, WANs, metropolitan-area networks (MANs), optical devices, and storage devices.
- Familiar and easy-to-use interfaces in the form of GUI, CLI, and SNMP.
- Optimal performance and reliability.
- Enhanced security in the form of access control lists (ACLs).
- High scalability and potential of future growth.

Figure 4-12 depicts a Fibre Channel router.

Figure 4-12 *Fibre Channel Router*

| NOTE | For more information on Cisco SN 5420 storage routers, refer to the site www.cisco.com/warp/public/cc/pd/rt/5420/index.shtml. |

Cisco 7200 Series Internet Routers

The 7200 series Cisco routers provide scalable solutions based on the differing requirements of performance and availability. These routers provide a rich range of IP services over varied interfaces including OC-3, DS-3, Fast Ethernet, Gigabit Ethernet, ATM, and so on.

NOTE   For more information on Cisco 7200 Series Internet routers, refer to the site
www.cisco.com/warp/public/cc/pd/rt/7200.

Cisco 7600 Series Routers

The 7600 series Cisco routers offer high-speed optical WAN and MAN solutions that help
service providers gain the competitive edge. Similar to the 7200 series Internet routers,
7600 series routers offer seamless integration of IP networks with interfaces such as OC-3,
DS-3, Fast Ethernet, Gigabit Ethernet, ATM, and so on.

NOTE   For more information on Cisco 7600 Series Internet routers, refer to the site
www.cisco.com/warp/public/cc/pd/rt/7600osr.

Storage Devices

High-performance and reliable storage infrastructure forms the basis of storage networks.
SANs support a rich variety of storage devices that you can use to store large amounts of
data and ensure the high-speed retrieval of data. The most commonly implemented Fibre
Channel storage devices are the following:

- Disk arrays
- JBODs
- Tape libraries and subsystems
- Storage servers

The following sections describe each of these devices.

Disk Arrays

A disk array, also referred to as a Redundant Array of Inexpensive Disks (RAID) disk array,
is a set of high-performance, high-speed storage disks that can store up to several terabytes
of data. The main features of disk arrays include the following:

- **High-speed data transfers**—Disk arrays do not store data serially. Rather, large
  blocks of data are stored in parallel on several storage disks. When a large amount of
  data is accessed from or stored on the disk array, high transfer speeds are achieved by
  accessing or storing data from or to multiple storage disks in parallel.

- **High reliability**—Disk arrays offer high reliability. Even if a large number of components of the disk array fail, the overall device continues to function. Moreover, disk arrays support multiple paths to the network. As a result, problems related to a single point of failure are avoided successfully by the implementation of disk arrays.

NOTE   For detailed information on RAID technology, see Appendix A, "RAID Technology and Fibre Channel Vendors."

Disk arrays are costly Fibre Channel devices. The cost of a typical disk array ranges from $18,000 to $50,000 and up. HP, IBM, Adaptec, Veritas, and Sun Microsystems are some of the vendors of disk arrays.

JBOD

A *JBOD* is a set of multiple storage disks that you implement as one single logical volume. Data is stored redundantly on multiple disks. The use of multiple disks as one volume is referred to as *spanning*. However, the vernacular and more famous term associated with spanning in the field of storage devices is JBODs.

Unlike disk arrays, JBODs are not configured for RAID levels. As a result, they do not offer fault tolerance. Although treated as a single logical entity, JBODs do not offer high-performance in terms of access speed when compared to the independent use of constituent disks.

The price of JBODs ranges from $500 to $2000. HP, Hitachi, Compaq, Dell, Network Storage Solutions, and IBM are some of the JBOD vendors.

Tape Libraries and Subsystems

Tape storage is one of the most cost-effective and reliable backup technologies. It offers a huge storage capacity that ranges from 10 GBs to 1000 TBs. A tape library consists of a set of tape cartridges that are used to store data. In addition to the tape cartridges, a tape library also consists of a tape subsystem that includes the hardware interface to facilitate communication between the host processor and the library.

In addition to the large amount of data space that tape libraries offer, the tape cartridges are capable of mounting and dismounting automatically. This makes them highly manageable and administrator-independent.

IBM, HP, Compaq, Quantum Corp., and Compaq are some of the most well-known vendors of tape storage. Despite the huge storage space they offer, the prices of tape storage are low as compared to other storage devices. The price of tape storage ranges from $2500 to $10,000.

Storage Servers

Storage servers are the focal point of any storage infrastructure that can support a wide range of clients. These servers are high-performance, highly reliable, and scalable storage devices that can store up to several terabytes of data. You can integrate additional storage servers into the existing storage network without the need of costly upgrades.

The price of storage servers ranges from $2000 to $10,000 and up. IBM, HP, Compaq, and Cisco are some well-known storage server vendors.

Summary

Fibre Channel technology offers high-performance solutions that are a prerequisite of any SAN. In fact, most of the SANs that are built today are based on Fibre Channel devices. However, to build a successful SAN that fulfills all or most of the business requirements of a corporation, each device must be chosen with care and understanding. An intelligent mix and match of compatible products will help you as a SAN designer to build a cost-effective and high-performance storage solution.

In this chapter, you will learn about the following:

- Copper-based cabling
- Fiber-optic cabling

CHAPTER 5

Fibre Channel Cabling

Cabling is the backbone of any network, including a storage area network (SAN). Similar to any other network, if cables in a storage network haven't been implemented properly, your network can fail to live up to its expectations, no matter how sophisticated or high the performance of your infrastructure or other SAN components is.

You can use two types of Fibre Channel links in storage networks—copper-based and fiber-optic. You must understand the two types of media thoroughly to build a high-speed and high-performance SAN. In this chapter, you'll explore the two types of Fibre Channel media.

Copper-Based Cabling

Copper has been one of the most popularly used media in normal networks. The main reasons behind its popularity are that it is inexpensive, easy to implement, and capable of supporting considerably high data transfer rates. Currently, copper-based cables are used to implement Gigabit Ethernet networks, where the average data transfer rate is 1 Gbps and higher. Because of their ability to support high data transfer rates, copper-based links are also used in storage networks. However, copper-based links do not enjoy the same popularity in SANs as fiber-optic links.

NOTE   You will learn about the reasons why fiber-optic links enjoy more popularity in storage networks as compared to copper-based links later in this chapter.

Copper cables and copper-based Fibre Channel devices are attached to other Fibre Channel devices through two types of connectors:

- Copper Gigabit Interface Connectors (GBICs)
- Media Interface Adapters (MIAs)

These connectors are discussed in the following sections.

Copper GBICs

GBICs allow a wide range of copper-based transmission media to be connected to optical Fibre Channel devices. GBICs are hot-pluggable connectors that can be inserted into or removed from a Fibre Channel device while the device is still operational. They can be attached to Fibre Channel devices by using two types of connectors:

- DB-9
- High-Speed Serial Data Connectors (HSSDCs)

NOTE DB-9 connectors are also popularly called Style-1 connectors and HSSDC connectors are known as Style-2 connectors.

Figure 5-1 shows the two connectors.

Figure 5-1   *DB-9 and HSSDC Connectors*

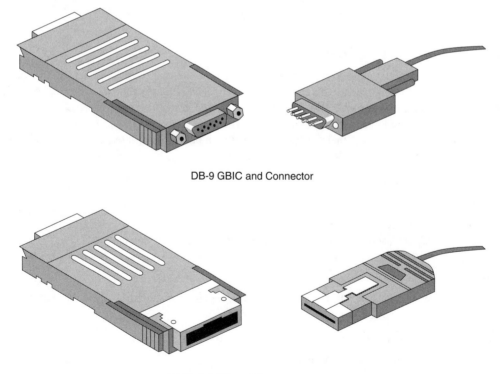

DB-9 GBIC and Connector

HSSDC GBIC and Connector

There are two types of copper GBICs—*intracabinet GBICs* and *intercabinet GBICs*. As the name suggests, intracabinet GBICs are used to connect devices located within a cabinet. The short distance between the devices and inside the cabinet connectivity helps in lowering the maximum transmitter voltage for short-length cables. The lowered transmitter voltage, in turn, brings down the problems of Electro-Static Discharge (ESD) and Electro-Magnetic Interference (EMI) that are common problems with copper transmission media.

You should use intracabinet GBICs in the following instances:

- You need to connect Fibre Channel devices that are placed in close proximity, not more than 13 meters apart.
- You do not need to provide intercabinet connectivity.

Intracabinet GBICs are low-cost GBICs that are commonly referred to as *passive GBICs* because they are not capable of regenerating or amplifying transmitted signals. This is due to the lack of corresponding circuitry. They merely pass the signals amplified by a hub or a switch to the attached Fibre Channel devices. The other reason that they are referred to as passive GBICs is because they are not capable of reporting transmission faults or signal losses. This is because TX_FAULT and RX_LOS signals of these GBICs are disabled. As a result, they fail to report any signal loss or transmission errors to the attached Fibre Channel hub or switch.

Intercabinet GBICs are used to connect Fibre Channel devices that are located outside a cabinet. As a result, these GBICs allow cable lengths beyond 13 meters. In fact, shielded twisted-pair (STP) cables can be extended up to a maximum distance of 25 meters and TW-style cables can be stretched to a maximum length of 33 meters. However, any copper cable whose length is greater than 25 meters must have a 22 or 24 wire gauge, as per intercabinet specifications. In addition, these connectors must have an equalization circuit and buffer circuitry to support higher levels of Positive Emitter Coupled Logic (PECL) signals that are transmitted by Fibre Channel devices.

You should use intercabinet GBICs in the following instances:

- The length of the cable can be more than 13 meters.
- Cable connecting the devices must have 22 or 24 wire gauge.
- ESD and EMI emissions must be at a minimum.

Intercabinet GBICs are also commonly referred to as *active GBICs*. This is because they are not only capable of regenerating the signals that they receive from attached hubs and switches, but are also capable of reporting transmission faults and signal losses. As a result, they can be managed by the attached hubs or switches.

Because intercabinet GBICs provide long-distance connectivity, extremely low ESD and EMI, and actively participate in transmissions by regenerating signals and reporting errors, they are much more expensive than passive GBICs. In fact, their cost is comparable to shortwave optical GBICs.

Table 5-1 provides at-a-glance information regarding considerations and recommendations while using intracabinet and intercabinet GBICs.

Table 5-1 *Intracabinet and Intercabinet GBICs—Recommendations and Considerations at a Glance*

	Recommendations	**Considerations**
Intracabinet GBICs	• You should use intracabinet GBICs when you need to connect Fibre Channel devices that are placed in close proximity, not more than 13 meters apart. • You do not need to provide intercabinet connectivity. • Cost of implementation is a consideration because these GBICs are less expensive.	• High EMI and ESD emissions. • Low performance.
Intercabinet GBICs	• You should use intracabinet cables when the length of the cable should be more than 13 meters. • Cable connecting the devices must have 22 or 24 wire gauge. • You should use these GBICs if you need to ensure high performance and low EMI and ESD emissions.	• Expensive. In fact, their cost is comparable to optical GBICs.

NOTE   For more information on considerations and recommendations for implementing copper GBICs, refer to the white paper, "Guidelines for implementing Fibre Channel with copper" by Rick Swanson. The URL of the Web site where you can find this white paper is www.vixel.com/whitepapers/whtppr1.pdf.

You will now learn about the second category of connectors that are used to connect copper-based cables to Fibre Channel devices in a storage network—MIAs.

Media Interface Adapters

Media Interface Adapters (MIAs) are used to attach Fibre Channel devices that use copper-based HBAs to optical fiber links. MIAs are used when you need to extend the distance of a Fibre Channel link to the corresponding hub or switch beyond the stipulated length of 33 meters. Unlike GBICs that can be attached to Fibre Channel devices either through DB-9 or HSSDC connectors, MIAs can be attached to Fibre Channel devices only through DB-9 connectors.

Beyond extending the length of copper-based cables and converting the Fibre Channel copper interface to an optical interface, MIAs have more disadvantages associated with them than advantages. The major disadvantages of MIAs include the following:

- No support for the popular HSSDC interface
- No protection from high EMI
- No capability of reporting signal losses and transmission errors
- High cost of implementation, which increases the Total Cost of Ownership (TCO) of the storage network without justifying the high cost

Although more expensive than copper-based cables, fiber-optic cables are the preferred means of linking Fibre Channel devices in a SAN. The following section looks at fiber-optic cabling in detail.

Fiber-Optic Cabling

Copper-based cabling solutions were preferred in normal networks until a few years ago. However, due to the fast emergence of speed- and data-intensive transactions over local networks, intranets, and the Internet, fiber-optic has been replacing copper-based cables. In fact, fiber-optic cables have emerged as the undisputed choice in the field of Fibre Channel-based networks.

To understand why fiber-optic cabling has replaced copper in the present scenario, you need to understand the basics of fiber-optic technology. A fiber-optic cable consists of a *core*, *cladding*, and a *plastic encasement*.

The core is the innermost part of the cable, which provides the path for the transmission of a light wave. Therefore, the core is also referred to as a *waveguide*.

The cladding is the tough and resilient sheath that covers the core. It is made up of multiple layers of glass, where each layer has a different refractive index. As a result, the light signals are refracted back into the core and are prevented from being leaked out.

NOTE   Core and cladding are considered as *active components* of a fiber-optic cable because they are actively involved in signal transmissions.

The core and cladding are encased in a plastic sheath, which can tightly or loosely surround the cladding. This sheath provides the necessary cable strength and protects the cladding and core of the fiber-optic cable from elements, such as excessive heat, bending, stretching, or breaking.

If the encasement is fitted loosely around active components, the outer protective sheath is filled with a gel. This gel provides the extra strength and protection to the cladding and the core. The tightly fitted outer sheath contains strength wires that completely surround the active components. These strength wires are generally made up of Kevlar, which is used in manufacturing bulletproof jackets. This makes the optical cable more tensile.

Figures 5-2 and 5-3 depict the loose and tight configurations along with the main components of a fiber-optic cable.

Figure 5-2   *Fiber-Optic Cable with Loose Configuration*

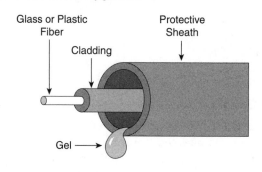

Figure 5-3   *Fiber-Optic Cable with Tight Configuration*

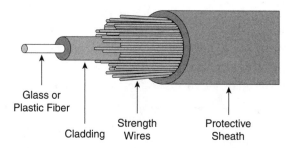

In the next section, you'll learn about the two types of fiber-optic cables—single-mode and multimode cables.

Types of Fiber-Optic Cables

Depending on the diameter of the core of the fiber-optic cable, there are two types of optical cables—single-mode and multimode. Both of these are discussed in the following sections.

Multimode Fiber-Optic Cables

Multimode cables provide multiple paths for the passage of light signals. The different refractive indexes of various layers of the cladding reflect the light at different angles. This is known as *mode dispersion*. Because of mode dispersion, the original light signal is bent at different angles, which causes the signal to be broken into parts.

In addition, the refractive index and physical properties of the layers of cladding ensure that the separated parts of the signal arrive simultaneously at the destination. Therefore, the recipient always receives a single signal. Figure 5-4 depicts the propagation of a light signal in multimode fiber-optic cables.

Figure 5-4   *Propagation of a Signal in a Multimode Fiber-Optic Cable*

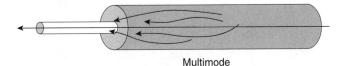

Multimode

There are two types of multimode fiber-optic cables—*50/125 micron* and *62.5/125 micron*. Figures 5-5 and 5-6 depict the cross-section of 50/125 and 62.5/125 micron multimode cables. The parameters of these two multimode optical cables are specified in Table 5-2.

Figure 5-5   *50/125 Micron Multimode Fiber-Optic Cable*

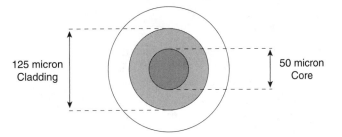

Figure 5-6   *62.5/125 Micron Multimode Fiber-Optic Cable*

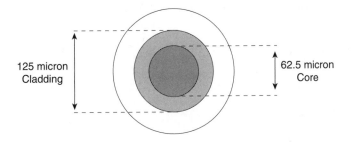

Table 5-2 *The Parameters of 50/125 and 62.5/125 Multimode Cables*

Cable Type	Core Diameter	Cladding Diameter	Maximum Distance	Data Transfer Rate
50/125	50 micron	125 micron	500 meters	133 Mbps
62.5/125	62.5 micron	125 micron	Approximately 250 meters	133 Mbps

NOTE There is a third category of multimode cables—*100/140 micron*. Cables of this category are not popular anymore because of the better performance of its other two counterparts.

As you can infer from Table 5-2, the smaller the diameter of the core of the fiber-optic cable, the further the signal is propagated. This is because a light wave enters the fiber as a focused beam consisting of millions of rays. These light rays hit the internal walls of the core at an angle and are reflected back into the core at the same angle. At the same time, the light ray also undergoes refraction (scattering, in layman's terminology). The bigger the diameter of the core, the more scattered the light rays will be. As a result, light loses some of its intensity. On the other hand, the smaller the diameter of the core, the less scattered the light ray will be and the greater its intensity.

Single-Mode, Fiber-Optic Cables

These fiber-optic cables provide a single path for the propagation of light waves. This is because the core of single-mode optical cables is made up of a uniform index. At the same time, cladding has a lower index of refraction. As a result, only a single mode of signal propagation is possible and the light wave is not broken into parts, as in multimode signal propagations. Figure 5-7 depicts the propagation of a light signal through a single-mode, fiber-optic cable.

Figure 5-7 *Propagation of a Signal in a Single-Mode, Fiber-Optic Cable*

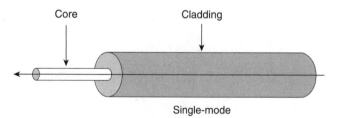

Core   Cladding

Single-mode

The physical characteristics of a single-mode, fiber-optic cable are the following:

- Core diameter: 9 micron
- Cladding diameter: 125 micron
- Maximum distance: 10 kilometers
- Data transfer rates: 1.063 Gbps

Figure 5-8 depicts the cross-section of single-mode, fiber-optic cables.

Figure 5-8   *Single-Mode Fiber-Optic Cable*

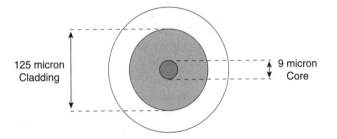

In the next section, you learn about the connectors used in fiber-optic cabling.

Fiber-Optic Connectors

The two fiber-optic connectors that are predominantly used with optical cables are *568SC connectors* and *optical GBICs*.

Standardized by ANSI TIA/EIA-568A under X3T9.3 specification, 568SC connectors are color-coded duplex connectors that allow for easy connections and reconnections. These are push and pull type connectors and are keyed to prevent cross-mating or incorrect connection of connectors. According to the color code used in these connectors, multimode connectors and adapters are identified by beige color, whereas single-mode adapters and connectors are blue in color. Figure 5-9 depicts a 568SC connector.

Optical GBICs are used with fiber-optic cables to convert optical signals to electrical signals and vice versa. Figure 5-10 depicts an optical GBIC. *Shortwave* and *longwave* optical GBICs are available. Shortwave GBICs are used to connect multimode optical cables that can extend up to a distance of 240 meters in the case of 62.5/125-micron cables and 500 meters in the case of 50/125-micron cables. Longwave GBICs are used to connect single-mode cables that can extend up to a distance of 10 kilometers.

Now that you are familiar with the basic components of fiber-optic cabling, in the next section you'll learn to plan and implement them.

Figure 5-9   *568SC Connector*

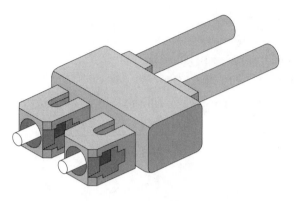

Figure 5-10   *An Optical GBIC*

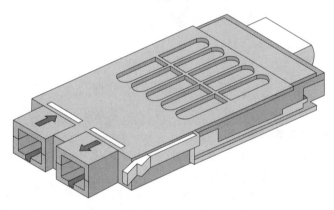

Planning and Implementing Fiber-Optic Cables

When implementing the fiber-optic cabling system, you need to ensure that it is compatible with the existing infrastructure as much as possible. At the same time, you must ensure that the cabling justifies its high cost of implementation. Cabling also plays an important role in the future growth of a network. Therefore, planning is one of the most important aspects of implementing the cabling system.

You need to answer the following questions while planning to implement fiber-optic cables in a storage network:

- At what rate approximately will the network grow?
- Will you need to reshuffle the equipment a lot?
- How often will you need to add or upgrade the equipment?
- What type of cabling do you require?
- How will you trace cables?

There are no common answers to these questions, and answers vary from one organization to another and from one situation to another. You'll need to assess the organization's requirements, budget, and future growth prospects thoroughly to be able to answer these questions correctly. The following sections consider some of the factors involved in implementing fiber-optic solutions.

Fiber-Optic Cabling Considerations

In addition to answering the preceding questions, you must consider the following facts to install fiber-optic links that can support any protocol successfully along with the high speed of data transactions:

- Connectors must be chosen keeping losses, back reflectance, and performance in mind. If you fail to choose the right connectors, attenuation of the optical signal is possible because of scattering or absorption.

NOTE   Back reflectance is the scattering of a light wave in the direction opposite to its direction of propagation so that the scattered light portion reflects back to the input end of the cable. The term loss in fiber-optic terminology refers to a decrease in the strength of an optical signal caused by absorption and scattering. Loss is measured in dB/Kilometer.

- Multimode fiber-optic links cannot contain mixed fiber diameters in the same link. They cause high signal losses.
- Different protocols being used in SANs demand different drive specifications and link budgets over the same fiber-optic link. You should consider these requirements carefully before choosing the type of cable for your network.
- The use of fusion or mechanical splices must be considered carefully because they can further add to the cost of the implementation of the SAN.
- Many fiber-optic links, especially the ones that use duplex connectors, require that the transmitter end of a device be connected to the receiver end of the other device and vice versa. However, other cabling systems that are more generic and that do not use duplex connectors might not support this polarity. Therefore, it is important to test cables to ensure correct polarization while implementing fiber-optic cabling for your storage network.
- With the quantum development in the field of laser technology, the old LED-based infrastructure might not be able to support new Fibre Channel protocols seamlessly. However, a mismatch between the two technologies might lead to an extensive loss of signal strength and data if not implemented properly.

With these considerations in mind, you can now plan for your fiber-optic cabling. The following section provides recommendations.

Fiber-Optic Cabling Recommendations

This section reviews some recommendations to help you plan for a stable and resilient fiber-optic cabling system. Following are some recommendations and best practices:

- Ensure that you obtain complete documentation and performance parameters from the manufacturer or vendor of the cable that you are using. This will help you get acquainted to the product, and determine and implement the optimal parameters according to your organization's requirements.

- Ensure that you provide detailed documentation that contains extensive information about the cabling scheme, labeling strategy of the cables, how to trace cables in case problems arise, vendor-supplied cable parameters, and so on. A detailed documentation helps you to locate faults quickly and troubleshoot them without having to waste additional time. Documentation also proves to be helpful for other people while troubleshooting or understanding the cable layout in your absence.

- Use jumper cabling for small storage networks that have little chance of large-scale future growth. This is because jumper cabling uses a large number of cables. If used in a large network, the sheer number of cables would become unmanageable.

- Use jumper cabling if you need to ensure consistent performance and loss characteristics throughout the cabling system. However, you must use high-quality, factory-terminated jumper cables. This is because, no matter how much expertise you might have, there is a slightly greater possibility of signal loss if you terminate the cables on site. However, the signal loss in factory-terminated cables is minimal because cables are terminated according to the exact specifications. There is also less chance of human error.

- Implement structured cabling if the future growth of a storage network is probable because it is far easier to add new devices without the headache of re-cabling the entire setup.

- Implement structured cabling for large-scale storage networks because the volume of cables that must be managed in structured cabling is significantly less than in jumper cabling.

NOTE   Against popular belief, structured cabling is also highly recommended by experts for small-scale storage networks. Before deciding between jumper and structured cabling, remember that no network is static in nature. New devices and techniques will continue to be implemented into the network over time. Your organization might save a lot of expense at the moment by implementing jumper cabling, but because of the scope of future growth, easy manageability, and the restructuring capability that structured cabling has to offer, structured cabling outweighs its cost of implementation. As a result, structured cabling might prove to be an intelligent solution in the long run.

The next section sheds light on the reasons that have made fiber-optic cabling a success story.

Advantages of Fiber-Optic Cabling

There are many reasons behind the undisputed success of fiber-optic technology in the arena of storage networks. Some of the most important advantages that fiber-optic cables offer are listed here:

- **Immunity from EMI, RFI, and ESD**—EMI, ESD, and RFI, which are the major causes of signal loss in copper-based cables, are nonexistent problems in fiber-optic cabling. This is because these cables do not operate on electric signals. Fiber-optic cables operate on optical signals that are insusceptible to cross talk, electromagnetic field, electrostatic discharge, or Radio Frequency Interference (RFI). As a result, fiber-optic cables can be run through severe electrical environments without deteriorating the quality of signals. This is the reason why fiber-optic cables are used in and around manufacturing and industrial sites. For the same reasons, fiber-optic cables are predominantly used in airports.

- **Low attenuation**—*Attenuation* is the property of an electrical signal to become progressively distorted and weakened during a transmission. The longer the distance the signal has to traverse, the more distorted it becomes. This is because the energy of electrical signals is absorbed by the medium and surrounding environment. Fiber-optic cables, however, being optical signals, have lower attenuation rates. Multimode cables have an attenuation rate of 1 dB per kilometer, whereas single-mode cables have an attenuation rate of 0.2 dB per kilometer, as compared to the attenuation rate of 10 dB per kilometer in copper cables. As a result, optical signals can traverse longer distances without much loss in signal strength. In addition, attenuation in copper cables increases proportionately with an increase in frequency. On the other hand, fiber-optic cables boast a flat rate of attenuation. This means that the attenuation rate in fiber-optic cables remains almost constant despite any increase in signal frequency.

- **High bandwidth**—Fiber-optic cables offer high bandwidths that range from 100 Mbps to 2 Gbps. These high bandwidths are possible because of the high frequency, low wavelength photon properties of light signals that are used in fiber-optic cables.

- **Reliable and safe transmissions**—The error rate in fiber-optic transmissions is 10^{-12}, which means one error per trillion bits! This extremely low error rate in the fiber-optic medium is attributed to the fact that light signals are least susceptible to EMI, ESD, or atmospheric disturbances. Therefore, optical cables are considered to be extremely reliable transmission media. Moreover, it is extremely difficult to electronically eavesdrop into optical cables because they do not emit radiations or electromagnetic pulses. Therefore, fiber-optic cables also offer high levels of transmission security.

- **Safety from electrical hazards**—Electrical hazards, such as short-circuits, sparks, and spark-induced fires, are commonplace in copper-based cables. However, because electrical signals are not used in optical cabling, such hazards are nonexistent.

- **Easy maintainability**—In addition to high bandwidth, high data transfer rates, reliability, and transmission security, fiber-optic cables are not susceptible to moisture, corrosion, or degradation. Therefore, fiber-optic cables require less maintenance than copper wires. In addition, fiber-optic cables are capable of tolerating temperatures within a wide range—from –40˚F to 200˚F.

- **Cost-effectiveness**—Fiber-optic cabling is definitely more expensive than copper-based cabling systems. However, because of all the advantages they offer, the implementation of fiber-optic cables amply justifies the slightly higher cost of implementation. Intense competition among fiber-optic vendors and rapid advancement in the field of optical cables has led to a considerable reduction in the cost of fiber-optic cables. Therefore, fiber-optic cabling is proving to be more cost-effective than ever.

Fiber-optic vendors and industry experts are working toward cost-effective, easy-to-install optical cabling solutions. Given the rate at which fiber optics is taking over network implementations, copper-based cabling will soon become obsolete in storage networks where high-speed transactions, minimum error rate, and security of data in transit is not just desired but is a necessity. Moreover, copper-based cabling is not at all effective for long-distance connectivity (tens and hundreds of kilometers). Despite popular belief, the implementation of optical cables is not difficult, if not downright simple. Moreover, optical cables in your SAN would allow an unhindered growth and expansion of your storage networks in the near future.

Types of Fiber-Optic Cabling

You can implement fiber-optic cabling in your storage network in two ways. You can use jumper cabling or structured cabling, as discussed in the following sections.

Jumper Cabling

In this cabling system, jumper cables are used to connect one Fibre Channel device directly to another. Because individual cables are used to connect Fibre Channel devices, the number of cables in this system is large. As long as the storage network is small in size, it is fairly easy to manage the cables in the network. However, consistent expansion and growth of the network makes the addition or relocation of cables running under the floor a difficult task. After a while, the sheer number of cables can grow to such an extent that their management could become a full-time task. Figure 5-11 depicts an example of a typical jumper cabling setup.

Figure 5-11 *Jumper Cabling*

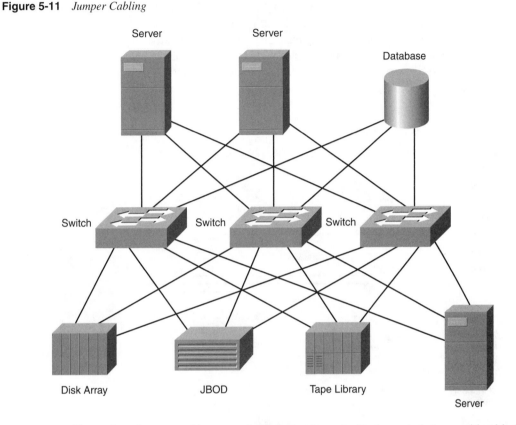

The major advantage of jumper cabling is that it can be implemented at a considerably low cost, as compared to the other method of fiber-optic cabling—structured cabling.

Structured Cabling

In this cabling system, fiber trunk cables, patch panels, and patch cables are used extensively to reduce the number of individual cables running under the floor. For example, instead of 36 individual cables running from various Fibre Channel devices to a single destination, all the cables can be connected to a 36-channel trunk cable. This single-trunk cable, in turn, can be connected to the destination device. As a result, instead of a large number of cables crowding the entire installation, only a few cables need to be extended over longer distances. This not only makes the cabling system highly manageable, but also brings down the cost of implementation of the storage network.

NOTE   Besides the more popular 36-channel version, trunk cables are also available in 6-, 18-, and 72-channel versions. IBM also offers a 256-channel trunk cable.

The *Central Patching Location (CPL)* plays an important role in structured cabling. A CPL generally consists of numerous cabinets. These cabinets contain patch panels, to which Fibre Channel devices are connected. Short jumper cables are used to connect Fibre Channel devices to one of the duplex ports of the patch panel. Finally, trunk cables are used to connect to destination device(s). Figure 5-12 depicts a typical example of structured cabling.

Figure 5-12 *Structured Cabling*

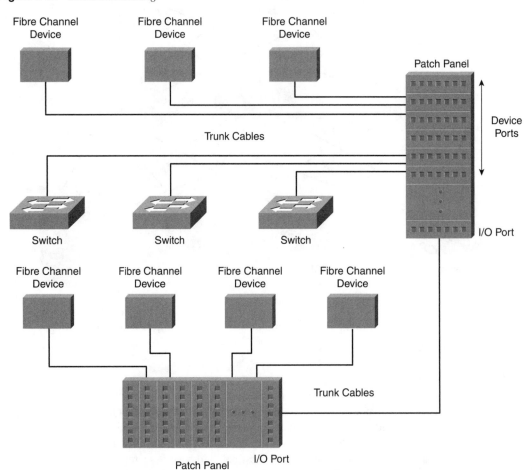

This cabling system is extremely effective in long distance campus connectivity, where trunk cables can be extended from one building to another. With the advancement in fiber-optic technology, structured cabling systems will soon be used to provide connectivity solutions for geographically dispersed locations. Other major advantages of structured cabling include the following:

- Drastic reduction in number of cables in the entire setup
- Easy manageability and traceability of cables that facilitate the troubleshooting of cable-related problems
- Easy accommodation of the extensive future growth of the network
- Cost-effective implementation of cabling that reduces the TCO of the entire SAN
- Quick and easy installation
- Ease of reconfiguration

You will now look at how you can implement structured cabling in your storage network. Figure 5-13 depicts an example of fiber-optic connectivity in a storage network.

Figure 5-13   *Structured Cabling in a Storage Network*

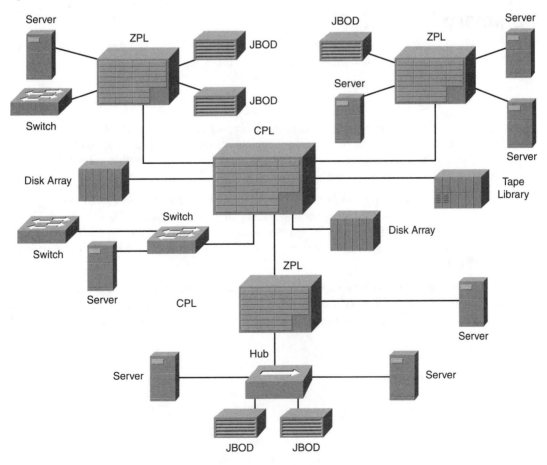

Figure 5-13 shows a storage network where fiber-optic structured cabling has been implemented. The CPL acts as the focal point of the entire cabling system. The CPL is directly connected to a few SAN devices and connected to several Zone Patching Locations (ZPLs), which are used to segregate the SAN into various zones.

A zone is a logical division of a SAN and can consist of several SAN devices, which can communicate with each other. However, inter-zonal communication is restricted to a minimum as a security measure. See Chapter 8, "Implementing SAN Security," for more information on zones.

The SAN depicted in Figure 5-13 is geared up to accommodate future growth. Whenever a new device is introduced into the storage network, it can be directly connected to either the CPL or to any of the ZPLs in the storage network. If a large number of devices are added to the network, they can be easily accommodated; you just need to connect more ZPLs to the CPLs.

Summary

In this chapter, you learned about the two ways of implementing Fibre Channel links in a storage network. These include the use of the following:

- Copper-based cabling
- Fiber-optic cabling

Copper-based cables work with the help of copper GBICs and MIAs. However, copper links do not satisfy the inherent requirements of high-speed, error-free, and secure transactions because they can be tapped into and are extremely susceptible to EMI, ESD, RFI, cross talk, and atmospheric conditions.

Therefore, fiber-optic cabling has emerged as the unrivalled cabling option in storage networks. Fiber-optic cables not only satisfy all the requirements of a SAN, but they are also largely unaffected by atmospheric conditions. However, there is a slight hitch. Fiber-optic cables are extremely expensive in comparison to copper cables and require special skills to handle.

Fiber-optic cables can be implemented in two ways—jumper cabling system and structured cabling system. Of the two, the structured cabling system has become the darling of administrators and experts because it is much easier to manage and provides ample future growth opportunities.

In this chapter, you will learn about the following:

- Point-to-point topology
- FC-AL topology
- Fibre Channel switched Fabric topology

CHAPTER **6**

SAN Topologies

A *storage area network (SAN)* is based on Fibre Channel technology. Therefore, the three SAN topologies—point-to-point, Fibre Channel-Arbitrated Loop (FC-AL), and switched Fabric—are the same as Fibre Channel topologies. Of these three, FC-AL and switched Fabric are implemented more commonly because they are cost-effective, high-performing, and scalable. Although the point-to-point topology offers the best performance of the three, it incurs high costs and, therefore, is used only in specialized cases. An effective mix of these three topologies can be implemented to meet the specific requirements and needs of a corporation.

Point-to-Point Topology

The point-to-point topology is the simplest and the fastest of the three SAN topologies. In this topology, a Fibre Channel link connects two nodes, as shown in Figure 6-1. The maximum length of the link depends on the type of cabling you use. If the Fibre Channel link is copper-based, the maximum length of the link is barely 30 meters. However, the use of optical fiber cables can stretch the link beyond 100 kilometers.

Because the point-to-point topology provides a dedicated connection between two devices, other network traffic does not affect the communication. This allows the devices sharing the point-to-point connection to use the full bandwidth of the link.

Before the two devices in the point-to-point topology can communicate successfully, the link needs to be initialized. Link initialization is important because unique port addresses are assigned dynamically to the two devices during link initialization.

Point-to-point topology is not very cost-effective because separate Fibre Channel links must be established between nodes, which is a very expensive exercise. This topology is best suited for specialized situations where two nodes communicate with each other frequently and the data being transferred between the two nodes is bandwidth-intensive. For example, a server might need to frequently communicate with a storage device so that the server can forward data to its clients.

Figure 6-1   *Point-to-Point SAN Topology*

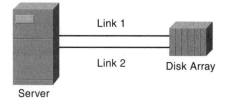

Extending Point-to-Point Connections

As shown in Figure 6-2, the point-to-point topology allows a node or a storage device to be connected to more than one node at the same time. However, this is possible only when the node or the storage device supports more than one Node Port (N_Port). In this case, each connected device enjoys a dedicated connection. This dedicated connection means that simultaneously occurring communications do not interfere with a point-to-point communication. However, if a node that is connected to multiple nodes is not high-performance, simultaneous connections can adversely affect the performance of the node because a low-performance processor cannot take the high load and slows down considerably. This in turn can bring down the performance of other high-performance nodes connected to this slow node.

Figure 6-2   *A Node Supporting Multiple Point-to-Point Connections*

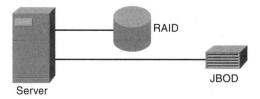

FC-AL Topology

Fashioned after the Token Ring topology used in a local-area network (LAN), FC-AL is a cost-effective method of connecting up to 126 nodes to a Fibre Channel link. All the connected nodes share the available bandwidth. Similar to the Token Ring topology, frames can travel only in one direction. A typical FC-AL topology setup is shown in Figure 6-3.

All the connected nodes must arbitrate for access to a loop. After a node gains control of the loop, it establishes a virtual point-to-point connection with the intended destination and begins data transfer. Because of the virtual point-to-point connection, the communicating nodes can use the full bandwidth of the Fibre Channel link. When a connection is terminated, the loop becomes available to other nodes. After the data transfer is complete, the node need not give up control of the loop. However, FC-AL protocols ensure that all the nodes connected to the loop have a fair chance of controlling the loop.

Figure 6-3   *FC-AL SAN Topology*

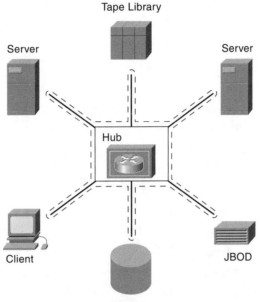

Because loop operations demand high performance, fiber-optic links are predominantly used in FC-AL. Therefore, the maximum length of the link that forms the loop is 10 kilometers. However, because of the increased overhead generated by arbitration, the larger the number of nodes supported by the loop, the lower its overall performance.

The arbitration to gain control of the loop and other shared functions are controlled by *loop protocols*, such as SCSI-3. These protocols are responsible for the following:

- Initializing the loop
- Assigning addresses to the loop nodes
- Controlling loop arbitration
- Ensuring that each loop node has a fair opportunity of gaining control of the loop
- Establishing a virtual dedicated connection between two communicating nodes
- Terminating a connection

The FC-AL topology is generally used in the following cases:

- Situations where you need to interconnect storage devices
- Situations where multiple nodes that require high-bandwidth connections need to be supported by the link

Fibre Channel loops can be categorized on the basis of their connectivity or non-connectivity to the rest of the Fabric. The following section discusses various Fibre Channel loops.

Types of FC-AL Loops

Fibre Channel loops are of two types—*private* and *public*. Private loops are not connected to the Fabric. Therefore, the nodes of a private loop are inaccessible to the nodes that do not belong to the loop. Figure 6-4 shows a private loop.

Figure 6-4   *A Private Loop*

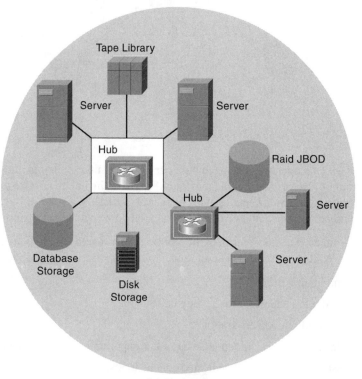

Private Loop

NOTE   The two left-most bytes of addresses of the nodes belonging to a private loop are always 0.

Public loops, in contrast to private loops, are connected to the Fabric through at least one FL_Port. Hence, they are accessible to other nodes that are not a part of the loop. Figure 6-5 shows a public loop.

Figure 6-5   *A Public Loop*

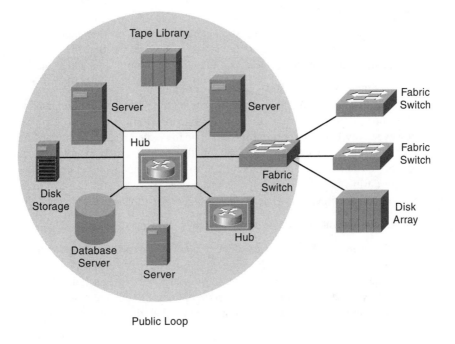

Public Loop

NOTE   The two left-most bytes of addresses of the nodes that belong to a public loop contain a positive value other than 0.

States of FC-AL Loops

The operations of a loop are associated with five states—*loop initialization*, *loop monitoring*, *loop arbitration*, *open loop*, and *close loop*. Each of these states is discussed in the following sections.

The Loop Initialization State

When a new node is introduced into a loop or when a port becomes active, the loop enters the loop initialization state. The loop initialization process consists of the following:

- Allocating an Arbitrated Loop-Physical Address (AL-PA) to all the loop ports
- Gathering information about the new device, or node, that has been added to the loop

The AL-PA and other information gathered about all the existing loop ports and the new node or port that has been introduced into the loop is maintained in the form of *positional maps*. A positional map contains the total number of active loop ports, their addresses, and the physical positions of all the ports in the loop.

Only after a loop has been initialized can it begin with normal loop operations. The process of loop initialization is completed in a matter of few milliseconds. However, loop initialization can take slightly longer if the number of ports attached to the loop is large.

The maximum number of nodes in a loop is limited to 127. This is because the AL-PA is a dynamically assigned address, which is used by the ports for communication and loop arbitration purposes. Because an AL-PA is one byte long, it can have 256 possible values. However, only 127 values are considered valid to maintain neutral Running Disparity (RD), which is required by the 8B/10B coding method. Therefore, if the total number of nodes connected to the loop is greater than 127, some of the nodes might not be assigned an AL-PA during loop initialization. As a result, these ports cannot take part in the arbitration process and are prevented from establishing a connection or transferring data.

The loop initialization process consists of the following steps:

1   When an NL_Port becomes active or a new node (or port) is added to the loop, they issue *Loop Initialization Primitives (LIPs)*. The LIPs consist of at least three identical ordered sets that trigger the loop initialization process. Each downstream node that receives the LIP suspends any current operations and enters the *open-init* state. The loop initialization process cannot begin until all the loop nodes enter the open-init state.

2   After all the current loop operations have been suspended, all NL_Ports start transmitting the *Loop Initialization Select Master (LISM)* frames. These frames initiate the process of selecting a temporary *loop master*, which is responsible for further initialization, management, and closure of the loop. If the loop is a public loop, the Fabric is selected as the temporary loop master. Otherwise, the port with the lowest Port_Name identifier, also known as *World Wide Port Name (W-WPN)*, is selected as the loop master. When a loop master has been selected, the loop master issues a special ordered set to notify other loop nodes that it will act as the temporary loop master.

3 After the loop master has been selected, all loop ports (NL_Ports attached to the loop) select an AL-PA. The loop master issues an AL-PA bitmap frame that contains all the valid 127 AL-PA addresses. Each downstream port that receives this bitmap frame selects the value that will act as its AL-PA and places the frame back on the loop for the next node. When all NL_Ports have selected an AL-PA (that is the bitmap frame has visited all loop ports), the frame returns to the loop master.

NOTE   After receiving the bitmap frame, the loop master can issue two additional frames if they are supported by all the loop nodes and ports. The *Loop Initialization Report Position (LIRP)* frame traverses the entire loop to determine the position of all NL_Ports in relation to the position of the loop master. The *Loop Initialization Loop Position (LILP)* frame allows each loop port to know its position on the loop based on information collected by the LIRP frame.

---

4 After each port has been assigned a valid AL_PA, the loop master issues the CLS primitive signal to notify the end of the loop initialization process. This primitive signal allows all the loop ports to resume normal loop operations.

After the loop initialization process is completed, the loop ports enter the loop monitoring state. This state is discussed in the following section.

The Loop Monitoring State

No activity occurs in the loop monitoring state. Idle primitives traverse the loop. The loop ports merely forward these primitives to the next downstream port. The loop is considered to be closed in this state, allowing ports to arbitrate for loop control if they need to transmit data to another port. When a port notifies the rest of the nodes about its intention to gain control of the loop, the loop enters the loop arbitration state.

The Loop Arbitration State

A port must arbitrate to gain control of the loop before it can communicate with another port. To do so, it transmits the Arbitrate primitive signal, ARB(x). Here, x is the AL-PA of the port that issued the arbitrate primitive signal. If the signal traverses the loop and returns to the originator port, the port has successfully gained control of the loop and can begin communication with the intended destination port.

If more than one port is arbitrating to gain control of the loop, their AL_PA plays an important role in deciding which port ultimately controls the loop. When an arbitrating port issues its ARB(x) signal to notify others about its intention to gain control of the loop, the signal is passed down from port to port. When another port that needs to arbitrate for loop control receives the signal, it compares the value of x (AL-PA) received in the signal with its own AL-PA. The ARB(x) signal with the lower value of x is forwarded, while the ARB(x) signal with the higher value of x is blocked. This procedure takes place at all the nodes that are arbitrating for loop control. Finally, only the arbitrating port with the lowest value of x receives its own ARB(x) signal back, thus gaining control of the loop.

After a port has gained control of the loop, it opens the loop at its end to prevent further arbitration.

The Open Loop State

After a port gains control of the loop, it sends the Open (OPN) primitive signal to the destination port with which it wants to communicate. This signal can be in either of the following two formats:

- **OPN(y, x)**—This signal notifies the destination port that the connection being requested is full duplex.

- **OPN(y, y)**—This signal notifies the destination port that the connection being requested is half-duplex.

NOTE   Here, y is the AL-PA of the destination port, whereas x represents the AL-PA of the source (or originator) port.

On receiving the OPN primitive signal, the destination port enters the open state by physically opening the loop at its end. When both the source and the destination ports have opened the loop, a logical point-to-point connection is established between the two ports. The dedicated point-to-point connection allows the full use of link bandwidth because no other transaction can take place while the loop is in the open state.

NOTE   After a transaction is complete, the source port need not give up loop control. This indicates the channel characteristic of the Fibre Channel. However, loop protocols ensure that a port does not regain loop control until all the other nodes have had a fair chance to access the loop.

The Close Loop State

After a transaction is complete, either of the communicating ports can initiate the procedure to close the loop. To do so, the port must send the Close (CLS) primitive signal to the other port. After issuing the CLS signal, the port cannot transmit any more frames. However, the other end can continue to send frames until it finishes the current operation. It then responds to the earlier CLS signal with its own CLS primitive signal. When both the communicating ends receive the CLS signal from the opposite end, the ports close the loop and return to the monitoring state.

Loop Addressing

To identify a node in a LAN, a 48-bit (six-byte) Media Access Control (MAC) address is used. This MAC address is permanent and is hard-coded (embedded) into the node's network interface card (NIC). In contrast, Fibre Channel uses a three-byte native address identifier to identify a port. This address is formed dynamically during the loop initialization process or Fabric login.

In arbitrated loops, the first (upper or left-most) two bytes represent the loop identifier. If the loop is private, these two bytes of address identifiers of all the loop ports contain 0s. In case of public loops, the two left-most bytes represent the *loop identifier*, which identifies a loop in the Fabric. The loop identifier is common to all ports that are attached to a given loop. Therefore, the upper two bytes of all ports that belong to a given loop are the same.

NOTE   Addresses in the range of Hex FFFFFE to Hex FFFFFF are referred to as *well-known addresses* and are reserved for well-known components of a SAN, such as Fabric, multicast servers, and alias servers. Hex FFFFFF is reserved for Fibre Channel broadcasts.

The last byte of a port address in public and private loops is formed by an *AL-PA*. An AL-PA is an 8-bit address, which means 256 (2^8) values of the address are possible. However, according to the 8B/10B encoding method, values must have a neutral RD. This leaves only 134 valid values out of the original 256. Of these 134 values, only 127 values are available for AL-PA addresses. The rest are used as control functions.

The AL-PA addresses are dynamically allocated to the ports during initialization of the loop. The loop master sends a bitmap frame of 127 addresses to all the attached ports. Each port selects a value and passes the frame to the next downstream port. The frame continues to traverse the loop until all the loop ports have been assigned an AL-PA. In private loops, an AL-PA assigned to a port during the loop initialization process remains unchanged until the next loop initialization. However, a Fabric switch can modify the AL-PA of a port belonging to a public loop when the port attempts Fabric login.

The lower the value of an AL-PA, the higher its priority during the arbitration process. For example, a port with AL-PA value 00000001 has better chances of gaining loop control than another port whose AL-PA value is 00000101. Generally, servers in the loop are assigned lower AL-PAs to ensure them high priority. However, storage devices, such as Just a Bunch of Disks (JBODs) and disk arrays, are assigned higher AL-PAs (lower priority). Figure 6-6 represents the loop-addressing scheme.

Figure 6-6 *Loop-Addressing Scheme*

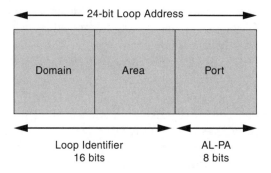

Loop Logins

Fibre Channel supports two types of login procedures that allow a port to communicate with other ports through the underlying Fabric. These login procedures include *port login* and *Fabric login*.

- **Port login (PLOGI)**—The PLOGI procedure establishes a session between two N_Ports before the two can communicate. The port that originates the connection sends a PLOGI frame to the destination port. The destination port, in response, sends an Accept (ACC) frame to the originator port. Service parameters are exchanged after the two ports identify each other successfully. PLOGI also establishes the classes of service that are mutually supported along with the flow control mechanism.

- **Fabric login (FLOGI)**—The FLOGI procedure helps a Fabric switch to identify N_Ports and NL_Ports that are attached directly or indirectly to it. The port that initiated the FLOGI procedure sends a FLOGI frame to the well-known address, Hex FFFFFE. At the same time, the port identifies itself with the hexadecimal address

000000, which indicates that the port still needs to be assigned a Fabric address. This FLOGI frame contains the Node_Name of the source port (N_Port or NL_Port), Port_Name of the source port, and expected service parameters. When the switch accepts the login, it responds with an ACC frame. If the switch does not support any of the requested parameters, it notifies the source port by setting the appropriate bits in the ACC frame.

NL_Ports are already assigned an address during the loop initialization process. Therefore, when they log on to the Fabric, the switch verifies whether their port address is unique. If the NL_Port address is unique, the port is successfully logged in. If not, the NL_Port initiates another loop initialization process to obtain another port address, after which it re-attempts the FLOGI procedure.

NOTE	Until the FLOGI procedure, the N_Ports are not assigned port addresses. Therefore, the Fabric assigns a unique port address to these ports and notifies them about the same through the ACC response frame.

Process login (PRLI) is a third type of login procedure that is supported by N_Ports. This login procedure establishes the environment between two communicating processes that are located at the respective ports. System and high-level applications are examples of processes that are involved in the PRLI procedures.

Extending the Loop

The FC-AL topology is based on hubs, which are used to connect all loop devices. Figure 6-7 depicts the simplest FC-AL, where a single hub is used. In Figure 6-7, the disk array and the database are connected to the hub by using an additional backup link. The backup link is redundant and takes over if the main link fails. In this manner, the backup link is used to ensure full-time connectivity of these devices to the hub (and therefore the loop).

Because the number of ports offered by a FC-AL hub are limited, the loop can support only a specific number of devices. You can extend an existing loop by adding more hubs. Figure 6-8 and Figure 6-9 depict a loop where two hubs are used. In these figures, the loops are *non-cascaded*. This means that although the hubs are connected to each server and storage device, they are not interconnected. Figure 6-8 depicts a short-distance loop, whereas the loop depicted in Figure 6-9 extends at least one kilometer.

Figure 6-7 *Simplest FC-AL Using a Single Hub*

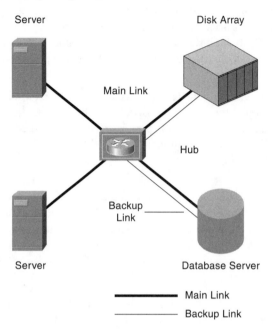

Figure 6-8 *Short-Distance, Non-Cascaded Loop*

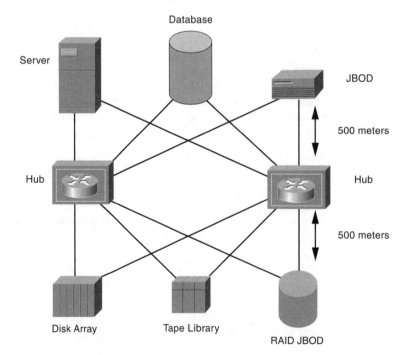

Figure 6-9   *Long-Distance, Non-Cascaded Loop*

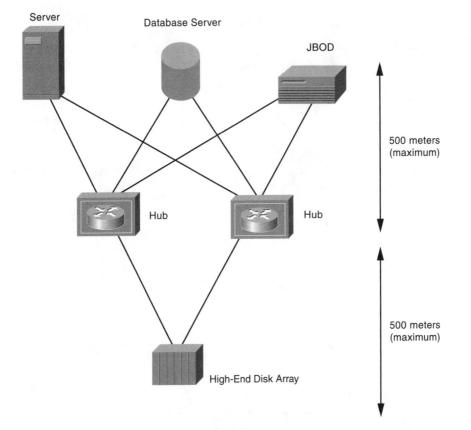

You can extend the scalability of a loop and the maximum distance it can span by inter-connecting hubs. This interconnection of hubs is known as *hub cascading*, where at least one port on each hub is used for hub-to-hub connection. Figure 6-10 depicts a simple cascaded connection.

Figure 6-11 depicts an extended cascaded loop.

Although the FC-AL topology uses hubs predominantly, Fibre Channel switches can also be employed. The use of switches increases the bandwidth available to loop nodes. In addition, a loop node can be disconnected from the loop without forcing other loop devices to be down. When you use switches to interconnect individual devices, the setup is referred to as *Fabric* and the topology is known as the *switched Fabric* topology.

The switched Fabric topology is the third and most popular topology. The following section discusses the switched Fabric topology in detail.

Figure 6-10 *Simple Cascaded Loop*

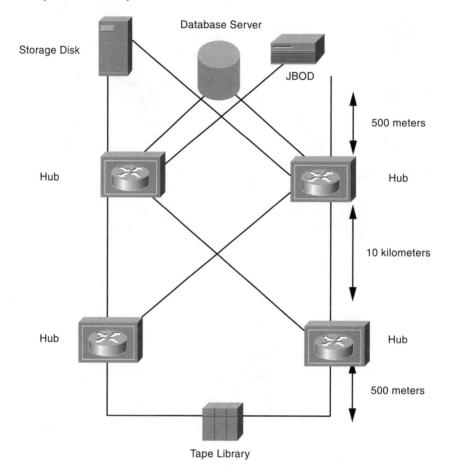

Figure 6-11   *Extended Cascaded Loop*

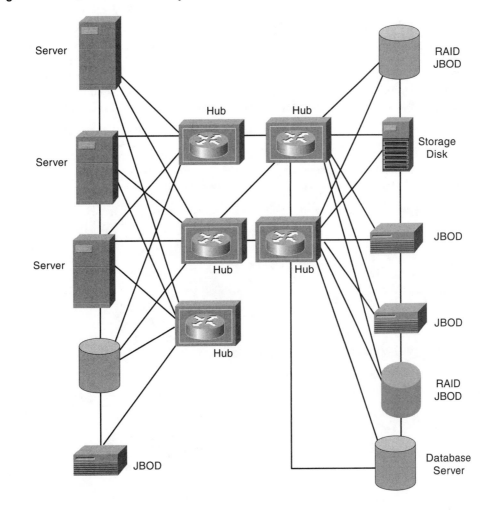

Switched Fabric Topology

The term switched Fabric refers to an intelligent infrastructure that can efficiently switch bandwidth-intensive data between communicating nodes and ports. Despite the fact that the switched Fabric topology allows an interconnection of 2^{24} ports, each individual port that is connected to the Fabric is allocated 100 Mbps full-duplex, dedicated bandwidth.

Each logical connection that is established using the Fabric actually helps in increasing the overall bandwidth of the switched Fabric network. This is because each connection is allocated a dedicated bandwidth. Therefore, overall network bandwidth is equal to the product of the average bandwidth used by one connection and the total number of current connections. In fact, the higher the number of connections at a given time, the greater the overall bandwidth of a switched Fabric SAN. Thus, where each new device that is connected to the arbitrated loops leads to the further reduction of shared bandwidth, addition of a new node or a port to the switched Fabric increases the overall bandwidth.

Figure 6-12 depicts the simplest switched Fabric setup, which is purely based on switches.

Although switches are more powerful and versatile than hubs in terms of performance, SAN designers use hubs extensively in the switched Fabric topology. Figure 6-13 depicts the switched Fabric setup where a mix of switches and hubs is used.

Next, you will learn about the node addressing scheme in the switched Fabric topology.

Figure 6-12   *Simple Switched Fabric Setup*

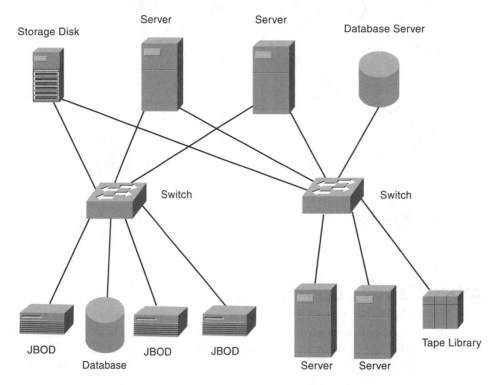

Figure 6-13   *Switched Fabric*

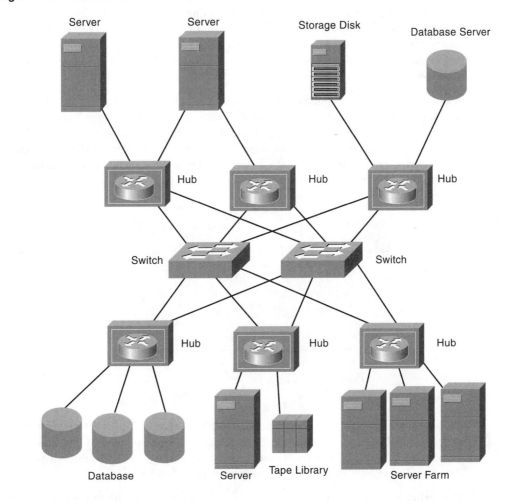

Switched Fabric Addressing Scheme

Every Fibre Channel device is shipped with a 64-bit Node_Name (or Name_Identifier) that the manufacturer assigns. The Institute of Electrical and Electronics Engineers (IEEE) has allocated to all the Fibre Channel vendors a range of these addresses for their exclusive use. Therefore, these 64-bit addresses are also known as *WWNs*. Each port of a Fibre Channel node, in turn, is also assigned a 64-bit port address known as a *Port_Name*, or *WWPN*.

However, a 64-bit address is quite lengthy and can slow down the speed with which a switch routes frames through the Fabric. To make the routing decisions faster, a 24-bit address is assigned to each port by the corresponding switch. Loop ports (NL_Ports) need not be assigned the 24-bit address because they are assigned an address dynamically during the loop initialization process. However, until a non-loop port, N_Port, logs into the Fabric, it is not assigned a 24-bit address.

In addition to assigning unique addresses to ports that attempt Fabric login, a switch also maintains a table that maps 24-bit addresses of all the ports that have logged into the switch with the corresponding WWPN and WWN of the node to which the ports belong. A Fibre Channel switch uses one of its components called *Simple Name Server (SNS)* to maintain these mapping tables.The 24-bit addresses assigned by a Fibre Channel switch consist of three parts—*domain*, *area*, and *port*. Figure 6-14 shows the switched Fabric addressing scheme.

Figure 6-14 *Switched Fabric Addressing Scheme*

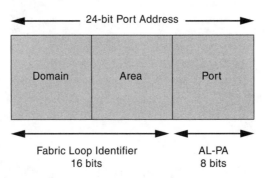

The left-most eight bits of the port address represent the domain. The domain represents the switch to which the port is connected. Because the value of a domain is 8 bits, 256 values are possible. Of these 256 values, 17 are reserved. Therefore, only 239 valid values are available. This implies that a SAN can support up to 239 switches.

The next eight bits (area) are used to identify an FL_Port that is connected to a loop. This part of the port address can also identify a group of F_Ports. Being eight bits long, the area field can have any value from a set of 256 possible addresses.

The right-most eight bits of the port address identify the N_Ports or NL_Ports. Again, being eight bits long, this field can have any value from a set of 256 addresses.

NOTE   The three parts of 24-bit port addresses determine how many addresses are available in the switched Fabric topology. In other words, these three parts define the number of ports that the switched Fabric SAN can support. Domain allows 239 valid addresses, whereas the area and the port part of the address allow 256 valid addresses each. As a result, the total number of available addresses in a switched Fabric SAN is $239 \times 256 \times 256$, which is approximately equal to 16 million.

Switched Fabric Switching

The data travelling over a SAN is generally bandwidth-intensive and time-critical. Therefore, the switched Fabric topology must be capable of switching frames to their destination quickly and efficiently. If the frames are not switched quickly, there is a high possibility of network congestion that can, in the worst cases, lead to network crashes.

Switched Fabric switches ensure the high-speed switching of frames by the use of a *cut-through switching mechanism*. The 24-bit port addresses also play an important role in improving the performance of switched Fabric switches.

The switched Fabric topology uses the cut-through switching mechanism to route frames, because the speed with which frames are routed to the destination ports is very high. In fact, as soon as a frame enters the Fabric, the switch makes the switching decision and forwards the frame to the destination port.

In the cut-through switching mechanism, the switch only examines the destination address of the frame and makes a routing decision on the basis of this address. The destination address is available in the first four bytes of the frame header. As a result, the switch does not need to examine the entire frame. This helps the switch make faster routing decisions.

The use of 24-bit, switch-assigned port addresses also helps in the high-speed switching of frames to their destinations. Because port addresses consist of three parts, routing decisions can be made on the basis of a given part. For example, on the basis of domain value, a switch can forward a frame to the destination switch, which in turn is responsible for forwarding the frame to the destination port.

A switched Fabric SAN is made up of one or more switches that are interconnected to each other through E_Ports to form a mesh. Therefore, multiple paths can exist between the source and destination nodes. This might cause each frame to take a path independent of its predecessor(s). Thus, there is a high possibility that frames are delivered to the destination port out of order. Fabric switches employ the *Fabric Shortest Path First (FSPF) protocol* and *spanning tree algorithm* to ensure in-order delivery of frames.

Switched Fabric switches use the FSPF protocol for path selection. According to this protocol, all paths are established at boot time. However, a primary path to the destination port is selected at the time of communication. If the primary path fails, a new shortest path is selected from the set of available paths for further communication until the primary path becomes available again. However, all the frames traveling through the primary path at the time of failure cannot be delivered to the destination, thereby causing frame congestion. As a result, frames delivered over the new path might arrive at the destination port before their predecessor frames, leading to the out-of-order delivery of frames.

The spanning tree algorithm is employed by the switched Fabric switches to prevent frames from being delivered out-of-order. This switching algorithm calculates the shortest path (in terms of hops) to the destination port, while all the other available paths are blocked. Therefore, frames sent by the source port must traverse one single path to the destination port. As a result, frames are delivered in the same order as they are transmitted. The blocked paths are not ignored and are held as reserved paths in case the primary path fails.

Fabric Services

Fabric is associated with many services that it provides to all the nodes that are directly or indirectly attached to it. The Fabric services help Fibre Channel nodes to locate other nodes in the storage network quickly and efficiently. Basic Fabric services are the following:

- **Fabric login**—A Fabric can support approximately 16 million Fibre Channel nodes. Therefore, it is extremely difficult for the Fabric nodes to resolve addresses on their own, such as the nodes in Fibre Channel loops. Here, Fibre Channel switches play an important role in address assignment and resolution in the switched Fabric topology.

  When a node needs to communicate across the Fabric with another node, it must log in to the attached switch at the hexadecimal address FFFFFE. While logging in, the node identifies itself by the hexadecimal address 000000, indicating that it needs to be assigned a Fabric address. The switch responds to the login request by sending the ACC acknowledgment. If the login was successful, the ACC frame contains a unique three-byte Fabric address. The switch sends a negative acknowledgment to the port if the login was unsuccessful. In that case, the port must re-attempt the login. During Fabric login, besides address assignment to the port, mutually supported service parameters can also be negotiated between the port and the switch.

- **SNS**—Fibre Channel switches offer the SNS functionality that helps a source node to discover the destination node quickly and efficiently. SNS is implemented as a database that contains the WWN of the attached nodes, their Fabric addresses, and the supported types of ports. The SNS also contains the upper-layer protocols and service parameters that are supported by each node. A node registers with SNS during PLOGI, after it has successfully logged into the Fabric.

When a node needs to communicate with another node, it queries the SNS of the switch it is attached to. If the source and destination nodes are attached to the same switch, the node can start the PLOGI procedure to log into the destination port. If the destination node is not attached to the given switch, the query is forwarded to all the other switches attached to the given switch. After the destination node is located, the source port can log in to the destination port and begin communication.

- **Fabric Address Notification (FAN)**—An ongoing transaction might be disrupted before completion. For example, the loop initialization process can temporarily stop all the current transactions in a loop. The FAN service enables nodes to verify the status of the transactions that were temporarily halted and to resume them when normal operations are restored.

- **Registered State Change Notification (RSCN)**—The RSCN service notifies Fibre Channel nodes about changes in the existing topology. These changes include the addition of new nodes to the current setup or change in the status of a node. RSCN is not a default service and the interested N_Ports and NL_Ports must register with the Fabric to be notified about changes in topology. This service is especially beneficial for servers in the storage environment because they must keep track of all the resources in terms of availability.

- **Broadcast server**—This service facilitates the address resolution between Fibre Channel addresses and the upper-layer protocols, such as IP. When a non-Fibre Channel host issues a query to locate a device, the query is broadcast to all the attached ports until the device is located. The destination host then responds with information about itself. This information is used by the Fabric switches to build up the SNS database.

Maintenance and management of large-scale storage networks is a difficult task. Segmentation of a large SAN not only makes management and maintenance simpler, but it also enhances the efficiency of the storage network. You will now learn how a SAN can be effectively segmented.

Segmenting the Switched Fabric

Switched Fabric switches employ two methods of breaking a large Fabric into smaller segments for the efficient functioning of the Fabric. These methods include *zoning* and *Logical Unit Number (LUN) masking*. Both methods are discussed in the following sections.

Zoning

Zoning is the process of segmenting the switched Fabric into various zones. In zoning, only the members of a zone can communicate with each other. Inter-zone communication is strictly prohibited.

Generally, these zones are created to segregate different environments, such as Windows, UNIX and Linux, Macintosh, AIX, and so on, whose file systems might be incompatible with each other. Moreover, GUI-based operating systems such as Windows tend to require more memory and storage resources than non-GUI operating systems. Zoning also helps in segregating storage-intensive environments from other environments that make lesser demands on memory and storage.

You can also use zoning to segregate a server cluster that stores confidential information from unauthorized access, including unauthorized internal access. For example, HR information of a corporation must not be accessible to everybody. Therefore, it makes sense to segregate the storage devices that store the confidential HR-related data from the rest of the network as a separate zone.

The two methods of implementing zoning are *hardware zoning* and *software zoning*. Hardware zoning is a port-based zoning method where physical ports are assigned to a zone. A port can be assigned to either one zone or multiple zones at the same time. Because this is a port-based implementation, devices need to be connected to a particular port. If the devices are shifted to a different port, the entire zone might cease to operate.

Software zoning is a SNS-based zoning method. Because SNS can function on the basis of both WWN and WWPN, a device's physical connectivity to a port does not play any role in the definition of zones. Even if a device is to be connected to a different port, it will remain in the same zone.

Although SNS maintains a table of storage devices that are accessible to each member of a zone, a node can overrule the SNS entries by establishing a direct connection to a storage device, which is not accessible to it. Therefore, hardware zoning is more secure than software zoning.

LUN Masking

A LUN is a unique number assigned to each storage device or each partition that the storage device can support. Every node on a SAN can access a storage device or its partitions by using these LUNs.

The implementation of LUNs helps in segmenting a SAN effectively. A server or a set of servers can be allowed access to a storage device or a specified area (in the form of partitions) of the storage device on the basis of LUNs. When a storage device receives a request from a server to access information from a LUN, the storage device checks its access list to verify if the requesting server can access the specified LUN. If the server does not have the proper rights to access the given LUN, the request is rejected.

Extending the Fabric

The switched Fabric topology can be expanded with the help of switch cascading. Similar to the FC-AL topology, the switched Fabric topology can be either *cascaded* or *non-cascaded*. In the non-cascaded setup, the switches are not interconnected. Figure 6-15 depicts a simple non-cascaded switched Fabric setup.

Interconnection of switches in a SAN makes the Fabric cascaded. Figure 6-16 depicts the cascaded switched Fabric setup where switches are interconnected with each other.

Figure 6-15 *Non-Cascaded Switched Fabric Setup*

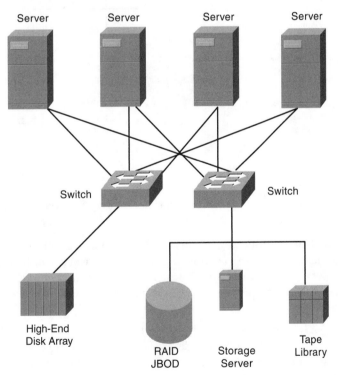

Figure 6-16 *Cascaded Switched Fabric Setup*

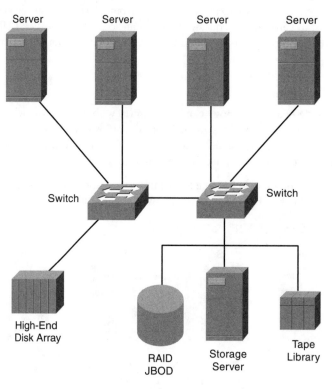

Summary

SANs are strongly based on Fibre Channel technology. The following list summarizes each technology:

- **Point-to-point topology**—This topology is the direct connection between two SAN devices. Because of the dedicated nature of physical connections, the point-to-point topology is the fastest, simplest, and easiest to implement and manage. However, the point-to-point topology is not commonly used to build an entire storage network because it is the costliest of the three.

- **FC-AL topology**—FC-AL is the most cost-effective topology of the three and can support up to 127 nodes and devices simultaneously. However, because the link bandwidth is shared among connected devices in this topology, its performance can degrade considerably if all 126 nodes are connected to it. Also, because of the shared nature of the loop, node loops need to arbitrate for loop control. After a node gains control of the loop, only one loop node can transmit data at a time. Therefore, this topology should be used in a SAN if the number of nodes is not high or transmissions are not time-sensitive. FC-AL supports two types of loops—public loops and private loops. Private loops have no connection to the rest of the Fabric in the SAN. However, public loops are connected to the Fabric.

- **Switched Fabric topology**—This topology is the most high-performing and reliable topology of the three. Also, it is not as expensive as the point-to-point topology. This topology consists of an interconnection of Fibre Channel switches that can support a staggering 16 million Fibre Channel devices. The high point of this topology is that despite the addition of devices to the Fabric, the aggregate bandwidth of the topology increases because Fibre Channel switches that form the backbone of the switched Fabric topology are high-performing, non-blocking devices.

You are not limited to implementing only one topology when building your storage network. An intelligent mix-and-match of these three topologies helps in achieving a cost-effective and efficient storage network, which meets organization-specific needs and business requirements in terms of scalability, required bandwidth, and traffic regulation.

In this chapter, you will learn about the following:

- SAN design considerations
- Designing a SAN
- Constructing a SAN
- SAN best practices

CHAPTER 7

Designing and Building a SAN

The design and implementation of a storage area network (SAN) is a complex process. You need adequate expertise, manpower, and a sufficient budget to develop a storage network that not only will address the current storage demands, but also will meet any future requirements. A SAN must be stable, secure, high-performance, scalable, and extremely resilient. At the same time, a SAN must justify its cost.

SAN Design Considerations

Although vendors offer standard solutions for the implementation of SANs, customized SAN designs are the norm. This is because custom designs allow organizations to tailor their storage networks according to their needs, requirements, and limitations. However, while implementing either of the solutions—standard or customized—certain design considerations must be evaluated in detail. The most important design considerations while designing a SAN include the following:

- Business requirements
- Performance
- Physical layout
- Data pooling
- Data availability
- Heterogeneity
- Storage requirement
- Connectivity
- Scalability
- Migration
- Security
- Manageability
- Resilience
- Routability

- Prevention of traffic congestion
- Backup and restore capability

Each of the previously stated requirements must be considered carefully. Each point should be evaluated while keeping in mind the future growth of the network and storage requirements. Depending on the individual requirements of each corporation, some considerations might be more important than others. These scenarios will be discussed in the following section.

Business Requirements

Your organization is a strong candidate for implementing a SAN if it fits into the following fields or if it is planning to venture into one these fields in the near future:

- **Online transaction processing (OLTP)**—OLTP refers to a set of applications that are used to process—input, save, and retrieve—information from a networked system in real-time. The speed with which data is processed in OLTP systems is extremely critical. It is vital that the system is not bogged down with incoming requests and that clients and users do not have to wait for their requests to be fulfilled.

- **E-commerce and e-business**—E-commerce refers to digital business transactions that are conducted over the Internet. These transactions include business-to-business (B2B) transactions and business-to-consumer (B2C) transactions. B2B transactions involve commerce between two or more commercial setups, such as companies; B2C represents sales of merchandise or information products to consumers and individual buyers.

NOTE   Initially e-commerce was restricted to the online sale and purchase of merchandise. However, e-commerce has evolved to encompass general business activities, such as advertising, marketing, public relations, and customer service.

- **Enterprise Resource Planning (ERP)**—ERP is a resource management technology that integrates the enterprise-wide resources of a company. These operations include human resources, financial operations, manufacturing, and distribution. ERP also connects an organization to its customers and suppliers. Because ERP applications are used for the online management of critical data and resources, it is highly critical that the related infrastructure support high-speed transactions.

- **Data mining and warehousing**—The data mining process involves the analysis of stored data to recognize significant patterns and hidden relationships in the data. With the help of these subtle patterns and hidden relationships, business experts can infer and predict future trends. For example, data mining helps in answering vague business-related queries, such as "which international customer gave us the biggest orders two years back." Data warehousing, on the other hand, is the process of collecting, organizing, maintaining, updating, and making the information (or data) available to data mining tools for analysis. Because both data mining and data warehousing deal with huge amounts of business-related data, that must be available at any time, it is important that the infrastructure be able to support high-speed, bandwidth-intensive transactions without other users on the network feeling the bandwidth pinch.

The previously listed fields and applications are extremely mission-critical. They demand 24×7 data availability and high-speed data transactions, in addition to a high level of data security during these transactions. The implementation of SANs can efficiently address these demands. However, SANs are extremely expensive solutions. The cost of each solution can vary on the basis of each port's implementation. As a result, you must thoroughly evaluate the after-effects of a SAN implementation on your organization's overall budget before making decisions about setting up a storage network. The implementation of a SAN must justify its cost.

Performance

Performance is one of the most important considerations of SAN design. However, performance is not a standalone consideration. Many other factors contribute to the performance of a SAN. These factors include the following:

- Physical layout of the storage network
- Placement of storage systems
- Data accessibility
- Data availability
- Connectivity
- Manageability
- Fault tolerance

If you plan for a high-performance storage network, you must remember that performance is directly proportional to the cost of implementation. This implies that the higher the performance of a network, the higher the cost of its implementation. Therefore, you must ensure a proper balance between the performance and the cost of implementing a SAN.

Physical Layout of the Storage Network

The physical layout of the corporate network is another factor that plays an important role in determining the best SAN design for your organization's storage requirements. The physical distance between campuses and the location of servers and storage devices within these campuses help to determine the most appropriate and cost-effective design for the SAN. Support for long distances throughout the SAN allows your storage network to easily accommodate future growth. However, you must remember that the implementation of long-distance SANs is extremely expensive.

Placement of Storage Systems

The placement of storage systems in relation to servers that access these storage systems also helps you to determine the most appropriate SAN design for your organization. In a storage network, the placement of storage systems largely depends upon the data-access approach. In a corporate network, data is generally accessed on a divisional/departmental basis or corporate basis.

Because corporate storage systems and data systems are accessed remotely, you should plan for low response-time, high availability, high level of security, and fast transaction speeds for these storage systems.

NOTE	Planning for low response time, high-availability, and fast transactions for remote connectivity is much more expensive than planning for the same attributes for local connectivity.

Because divisional or departmental storage data systems are generally accessed locally, you should plan for low response time, high availability, and fast transaction speeds. However, due to local access within a secure LAN environment, elaborate security measures are not as important as in remote access to corporate storage systems.

You can group the storage systems on the basis of divisional/departmental or corporate data accessibility and place these storage systems accordingly. The rule of thumb in both access approaches is that if a storage system is accessed frequently by a server or a group of servers, the storage system in question must be placed in the physical vicinity of these servers to ensure low response time and to reduce traffic over the network.

Storage Pooling

Storage systems can be grouped into three pools—*local pool*, *centralized pool*, and *distributed pool*.

- **Local pool**—Local pooling ensures one-to-one data access between servers and storage systems, where both entities are connected to the same Fabric switch. Figure 7-1 shows SAN components pooled locally.

- **Centralized pool**—Centralized pooling provides one-to-many data access between a centrally located storage system and multiple servers that access the storage system. Figure 7-2 depicts a centralized pool.

- **Distributed pool**—Distributed pooling provides many-to-many data access between multiple servers and storage systems. Figure 7-3 depicts a distributed pool.

Figure 7-1   *Local Pool*

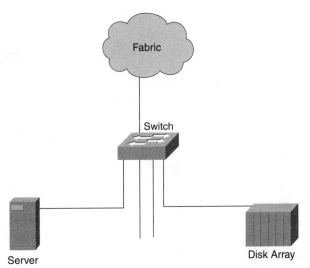

Figure 7-2   *Centralized Pool*

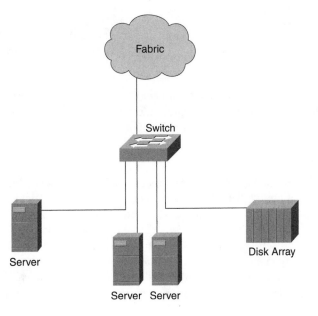

Figure 7-3   *Distributed Pool*

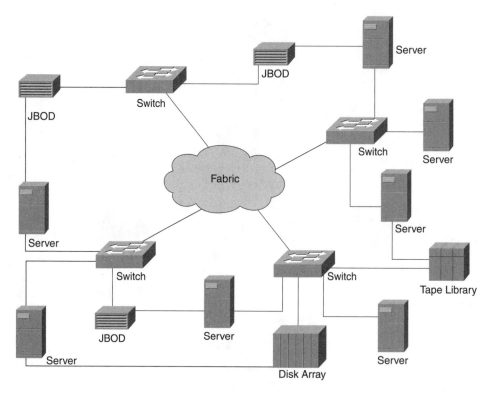

You should plan for local and centralized pools if you need to implement a local SAN. Distributed pools prove to be appropriate solutions for remote SANs.

Data Availability

You can avoid connectivity failures related to a Single Point Of Failure (SPOF) by planning for data availability. The use of Redundant Array of Independent Disks (RAID) and remote data mirroring are effective measures to provide high data availability. However, as the experts recommend, you can integrate these data availability requirements right into the SAN design itself rather than implementing external measures, such as remote data mirroring. By integrating the data availability solution into the SAN design, you can bring down the Total Cost of Ownership (TCO) of your SAN. This is because external solutions, such as remote data mirroring, are not only expensive, but also difficult to manage.

NOTE   For detailed information on RAID, see Appendix A, "RAID Technology and Fibre Channel Vendors."

You can integrate four levels of data availability—*Level 1*, *Level 2*, *Level 3*, and *Level 4*—into the SAN design. These levels allow you to tailor your data availability requirements while implementing the SAN. Of these four levels, Level 1 provides the lowest data availability and Level 4 ensures maximum data availability. The following are the four levels of data availability:

- **Level 1**—Each switch is connected to another switch in the Fabric through a single link. Similarly, servers and storage devices are also connected to the Fabric through a single link. In case of a link failure, connectivity between the two ends is disrupted. As a result, this level provides the least resilience to path failure in the Fabric. Figure 7-4 shows the Level 1 setup.

NOTE   A link between two switches is also referred to as an *Inter-Switch Link (ISL)*.

- **Level 2**—Each switch is connected to other Fabric switches through more than one link. However, storage devices and servers connect into the Fabric using a single link. Figure 7-5 shows a typical Level 2 data availability setup. Compared to Level 1, this level makes the Fabric more resilient to any failures between two switches because the data can be routed to the destination port or device through an alternate link.

Figure 7-4   *The Level 1 Setup*

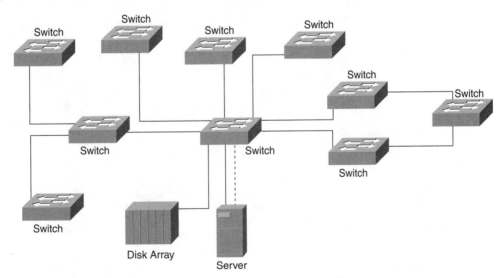

- **Level 3**—Each switch is connected to the other Fabric switches through more than one ISL as in Level 2. However, the storage devices and servers are also connected to the Fabric through more than one link (as shown in Figure 7-6). As a result, in case of a switch or link failure, transactions are re-routed to the destination through an alternate path. In addition to Fabric resilience, this level ensures increased data availability by providing multiple alternate paths to the destination.

Figure 7-5   *The Level-2 Setup*

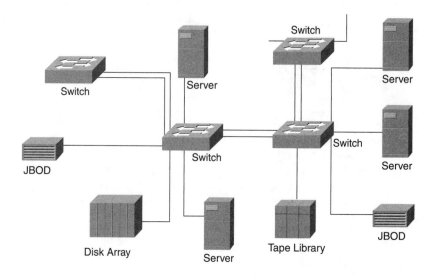

Figure 7-6   *The Level-3 Setup*

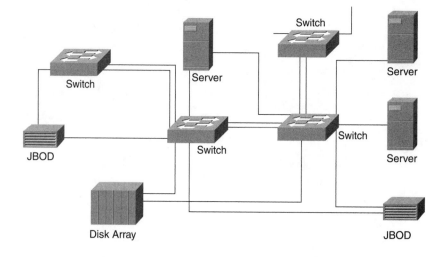
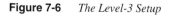

- **Level 4**—Each server and storage device is connected to the Fabric through multiple links. However, unlike previous levels that are based on a single Fabric, this level supports more than one Fabric. Figure 7-7 shows the Level 4 setup. This level offers maximum data availability because even if the maximum number of switches in a given Fabric fails, the transactions can be re-routed to the destination through an alternate Fabric. Therefore, this level provides NSPOF.

Figure 7-7   *The Level-4 Setup*

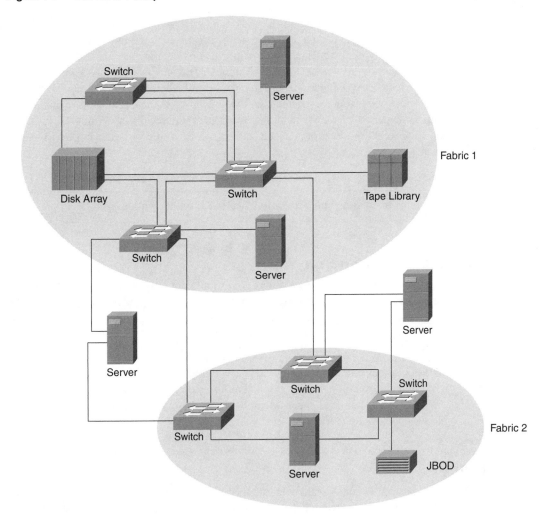

You can plan for any of the levels (or combination of levels) of data availability, depending on the criticality of the full-time availability of data to a given application or server. For example, to ensure $24 \times 7 \times 365$ access to a storage device that holds the database of all the users registered to an e-commerce site, you should preferably implement the Level 4 data-availability setup.

Heterogeneity

A wide range of multi-vendor platforms and operating systems are used in present-day networks. Therefore, you need to identify each platform and operating system that is used in a SAN, and individually evaluate each platform and operating system to determine its limitations and advantages in the SAN environment. This step is necessary in ensuring that your storage network will function more seamlessly and efficiently. For example, Windows NT tends to hog the resources available on the network. As a result, make sure that other operating systems, such as UNIX and Sun Solaris, are separated from Windows NT-based servers. To prevent this situation, it is advisable to place Windows-based and UNIX-based servers in separate zones.

NOTE   For more information on zoning, refer to Chapter 8, "Implementing SAN Security."

Future Storage Requirements

While planning for SAN implementations, you should not only consider present storage requirements, but also account for future demands that might be imposed on your storage network. If you consider increasing the storage capacity by simply adding additional disk devices or storage systems to the existing SAN, you might risk degrading the performance of your storage network, which defeats the entire purpose of the SAN.

One of the solutions recommended by experts is to replace the existing low-capacity storage system with a high-capacity alternative. The storage network performance of fewer high-capacity storage devices is considerably higher than the overall effect of a large number of low-capacity storage devices.

Connectivity

You should carefully consider the total number of Fabric switches and the total number of ports supported by each switch before building a SAN. This is because the cost of Fibre

Channel products, on which present-day SANs are based, is directly proportional to the number of ports supported by them.

At the same time, you must also keep future connectivity requirements in mind and choose a design that can be scaled or migrated to a better design and that is capable of providing higher storage capacity and performance, if required. While interconnecting the switches, you must ensure Fabric performance by providing the adequate number of ISLs between switches so that the Fabric meets the business and technical requirements of your organization.

Scalability

Future growth is one of the most important aspects of any network setup. Therefore, you must select a SAN design that will be able to accommodate future storage and connectivity requirements without the need for a major upgrade of the existing storage network.

Keeping the future scalability of your storage network in mind, experts recommend the implementation of the switched Fabric topology, because this topology can easily accommodate about 2^{24} connections without much degradation in the performance of the storage network. In fact, additional connections only tend to increase the accumulative bandwidth of the network. Although, implementation of switched Fabric might seem to be an extravagant move, it can prove to be an extremely prudent solution for accommodating future growth. The implementation of pure Fibre Channel loop topology is far less expensive than switched Fabric, but it can only accommodate a maximum of 127 connections. (This number is actually fewer than 127.) Moreover, every new addition tends to further degrade the performance of the network.

Migration

Migration is another growth path that helps to accommodate the future growth of a storage network. You must choose a SAN topology that can be migrated to a higher-capacity design without disturbing the current setup and without increasing expenditures. For example, if you have implemented a multi-Fabric (at least, two Fabrics) SAN that has no SPOF, you can migrate all the operations in one Fabric to another, with minimum need of re-cabling the setup.

NOTE   As an important precaution, it is highly recommended that you back up all data before undertaking any migration-related activity.

Manageability

Manageability is a major consideration while designing a SAN. The SAN administrator must be able to manage the storage network regardless of the physical layout and location of SAN components. SAN management tools must offer the following features:

- Easy implementation
- Easy-to-use management interface, preferably Graphical User Interface (GUI)
- Centralized management, preferably automated policy-based management
- Support for heterogeneous environment (by not being vendor-specific)

Various management tools available in the market can be broadly divided into four categories—*configuration tools*, *performance tools*, *access-control tools*, and *fault-control tools*.

Configuration tools allow the administrator to configure and control SAN components that make up the storage network. In addition, these tools also help in collecting information related to the status of SAN components.

Performance tools allow the administrator to manage the performance of SAN components so that they provide the expected quality of service (QoS). In addition, performance tools help in analyzing the traffic and behavior of applications in the storage network. Some performance tools also help the administrator to plan for future growth.

Access-control tools allow administrators to control user and device access to specified information. Generally, these tools are useful for implementing access control methods, such as Logical Unit Number (LUN), masking, and zoning.

Finally, fault-control tools allow the administrator to detect, isolate, and correct faults in a SAN. These tools are also responsible for creating and maintaining error logs that can help an administrator in case the problem occurs again.

Fault Tolerance and Resilience

While planning for a SAN, you should also plan for unforeseen failures and faults that can lead to catastrophic failure of the entire storage network. This situation can be disastrous in the case of businesses that depend on OLTP, e-commerce, e-business, ERP, and so on.

You must design your SAN in such a manner that critical data can be completely recovered without loss or corruption. Therefore, you should consider automatic remote data replication and maintenance of multiple copies of critical data at strategic locations. These measures could help your organization's SAN to be more fault-tolerant and resilient.

Prevention of Congestion

The ongoing data transfer between a pair of communicating devices must not affect other pairs that are engaged in simultaneous transactions or that need to begin a session of their own. Fabric switches might prove to be points of congestion if more than one device (or port) needs to communicate with the same device (or port) simultaneously over the same link. In this case, the built-in fairness algorithm in Fibre Channel switches ensures that the possibility of congestion is minimal. You can dramatically reduce congestion by providing multiple links between Fabric switches.

NOTE   A fairness algorithm provides fractional bandwidth to all devices (or ports) that need to communicate with the same device simultaneously over the same link. The provision of fractional bandwidth to all devices (or ports) ensures that all have a fair chance of transaction. However, the trade-off in this case is the degradation in the performance of the Fabric.

Routability

The more hops a data packet traverses during a transaction, the greater the probability of its corruption or loss in transit. This especially holds true in the case of remote transactions. Therefore, you must design your storage network in such a manner that the number of hops between two communicating ends is minimal.

Backup and Restore

Proper and timely backups add to the resilience of your storage network in case of disastrous situations, such as the failure of storage devices, which lead to data loss. Thus, proper backup and restoration capability increases the overall level of data availability to clients.

Unlike normal networks, SANs offer LAN-free backups. This means that you can back up or restore data at any point of time, whenever necessary, regardless of the time of day. The users working on the attached local network do not feel any bandwidth pinch. However, backup and restore operations are highly bandwidth-intensive. Therefore, you must provide sufficient bandwidth and connectivity (cabling) for these operations. If you fail to consider the requirements of these operations thoroughly, you might not be able to reap the full benefit of these applications.

Security

Data security—integrity and confidentiality—is one of the most fundamental issues while designing a SAN. The SAN design must ensure that data integrity is maintained and that data is not available to any server or user who is not authorized to access it, thus ensuring confidentiality.

You can design a secure SAN by using the following techniques:

- **Fabric zoning**—You can create a visual, private SAN by implementing *Fabric zoning*. Fabric zoning is also referred to as *zoning*. In zoning, several ports are grouped together to form a zone. Ports that belong to the same zone can communicate with each other. Inter-zonal communication is prohibited. In this way, all servers that can access a storage device or system can be zoned together, thus preventing any other servers that are not a part of a given zone from accessing data.

- **LUN masking**—Each logical unit (LU) in a SAN is uniquely identified by a LUN. You can control access to logical units in a SAN by using LUNs. These logical units can either be part of a storage device, such as device disks, or a set of storage devices.

  You can use the storage device's control program to specify the list of servers that can access a given LU. When a server needs to access an LU, the storage device verifies if the server is authorized to access the specified LU. Access requests from unauthorized LUs are rejected.

NOTE	Refer to Chapter 8 for more information on zoning and LUN masking.

In the next section, you learn the basics of designing a SAN.

Designing a SAN

After you evaluate the design considerations carefully, you can start designing your storage network. You might need to replace or upgrade the existing infrastructure or start from scratch. In either case, the SAN design phase consists of selecting an appropriate topology and selecting SAN components. The following sections discuss these two aspects of designing a SAN.

Selecting the Appropriate Topology

A well-planned topology helps an organization to meet its business and technical requirements efficiently and cost-effectively. The following decisions help you to arrive at the most appropriate topology for your organization's needs:

- **When and which SAN component to use**—Hubs, switches, bridges, routers, and gateways are the most fundamental building blocks of a SAN. The right choice of SAN components helps you to meet performance, storage, and cost requirements of your storage networks.

  — **Hubs**—You can use hubs to extend the maximum distance of a Fibre Channel link. They are best suited for the implementation of Fibre Channel-Arbitrated Loop (FC-AL) topology, as described in Chapter 3, "Fibre Channel Basics," and Chapter 6, "SAN Topologies." Fibre Channel hubs are of two types—managed and unmanaged. Although more expensive than unmanaged hubs, managed hubs offer intelligent manageability and a higher potential for supporting future growth. In addition, they can be effectively used for LAN-free backups, clustering, and remote disk mirroring.

    Unmanaged hubs are passive in nature and do not participate in protocol-related activities. They are simply the devices that are used to extend the Fibre Channel loop. Therefore, the use of unmanaged hubs is not recommended if you are planning to scale your SAN in the near future.

  — **Switches**—You use switches to implement the switched Fabric topology. In fact, what is commonly referred to as the Fabric is a collection of inter-connected switches. Switches allow you to implement a storage network where frames are routed efficiently through the Fabric at a high speed. Each switch port offers a bandwidth of 100 Mbps and can support a separate transaction without affecting the performance of other ports.

    In addition to the implementation of the switched Fabric topology, a category of switches, known as *loop switches*, allow you to connect an FC-AL loop to the Fabric. In this way, you can use switches to set up logical private loops. Use of switches in the loop topology improves the performance of Fibre Channel loops.

  — **Routers**—Fibre Channel routers allow you to integrate IP-based hosts with Fibre Channel nodes. Thus, the use of Fibre Channel routers increases the reach of SANs by allowing access to remote storage devices over IP WANs through ATM, ISDN, and T1/T3 lines.

Many vendors also offer routers that provide Fibre Channel-to-Small Computer System Interface (SCSI) interconnectivity. In addition, the use of intelligent routers allows the implementation of firewalls that can play an important role in preventing unauthorized access.

— **Bridges**—Fibre Channel bridges allow you to integrate legacy devices in a Fibre Channel network. You can bring down the total cost of implementation of storage networks by allowing the inclusion of existing expensive SCSI devices, such as legacy disks and drives, tape subsystems, and optical CD and DVD devices in Fibre Channel storage networks. Fibre Channel bridges also allow you to reduce network traffic by a rough estimate of 400 to 500 times.

— **Gateways**—Just as gateways are used in normal networks, you can use Fibre Channel gateways to provide interoperability between devices that operate on different protocols. Fibre Channel gateways act as the bridge between diverse protocols, such as SCSI, Ultra SCSI, and Fibre Channel, by providing protocol conversion, when necessary.

In other words, Fibre Channel gateways, such as Fibre Channel bridges, allow you to connect non-Fibre Channel devices to a Fibre Channel-based SAN. Additionally, many gateways also allow you to extend the maximum distance of Fibre Channel links while providing increased bandwidth and addressing capability.

— **Storage devices**—High-performance and reliable storage devices form the backbone of your storage network. The storage devices you choose should not only address your current storage demands, but should also be able to accommodate your future storage requirements.

• **How to build the Fabric**—Building an intelligent and efficient Fabric, even if it consists of only a few switches, is one of the most important aspects of designing a SAN. This is because all the data packets need to be routed by Fabric switches. If the Fabric functions efficiently, most of your business and technical requirements will be met. An efficient and well-planned Fabric design helps you to achieve high data availability, connectivity, manageability, fault resistence, congestion prevention, performance, and routability. A well-planned Fabric also helps you to address the affordability factor of a SAN. While building a Fabric, you should plan for the following components:

— **Alternate ISLs**—The higher the number of ISLs between switches, the higher the data availability and fault tolerance of your storage network. This is because ISLs provide alternate paths in case of a primary link failure.

You can keep adding ISLs to your Fabric as necessary. Adding new ISLs is quite simple as the routing and zoning information is automatically updated across the entire Fabric. However, addition of every new ISL generates an excessive amount of network traffic because the information must be conveyed to all the switches in the Fabric. Moreover, implementation of extra ISLs can increase the TCO of your SAN considerably. As per recommendations provided by experts (and vendors), the maximum number of ISLs between two switches must not exceed eight.

— **Alternate Fabrics**—One of the best methods for the implementation of redundant paths and switches is to set up alternate Fabrics. The setup of alternate Fabrics can be as simple and cost-effective or as elaborate and expensive as your budget allows.

The simplest alternate Fabric can be achieved by using two switches that are not interconnected. If one fails, the traffic is automatically rerouted through the other switch. If your SAN consists of redundant Fabrics, the alternate Fabrics can take over in case of the failure of the primary Fabrics.

— **Departmental Fabric approach**—One of the best approaches for building a secure and extremely resilient SAN is to break the entire storage network into smaller SANs. The best way of breaking a SAN into smaller SANlets is on the basis of various departments in the organization. As a result, each department will have its own Fabric that is interconnected to other Fabrics. This approach provides a large number of alternate Fabrics and, therefore, a large number of alternate paths through the network.

— **Number of hops**—You must design the Fabric in such a way that the maximum number of hops between any two switches is seven. If the number of hops is more than the recommended number, the probability of data loss is high. According to the findings of an IBM testing team, every extra hop causes an additional delay of 1.2 microseconds in the data packet reaching the destination.

— **Traffic over the Fabric**—You must thoroughly analyze and understand the nature of traffic that is transacted over the Fabric. This helps you to identify peak periods, choked paths, and probable bottlenecks. After you understand these problems, you can plan the Fabric setup accordingly to avoid traffic congestion and transaction delays. To avoid network congestions, a rule of thumb is that you should connect the servers to the switch they use most frequently.

Next, you learn about the facts that need to be considered while selecting various components that are used to build a SAN.

Selecting SAN Components

After you work out the topology of your storage network, you can begin selecting various SAN components—interconnects, cables, and storage devices—according to your requirements, while keeping the affordability factor in mind.

In a few cases, where the organization is implementing the storage solution for the first time, you need to start from scratch. However, most present-day organizations have their own small-scale storage solutions in place. Therefore, in most of the scenarios, you need to replace or upgrade the existing infrastructure to accommodate the new storage network.

If you are replacing or upgrading the existing setup, you must evaluate the existing infrastructure before actually setting up the SAN. Evaluation of the existing infrastructure will help you to identify the components and devices that you can possibly reuse in your storage network. For example, many organizations use fiber-optic cables in their normal networks. You can use these cables in the SAN after testing them to verify whether they meet your requirements. Although testing the existing infrastructure can be a tedious and time-consuming exercise, it can considerably reduce the total cost of implementation of your SAN. Similarly, storage devices, such as tape subsystems, can be reused effectively in SAN implementations, thereby reducing the TCO of the SAN.

After you identify the devices that can be reused, or if you are building your storage network from scratch, you now need to arrange for the rest of the SAN components. It is important that you consider products from various SAN vendors before deciding on each component.

While selecting components, you must balance your requirements with the total cost allocated for the implementation of the SAN. As a result, you might end up with a mix of products from various vendors as no one vendor offers the entire range of SAN products. In this case, you must ensure that these selected devices are compatible with each other because individual vendors offer individual solutions that may or may not be compatible with the products offered by other SAN vendors. Therefore, it is equally important that you also test these devices for interoperability with each other.

NOTE   The first time you implement a SAN, it is advisable to consult an expert who will help you make the right decisions while selecting the appropriate SAN components.

Constructing a SAN

After you have thoroughly worked out the design requirements, designed the Fabric, and selected SAN components, you can start constructing your SAN.

Before going ahead with the construction, you need to assemble the team that will implement the SAN. The team members must have the appropriate skills and extensive experience in the field of implementing complex and heterogeneous networks. Your team must have extensive knowledge of various operating systems and platforms, network and non-network applications, and databases. There should also be experts on the team who can handle the Fibre Channel cabling of the storage network.

With the help of your team and the design of the SAN that you have worked out, you can start with the SAN implementation phase. After setting up the SAN, you must document the entire SAN design and implementation for future reference. The documentation should contain the following information:

- **Business requirements**—Here, you should record the business-related reasons (such as benefits) for which the SAN was considered and implemented as a solution.

- **Design considerations**—Here, you must record all the considerations and rationale behind the present SAN configuration. You must also document any problems encountered while designing and implementing the SAN in detail for future reference.

NOTE	While planning and implementing, you might come across a problem that you could not find an answer to. You should record such problems. If and when you find the answer to the problem, you should document the solution because it will help you in the future when you come across the same problem.

- **Logical and physical layout**—Here, you must record the smallest details that are related to the design of your storage network. You can also use a detailed diagram of the entire setup. The logical layout of the SAN includes detailed information on various zones in the SAN.

- **Placement of storage devices and systems**—In addition to the detailed diagram of the SAN, this detail can help you easily track and locate a SAN component, especially while troubleshooting amidst the large number of SAN devices that might constitute your storage network.

- **Existing and planned infrastructure, including platforms and operating systems**—Here, you must record details about not only the existing infrastructure, but also any additions or upgrades planned in the near future. This should include details about the platforms and operating system.

- **Cabling**—Detailed information on the present cabling system will help you reduce the time for troubleshooting cable-related problems.

- **Zoning map that provides the implementation details of zoning (and LUN masking, if any)**—Here, you need to record details about all the zones and their zone members. You must also maintain a detailed record of any users or components that might have access to multiple zones. This documentation will help you to determine security measures for the SAN. It will also help you to track possible internal security breaches.

- **SAN applications and management tools**—Here, you should maintain a detailed record of what application is running on which SAN component. This will help you to track down software-related problems quickly and efficiently.

- **Training plan**—This should include the details of given or planned trainings related to the maintenance, usage, or implementation of the storage network. This practice will help you keep track of SAN-related trainings in the organization, budget training cost, and identify the trained personnel.

In the next section, you will look at best practices that will help you design a secure and high-performance SAN that can easily accommodate future growth.

SAN Best Practices

Best practices help you to achieve better results. In the following sections, you examine some best practices that you can follow while designing and constructing a SAN.

NOTE   Although the practices discussed in this section are referred to as best practices, an organization's business and technical requirements dictate the implementation of its storage network. Every organization has its own set of business and technical requirements. Therefore, these practices need not be followed verbatim to achieve best practice results.

The following sections discuss best practices for design and construction.

SAN Design Best Practices

Your SAN design should be such that it not only meets current requirements, but also addresses future requirements. The following practices will help you to design a SAN that can be expanded in size and capability over time:

- Plan for flexibility in your design so that it can accommodate future advancements, growth, and changes.

- Allocate an adequate amount of time to design the storage network. The more time you invest in the design phase, the easier and more hassle free the implementation of the SAN.

- Consider a topology that can be easily scaled and migrated to a high-capacity topology that supports better performance. Switched Fabric is one of the preferred topologies in this situation. This is because you can scale the Fabric extensively by simply replacing an 8-port switch with a 16-port switch.

- It is easier to plan, implement, and maintain smaller SANs. Therefore, implement several small-sized SANs and interconnect them according to the needs of your organization. Experts recommend that you have multiple Fabrics rather than one large Fabric. Keeping track of a large number of cables and devices in one Fabric is much more difficult than managing numerous small SANlets or Fabrics.

- Document the SAN design in detail. Proper documentation helps you to constantly evaluate your design and to work out trade-offs wherever necessary. You must make sure that the documentation is thorough and that it includes the cabling system, current design of the SAN, physical location of components, their names, and the current configurations.

In the next section, you learn about best practices that you should follow while constructing your storage network.

SAN Construction Best Practices

After you finalize the SAN design, you can begin the construction phase of your storage network. The following practices help you in achieving a stable, scalable, and high-performance SAN:

- Generally, all Fibre Channel products are pre-configured. However, before implementing SAN components, verify that components of the same type, such as all switches, are configured with the same parameter settings. This helps prevent numerous problems related to parameter mismatching.

- It is important that you label the Fabric switches relevantly because they form the backbone of the SAN Fabric, especially if you have a large-scale SAN on your hands. By doing so, you can easily track a switch. For example, the fourth switch in the first loop attached to Fabric1 can be named Fabric1-loop1-switch4. The name might be long, but it is extremely descriptive and helpful in understanding the makeup of your SAN's Fabric, which will aid in locating individual switches in the jungle of components.

- Label all SAN components by using an appropriate naming scheme. The naming scheme must be easily understandable and must convey the functionality of the SAN component. For example, a Unix server in loop1 can be named loop1-Unix1. You can also add the name of the zone, if any, to which the component belongs, to accurately identify a component. For example, DiskArray3 located in a zone called Finance can be named DiskArray3-Finance. Similarly, an AIX server in Fabric1 can be named Fabric1-AIX2. You also need to label all the ports in all the SAN devices. For example, you can label a port in an NT server called Sales-NT1, Sales-NT1_P2.

- Document the cable connections thoroughly. Maintain a repository (database or file) where you can record the details about each cable in the system. If you have numbered your cables, make sure that the details of the cable (to-from and cable-type) are also recorded.

- Label the cabling properly at each end of a connection so that you can identify a given cable in a set of cables without any problem. For example, a Fibre Channel link running from a Unix server called Loop1-Unix1 to DiskArray3-Finance (a disk array located in the Finance department) can be named as (FC)Loop1-Unix1/ DiskArray3-Finance. Although the name is long, you will instantly recognize the type of link and the devices it uses to connect. If you prefer short names, you can number each cable uniquely. Make sure that both ends of the cable bear the same number.

- Place a label on each SAN component that specifies the World Wide Identification Number (WWID) of the device. Most experts recommend that you also maintain a database, or at least a file, which records the WWIDs of all nodes and their physical locations.

NOTE   It is considered to be a good practice to label each Host Bus Adapter (HBA) with its WWID and to ensure that the label is in plain view. This practice reduces the time needed to track a malfunctioning HBA.

- Define zones on the basis of the zoning map and document any changes in the existing zones for future reference. While defining zones, you should use meaningful zone names (and aliases, if any). For example, if you have defined a zone based on the divisional/departmental approach, you might have a Finance, HR, or Sales zone. If you have created a server-based zone for Windows NT servers, you might name it NT (or NT-Zone, to be precise). Also, you must make sure that the naming convention remains consistent all over the network. This alleviates much confusion.

- Whenever scaling a SAN, ensure that new additions do not disrupt the current infrastructure. For example, if you need to accommodate more devices in your storage network, you can consider replacing the existing 8-port switch (or Fibre Channel hub) with a 16- or 32-port switch. This would barely cause any disruption in the existing setup. If you need to go in for a major scaling or upgrading exercise, you can consider adding a new Fabric rather than trying to fit in a large number of devices in the existing setup. You can also consider adding independent SANlets.

- While migrating the current SAN topology to a high-capacity topology, select a design that can be migrated without bringing about a major disruption in the existing setup. For example, migrating a meshed topology to a cascaded Fabric requires minimum changes in the existing infrastructure.

NOTE   Avoid relocating the SAN devices physically. This might result in unwanted repercussions related to the existing SAN design.

- Thoroughly review all SANlets before merging them to form a large SAN. This will prevent situations where the newly created SAN exceeds any existing SAN rules. Current zoning configurations are some of the most important things to consider while merging two independent SANlets. If both are zoned, the zone configuration database will be updated to include the zone configurations of each SANlet. However, if one of the SANlets is not zoned, any device in the non-zoned SANlet will be inaccessible until each constituent device of the non-zoned SANlet is added into the zone configuration of the zoned SANlet.

Now that you have the basic ideas behind planning and building a SAN, you can get into the practical aspects of implementing a storage network. Initially, you might have to request the help, support, consultation, and probably advice of your SAN vendor(s). However, you will gain expertise and experience over time.

Summary

The design and implementation of a storage network is a long and complex procedure. You need to do detailed groundwork if you want your SAN to last. Detailed planning is the key to success. However, before you even begin planning, you must analyze the organization's requirements thoroughly and decide whether an expensive SAN is required. It is possible that the organization doesn't need a SAN.

Some of the major design considerations while planning and designing the SAN include the following:

- Business requirements
- Physical layout
- Performance
- Data pooling
- Data availability
- Heterogeneity
- Storage requirement
- Connectivity

- Scalability
- Migration
- Security
- Manageability
- Resilience
- Routability
- Prevention of traffic congestion
- Backup and restore capability

In this chapter, you learned to consider and plan for each of the preceding design considerations.

While designing a storage network, you need to select an appropriate topology. A SAN's performance and ability to meet business and technical requirements depends, in part, on the implementation of the appropriate topology. In addition, the reuse of existing devices can help bring down the total cost of implementation of the SAN. Then, you learned how to construct a SAN on the basis of the design that you developed in the design phase.

You can follow certain best practices in the predesign (planning), design, and construction stages to build a cost-effective, high-performance, and fault-tolerant storage network. This chapter discussed these best practices, which you should follow while building your SAN.

In this chapter, you will learn about the following:

- General security guidelines
- Securing a SAN
- Securing business environments

CHAPTER 8

Implementing SAN Security

The end user expects the storage system to provide speedy data transactions 24 hours a day, 7 days a week, and 365 days a year. So, the prime focus of storage networks is high performance and 24/7 data availability. In addition to these requirements, the data stored in a storage network is highly confidential and valuable. According to a recent study, compromise of this data or a security breach can cost a small organization tens of thousands of dollars.

The fourth annual Information Security Survey by Information Week and Ernst & Young presented some more shocking statistics. According to this survey, more than 50 percent of 1300 IS executives surveyed across the U.S. and Canada indicated that they had suffered financial losses from security breaches and disaster recovery. Seventy percent were unable to calculate the loss they had to bear. More than 25 percent of medium-sized organizations estimated a loss of roughly $250,000. However, large organizations had to face losses of up to several million dollars. It is estimated that 90 percent of small businesses would go out of business in the case of a catastrophic event. These statistical figures reiterate the fact that security is not only important, but that it is another fundamental requirement of any storage area network (SAN).

However, security is one of the most neglected aspects of storage networks. Most SAN designers fail to realize the threats of snooping, unauthorized deletion or modification of data, compromised data, or inaccessibility to data because of hacking. These threats are as serious in the case of storage networks as in any other normal network. With the upcoming Internet Small Computer System Interface (iSCSI) and IP-based storage technologies that promise to connect SANs to the Internet, the security threat becomes even more real.

NOTE   The Internet has grown at an unprecedented rate. Since its advent in 1969, the Internet has expanded from merely four interconnected hosts to more than 80,000,000 interconnected hosts that form the core of the Internet—the World Wide Web (WWW). The security threat has grown proportionately. As per the latest report by the Computer Emergency Response Team (CERT), 34,754 security incidents were reported within the first three quarters of 2000-2001. This figure is staggering and warns just how real the security threat is in our wired world, and how important it is to protect mission-critical data stored in SANs if they are going to be interconnected over the Internet!

In this chapter, you will learn the basics of securing a storage network. You'll learn about the general guidelines that will help you secure a SAN. You'll also learn how to prevent SAN components and business transactions in divisional and enterprise environments from unauthorized access and hacking.

General Security Guidelines

As mentioned earlier, security is one of the most neglected aspects of SANs. The common security issues are as follows:

- Poor administration of the storage network.
- Lack of a comprehensive security policy.

NOTE   The security policy of a network contains directions on the management of user accounts. This includes detailed information about user accounts, user privileges, data categories and the associated safeguards, and a list of legal and prohibited activities.

- Absence of vulnerability analysis during the design and construction phase of the SAN.

NOTE   Vulnerability analysis helps an organization to re-evaluate and locate loopholes in its security policies.

The guidelines discussed in the following sections help to eliminate security threats and to implement a secure storage network.

Controlling Physical Access to the SAN and Its Components

You must first control physical access to the SAN and its components, which ensures the physical security of your storage network and its components. This is important because security threats by employees of an organization are common. The same study by Information Week and Ernst & Young estimates that employees pose 33 percent of the security threats for an organization as compared to a mere 17 percent of malicious attacks by outsiders. You can ensure better security of data and the network by implementing a strict check on the physical accessibility to the storage network and its components. Allow only authorized personnel to physically access the SAN and its components.

Implementing Passwords

Next, ensure that strictly confidential and valid passwords are used in the following cases:

- **All the SAN components directly connected to the attached local-area network (LAN)**—This is important because the security of IP-based networks is low. The most serious security threats are in the form of unauthorized access by using *IP spoofing*. IP spoofing is an access technique in which the intruder creates fake request packets from authorized IP-based clients. *IP sniffing* is another source of potential threat, where IP addresses are stolen by eavesdropping on the data packets while in transit. Harmful data are then stamped with trusted IP addresses and transmitted to the hosts within the LAN.

- **All the serial line connections using the EIA/TIA-232 interface**—This is important because Serial Line Interface Protocol (SLIP), which is gradually being replaced by Point-to-Point Protocol (PPP), does not provide for access security. In addition, ensure that serial line connection points are placed in physically secure locations and that only authorized personnel have access to these points.

NOTE	The RS-232 (Recommended Standard-232) has been replaced by the EIA/TIA-232 standard.

- **All the remote accesses**—It's important to prevent hackers (and crackers) from gaining access to the storage network and its individual components, such as routers and switches. Routers are especially vulnerable to unauthorized attacks from outside a SAN because they act as the periphery devices of a network and are used to connect remote SANlets. Similarly, access to switches in the SAN can also badly disrupt the functioning of the entire storage network. This is because switches form the Fabric of a SAN, and almost all the SAN devices and components are connected to each other through switches. Therefore, extra security measures must be taken to protect vulnerable components of the storage network, such as switches, hubs, routers, and so on.

NOTE	*Hackers* are unauthorized intruders who gain access to network resources and sensitive data stored in the network. A hacker might be a computer over-enthusiast trying to test their ability. The term *cracker* is also often used for a hacker, which refers to an individual whose goal is to gain access to a network and damage the stored information or to bring down the network and expose an organization's vital information to the rest of the world.

Disabling the Web Browser Management Interface

You should also disable the Web browser management interface, if possible. This helps decrease security threats because of unauthorized remote accesses.

Disabling Remote Management

You can also consider disabling remote management (using in-band and out-of-band connections) of hubs, switches, and other manageable devices for added measures of security.

Implementing Fiber-Optic Cables

The implementation of fiber-optic cables reduces the probability for eavesdropping and snooping of data during transmissions. It is extremely difficult to tap into optical cables because they are made up of fiber-optic glass and therefore do not emit radiation or electro-magnetic pulses. Therefore, fiber-optic cables offer a high level of transmission security.

NOTE   In addition to offering a high level of transmission security, fiber-optic cables have many more advantages to offer. These include support to high data transfer rates (1 Gbps and above) at much longer distances (100 kilometers and above). Also, fiber-optic cables are easier to handle than copper cables because they are much smaller and lighter in weight. Being made of fiber-optic glass, they are not subject to outdoor atmospheric conditions, corrosion, fire hazards, or electrical shocks. The biggest advantage of fiber-optic cabling is that it is immune to practically all kinds of interferences, such as lightning and electricity.

Refer to Chapter 5, "Fibre Channel Cabling," for detailed information on fiber-optic cables.

Implementing Perimeter Security

Ensure that perimeters of your storage network are secure from outside attacks. The proper implementation of a firewall system will help you achieve this target.

Firewalls are an effective way to protect a network from most outside security threats (intentional or otherwise). Besides preventing unauthorized access from other connected networks, firewalls play a significant role in preventing virus attacks, denying access to unauthorized sites by filtering URLs, and blocking unauthorized access to remote applications that might be unsafe for the network by filtering applications. When the network is under an attack, firewalls keep damage on one part of the network (for example, eaves-dropping, a worm program, file damage) from spreading to the rest of the network. Without firewalls, network security problems can rage out of control, dragging more and more systems down.

Securing In-Transit Data

The following measures must be firmly in place to bring down security threats faced in long-distance data transmissions:

- **Data must be transmitted in encrypted format**—Encryption based on IP Security Protocol (IPSec) should be used for this. Developed by IETF, the IPSec supports two data transfer modes to ensure secure transactions between the two sides exchanging data. In the first mode—known as the *transport mode*—the data portion, or the payload, of a packet is encrypted. However, the sender is not authenticated. The second mode, the *tunnel mode*, offers enhanced data security by encrypting the payload and authenticating the sender by using digital certificates. For data to be encrypted using IPSec, the exchanging devices must negotiate the IPSec parameters by using the Internet Key Exchange (IKE) standard.

NOTE   A digital certificate is an electronic document issued by a Certificate Authority that allows the parties involved in a transaction to establish their individual identities during an exchange. A digital certificate contains information such as name, address, and organization that establishes the identity of the sender or receiver. In addition, the digital certificate also contains the public key issued to the sender, dates of validity of the certificate, and the digital signature of the Certificate Authority.

- **Proper authentication and authorization measures must be implemented**—Use of digital certificates ensures the authenticity and confidentiality of the data transmitted. Digital signatures are obtained by a combination of public and private keys. Provided by a designated authority, a *public key*, as the name suggests, is known to everyone. The *private key* is a secret key shared between the parties involved in an exchange. The two keys—public and private—are related in such a manner that only the public key can be used to encrypt a given message and the corresponding private key can be used to decrypt the message. The best feature of this encryption methodology is that even if the public key were known to a third entity, it would be practically impossible to deduce the private key.

Implementing the Administration Policy

Auditing the network on a recurring basis helps you to ensure that the security policy of the organization is being enforced appropriately and that no irregularities have developed as the network has evolved. The results of these network audits can also be accumulated over a period of time, and can be used to modify the security policy and the technology implementation as needed.

Regular monitoring of system log files, automatic e-mail notifications that are triggered on the occurrence of an event, forwarding of messages to remote servers, and administration of security architecture of the storage network are a few more measures that help to ensure the security of data in a SAN environment.

Effective logging and log processing is the key method of monitoring the security of a network. System logs record a wide range of events that include hardware errors, failed logins, rejected connections, and possible intrusions from unauthorized (or untrustworthy) addresses. Processing the log entries through scripts provides network administrators immediate notifications if any event of interest occurs.

While installing management tools, make sure that the event-logging feature is enabled and functional. This feature can play one of the most significant roles in the maintenance of the security of any network, including a SAN. This is because they record any event—big or small—that occurs in the network. Regular monitoring of this event log, known as *SysLog* in most cases, helps to identify vulnerable points of your storage network in addition to detecting possible intrusions or intrusion attempts.

The SysLog facility runs a daemon known as *syslogd*. This daemon records events specified as severe. These include various categories of alerts and errors. This information about events of interest is either stored in ASCII files on the local system, forwarded to a remote system's syslog daemon, or mailed to the specified destination, as indicated in the syslog.conf file.

Restricting Access to Multiple Storage Systems

If possible, restrict user access to more than one storage system in the SAN. In other words, try to store related data on one high-capacity storage system. The more accessibility to various storage subsystems there is, the higher the risk there is for a security breach.

Choosing a Reliable Service Provider

Sometimes, you might have to enlist the services of a service provider for remote access. You must choose a reliable service provider and ensure that the Service Level Agreement (SLA) has a clear-cut definition of processes and the relationship between your organization and the service provider. More important, you must carefully go through the security services the ISP has to offer your organization. You might have to pay a little more for the enhanced security services, but it will definitely serve you better in the long run by ensuring improved security of mission-critical data.

NOTE	SLA is an agreement between the ISP and a customer regarding the services that the ISP will provide. Today, most of the organizations that request these services from their ISPs also measure them. Some of these metrics include percentage of the time promised services are available, help-desk response time for various classes of problems, and usage statistics.

Analyzing Vulnerability

Similar to any other network system, a storage network is also vulnerable to all sorts of attacks from within and outside the network. Vulnerability analysis done at regular intervals helps an organization to identify possible breaches in the existing security policies and to work out a proactive solution to security breakdowns.

A vulnerability analysis includes an in-depth analysis of network access rules for the network users, validity of passwords, and the weakest security link—internal hosts (FTP servers, Web servers, and routers) that are accessible publicly from outside the network. On the basis of the vulnerability analysis, a vulnerability report is prepared that contains the testing results and possible security solutions to eliminate the vulnerability.

Tools and techniques used by hackers (and crackers) to penetrate the security system of the network are used for vulnerability analysis to uncover weaknesses in the firewalls that are used in the system and router configurations. The determination of an acceptable time period after which the vulnerability analyses must be conducted also plays an important role in the effective monitoring of the security of a storage network. This time frame is determined on the basis of the size of the organization, resources, and security awareness.

Implementing the Management Policy

As specified earlier in this chapter, an average of 33% of an organization's data loss is the result of disgruntled employees and insiders. Therefore, the implementation of a well-defined management policy that keeps an eye on personnel also proves to be useful in ensuring security of your storage network.

Now that you know about the general guidelines you can implement to ensure security in your storage network, you will now examine how you can further secure your storage network.

Securing a SAN

Security of a storage network can be implemented at two levels—the hardware level and the software level. Security at the hardware level is implemented by ensuring the physical security of SAN components. Similarly, security at the software level is implemented with the help of various software applications that play a significant role in shielding data from security breaches and threats. These security breaches can be determined only in an after-the-fact method. Therefore, it is imperative that you maintain a running log file.

In the following section, you'll learn the basic techniques that will help you secure various SAN components.

Securing SAN Components

Securing individual SAN components is a major step toward ensuring the safety of confidential and valuable data that is stored in a storage network. The two most important components of a SAN that you need to provide maximum security for are the following:

- SAN Fabric
- Storage systems

The following sections discuss both of these components.

Securing the SAN Fabric

Fibre Channel switches form the backbone of the Fabric. These switches are also the most important components of a storage network because all SAN traffic has to pass through them. Aside from the general security measures discussed in the previous section you can secure Fabric switches from unauthorized access, eavesdropping, and other security breaches.

Storage networks offer a high level of data availability. Although a boon for users who can access information any time or any day, this feature is a potential nightmare for the administrators of storage networks. This is because increased accessibility leads to the need for increased security.

One of the best techniques for securing data stored in various storage systems in a SAN is *Fabric zoning*. Fabric zoning allows you to create logical subsets within a storage network. These subsets can be accessed either at device level or port level. As a result, devices or ports that belong to one zone can be easily restricted from accessing devices or ports from other zones.

In port-based zoning, individual ports of a single device can be assigned to different zones. Ports that belong to the same zone can communicate with each other. However, ports that belong to the same device but to different zones cannot communicate with each other. In device-based zoning, an entire device (regardless of the number of ports it has) belongs to a single zone. Switch-based zoning is the common implementation of device-based zoning. Figure 8-1 depicts the simplest implementation of switch-based zoning.

Figure 8-1   *Simplest Implementation of Switch-Based Zoning*

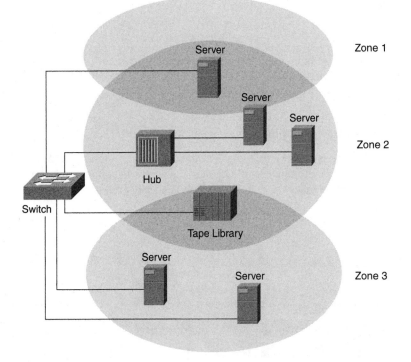

Zoning allows a device or a port to be a member of multiple zones at the same time. This allows selected nodes or ports to access data stored in other zones. Therefore, you must provide membership to multiple zones carefully. For example, you can create departmental zones in your storage network where employees of one department are restricted from accessing storage devices of other departments.

In addition, Fabric zoning allows you to create *virtual SANlets* within a SAN. A virtual SANlet is a logical portion of a storage network that is obtained by pooling or clustering a few SAN storage devices without having to re-wire or re-zone the entire storage network.

Although the SANlets derived from a large SAN can share resources (routers and switches) with each other, they have limited access to each other. Moreover, traffic in each SANlet is isolated from other traffic. This departmental approach not only reduces the transport overheads associated with IP-based routing, but also further enhances the data security of each department in the organization.

The next technique of Logical Unit Number (LUN) masking is a step beyond Fabric zoning in the quest of controlling access to a particular storage device in the network. LUN management software is run on each application server. DotHill's SANPath 3.1 and Dell's PowerVault 530F are two of the most commonly used LUN management applications.

These LUN management modules effectively mask LUNs that a server does not have rights to access. Only those LUNs to which the server has accessibility rights, are visible to the server.

NOTE   LUN refers to an individual storage unit of a storage network. For example, a disk in a disk array or a disk partition on a storage device can be assigned a LUN.

Figure 8-2 depicts the simple implementation of LUN masking.

LUN masking is also referred to as *Selective Storage Presentation (SSP)*. This technique not only reduces the chances of unauthorized access to confidential data to a considerable extent, but also makes the management of data access relatively simple.

Figure 8-2   *Simplest Implementation of LUN Masking*

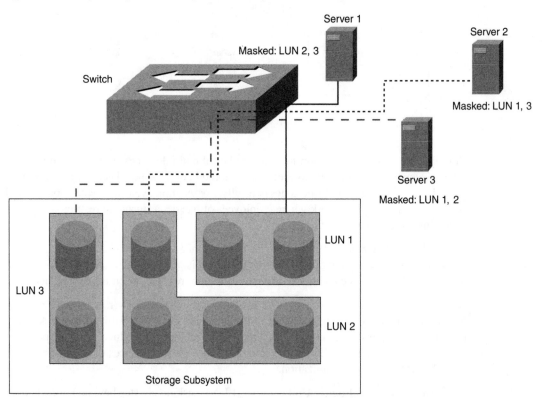

Components of a SAN can also be secured by disabling the management of switches using *SCSI Enclosure Services (SES)* for in-band connections. This measure increases the security of a Fibre Channel switch because it eliminates the possibility of unauthorized access through the in-band SES interface.

NOTE   When a SAN device communicates with the management console over the same Fibre Channel link that is used for data transport using the SES specification, the corresponding SAN management strategy is referred to as in-band management. For more information on in-band management, refer to Chapter 9, "Problem Isolation and Management of SANs."

In remote network management, *out-band connections* are used for the remote configuration of network devices and the diagnosis of hardware problems. In-band connections are basically used to monitor the status of devices. If not secured properly by using strictly confidential passwords, these management strategies can pose serious threats. You can ensure the security of SAN devices by disabling in-band and out-of-band connections in the following cases:

- Simple Network Management Protocol (SNMP) management of switches and other manageable SAN components

    NOTE   SNMP is a network administration protocol, which allows monitoring of network devices and traffic. The advantages of this protocol are that it uses a simple interface and allows the management of devices ranging from workstations, printers, servers, switches, routers, and so on. However, SNMP uses a single unencrypted string for authentication purposes. This makes it highly vulnerable to outside attacks. Once cracked, SNMP can supply detailed information about the network structure to the intruder.

- Web browser-based management of switches and other manageable SAN components

NOTE   Although password protected, most Web browser interfaces use Hypertext Transfer Protocol (HTTP) authentication, which is weak unless strong encryptions, such as digital certificates and Public Key Infrastructure (PKI), are implemented. As a result, if a SAN device is managed through the browser interface, it can be easily hacked.

In-band and out-of-band management can cause serious security threats. However, in some situations, remote management might be a necessity. For example, it might not be possible for the administrator to be physically present to troubleshoot a SAN device. In such cases, Telnet is the best option because it offers stronger authentication than most remote troubleshooting utilities. Therefore, you must ensure that Telnet connections for general data-access and remote-management purposes are password protected and that these passwords are strictly confidential. It is also advisable to change the passwords periodically. In addition, you must implement multiple levels of authentication and access control to the switches wherever possible.

In the next section, you'll explore the various methods that you can use to secure storage devices in a SAN.

Securing Storage Systems

Other than the SAN Fabric, storage systems are another important and vulnerable component of a storage network. They physically store the data. Therefore, they are another favorite target of hackers and data snoopers, if not protected adequately. You can ensure the security of storage systems in your storage network by implementing the following measures:

- **Presenting storage selectively**—The presentation of selective data to servers and users helps in reducing the security threat to data. You can use the concept of LUN masking to do so. For example, the personnel in the Finance or Sales departments do not require access to confidential HR-related data. Similarly, Sales personnel do not need to have access to financial data. To prevent unnecessary access to interdepartmental storage devices, a separate zone can be created for each department. If required, you can also make restricted personnel members of multiple zones, allowing them access to selected data of other departments. However, these personnel and requirements should be scanned thoroughly before making them members of multiple zones.

- **Controlling physical access**—Data is the most valuable asset of any organization in today's scenario. You must strictly control the physical accessibility to the storage systems and devices in the SAN. You must house the storage systems under lock and key and allow only trusted personnel to access these storage devices.

- **Controlling data access**—Use the concept of user rights and privileges extensively. Users must be able to access, query, or modify particular data only if they have rights to do so. Do not assign rights and privileges liberally. When used with other security techniques, such as LUN masking and Fabric zoning, proper data-access control measures help to enhance the security of your storage network.

- **Managing storage controllers**—Every storage system is controlled by a corresponding controller (or adapter sometimes). These controllers play an important role in the full-time accessibility and availability of data, in addition to the responsibility of the proper functioning of the storage device. However, in most of the storage devices, such as disk arrays and RAID subsystems, you can easily manipulate storage controllers with the help of various buttons located on front or rear panels. Therefore, it is necessary that you strictly control who can physically access and manipulate these controllers.

The next section discusses the various software-based security measures that help you tighten the security of your storage network.

Software-Based Security Measures

In addition to hardware security measures, you can also use software applications to manage the security and integrity of the data stored in your SAN. As opposed to hardware-level security measures, software-based security measures are dependent on user privileges. Also, software measures can be implemented at the level of files, folders, and volumes. This makes software-based SAN management much more flexible and simple compared to hardware-based security measures.

You can implement software-based security measures with the following applications:

- Data-access control applications
- Management applications

Data-access control applications, such as Compaq's Tru64 UNIX (compliant with the Windows platform), IBM's Tivoli SANergy File Sharing, and Availant's Availant Manager, allow users to be assigned access privileges. You can set access rights for every storage volume. Although most of these applications allow multiple reads from the same file or database, they allow only one user at a time to write to the file or to modify the existing data. Thus, these applications maintain the integrity of the data stored in the SAN.

Management applications, such as Tivoli Storage Network Manager, Compaq's SANworks Management Appliance, and StorageWorks Command Console Management Software, are more advanced ways of device management, especially remote management in SANs. These software appliances support elaborate authentication and authorization measures, which are sorely lacking in Web browser-based or Telnet-based remote management. In addition, most of the management applications implement data encryption during transactions, which makes device management and transactions more secure.

NOTE	Software-based SAN security measures do not work alone. They have to be augmented by elaborate hardware security measures to ensure the confidentiality and integrity of stored and in-transit data.

In the next section, you will learn the basics of securing business environments from threats—internal and external.

Securing Business Environments

Depending on the size of the organization, the storage network can be small-to-medium or large in size. Small- and medium-sized storage networks generally use the divisional approach, whereas large networks spanning great distances are based on the enterprise approach. However, irrespective of the size of the SAN, both the environments need to be adequately secured. The following sections discuss both of these approaches.

Divisional Security

In the divisional approach, the SANlets are created on the basis of divisions in the organization, as compared to the enterprise approach where the storage network is not divided into various zones on the basis of divisions. Security in the divisional environment is not as big a concern as in the enterprise environment. This is because personnel in the same division share similar goals and generally work on the same set of projects or tasks. All the employees in the same division more or less must access the same storage systems. Therefore, the implementation of security measures and the management of data access is comparatively simpler. However, there is still a possibility of the following security threats:

- Malicious attempt to break into the system by an employee
- Accidental access or modification of confidential information

Malicious attempts by an employee to access information for personal benefit or malicious intent can be prevented by restricting access to the storage systems, controllers, and other SAN components. Also, implementation of the SSP feature and password protected management interfaces reduces the possibility of such attempts.

Set the proper user privileges and activities to prevent accidental read access to confidential and prohibited information. You should also train employees to be aware of security breaches that they can easily prevent by reporting them. Performing regular security audits also exposes possible threats and security lapses.

Finally, restrict the disk quota for each user based on individual work requirements. By restricting the disk quota on a storage device for each user, you can reduce considerably the security risk. This is because when an intruder gains access to a storage device by hacking an authorized user's passwords and privileges, they can generate worms or codes that multiply on their own and that destroy the entire disk space of the given storage system. However, if the disk quota is restricted for each user, the damage is restricted to the user's disk space.

You can also train users to report attempted access to restricted files. This measure can prove effective in tracking users (internal and external) who try to access unauthorized information.

Enterprise Security

The enterprise environment encourages interdivisional transactions. Therefore, the level of trust is comparatively lower than the divisional approach. Also, there might be differences in the need of security requirements. As a result, the security requirements are more severe in this environment. The possible security threats here include the following:

- Malicious attempts to break into the system by an employee
- Accidental access or modification of confidential information
- Eavesdropping on data during transmissions

These security threats can be countered in the following ways:

- Restrict physical accessibility to SAN components. Password protect all the management interfaces and selectively present the data and resources to employees according to their needs and requirements.
- Place the storage network in a central location. This approach makes implementation of physical security measures and management of the storage fairly simple.
- Assign proper user privileges and activities. This prevents instances of accidental viewing of confidential and prohibited information.
- Implement optical cabling, which is difficult to eavesdrop on.
- Disable the in-band SES management interface to Fabric switches.
- Disable Web browser and SNMP management interfaces to Fabric switches. This reduces the risk of remote intrusions.
- Provide security awareness training to all employees. This training makes the employees aware of possible security breaches so that they will know to report these breaches when they occur.
- Regular security audits also expose possible threats and security lapses.
- As suggested for the divisional approach, you should restrict the disk quota for each user. According to work requirements, the disk quota for all users in the organization might not be the same.
- Perform routine user account management at the server side. Besides creating and deleting user accounts, user account management activities include analyzing individual user requirements, allocating disk quotas to users, and providing access rights to files and LUNs.

These measures help to bring down to a minimum the security threat to your storage network. However, remember that your storage network contains the organization's valuable, confidential, and mission-critical data. You have to be always on your toes to keep up with the latest trends—threats and preventive measures—if you want your storage network to justify the effort put into it and its cost of implementation.

Summary

Simply said, building and implementing a SAN is not enough. Your storage network contains the most important asset of your organization—the data. In this age of hackers and malicious crackers, your data is constantly under threat of being accessed and violated.

In this chapter, you learned about the general guidelines that you must religiously implement to ensure the safety and integrity of the data stored on the various storage devices. In addition to these storage devices, you also learned to secure fundamental SAN components, such as the Fabric (switches), routers, and storage systems. You also learned about software-based security applications that further help you strengthen the security of your storage network. Finally, this chapter discussed various measures that will help you secure business transactions in the divisional and enterprise environment.

In this chapter, you will learn about the following:

- Isolating and troubleshooting problems
- Managing SANs
- Disaster management

CHAPTER 9

Problem Isolation and Management of SANs

Problems are part of any network setup. A storage network is no exception. Despite choosing best-of-breed components, applications, and management tools, there is no guarantee that everything will function ideally. The challenge is in handling any problem quickly so that long-term harm to the network is avoided. How quickly you detect, isolate, diagnose, and troubleshoot the problem so that no ongoing operations are disrupted is critical to the management of a storage network. If operations are disrupted, the disruption must be short-lived.

Proper management can prove to be the most proactive method of avoiding a problem or disastrous situation. Management tools and applications allow you to control the network, monitor it, detect a problem before it reaches disastrous proportions, and provide assistance in troubleshooting the problem. Management tools and applications also play an important role in optimizing the performance of a storage network. In addition, many management tools can help you in planning, implementing, and configuring a storage area network (SAN).

Isolating and troubleshooting problems is not an instinctive art. It is an ongoing education that you gain from each experience. In this chapter, you will learn the basic techniques that set the groundwork for isolating and troubleshooting any problem in a storage network. You will learn about the management of SANs to help you to maintain and support a stable storage network. In addition, you will learn about one of the most critical aspects of any network—data backup and restoration. Proper data backup and restoration strategies help you recover data without potential corruption or loss, if you have to face network failure or data loss.

Isolating and Troubleshooting Problems

Most of the problems that occur in a storage network can be generalized into three broad categories. These categories are the following:

- Problems related to the physical connectivity of devices
- Problems related to the access of storage devices
- Problems related to the upper-layer protocols

Each category is discussed in the following sections.

Physical Connectivity Problems

SAN components can be either managed or unmanaged. Managed SAN components generally offer a graphical interface along with the capability of self- and remote-management. Because of this high degree of intelligence and the Graphical User Interface (GUI), connectivity-related problems are indicated in a user-friendly manner.

Unmanaged SAN components, on the other hand, use Light Emitting Diodes (LEDs) to indicate any connectivity-related problems. As a rule, each port on a SAN device, especially Fibre Channel hubs and switches, are represented by two LEDs—green and amber. The amber LED provides information about the bypass status of the port. At the same time, the green LED specifies the status of the link connection. They can also prove to be highly useful in identifying a connectivity problem.

The following combinations of LEDs are possible:

- **Amber off and Green off**—This combination indicates that no device is attached to the port. Therefore, the port is free.

NOTE   Copper cables do not use a Gigabit Interface Converter (GBIC) to attach a device to the port. As a result, they might not generate a port status despite the fact that a device is attached to the port.

- **Amber off/blinking and Green on**—This combination indicates that a device has been attached to the port and has been recognized successfully. This is the normal working condition of ports. However, if there is still a lack of proper communication, there is a possibility of one of the following problems:
    - Break in the cable
    - Incompatible cable
    - Bad quality cable
    - Bad connector
    - Protocol-related problem

The best way to verify a cable-related problem is to use a good cable in working condition in place of the existing cable. Similarly, bad connectors can be verified by replacing the current connector with a known working connector. If the problem is neither due to a cable nor a connector, verify that the device-end has been configured for the required device drivers because the problem might be due to upper-layer protocols.

- **Amber on and Green off/blinking**—This combination indicates that the GBIC connected to the port is either malfunctioning or is not connected properly to the port. Make sure that the GBIC is seated properly into the port. If the Green light still doesn't glow, connect the GBIC to another known working port. If the GBIC is bad, you'll have to replace it.

- **Amber blinking and Green blinking**—This combination indicates that the port is in maintenance mode. In the case of managed components, this mode can be started by the component itself. However, this mode can be evoked in unmanaged SAN components by an external management tool or application.

- **Amber on and Green on**—This combination provides information for different devices. In the case of unmanaged devices, this combination indicates that the device has been bypassed due to the lack of a proper signal. In the case of managed devices, this combination indicates that the port has been bypassed due to corruption of the data that is being received on the corresponding port. For a Fibre Channel switch, the same combination indicates failure in Fabric login. You will need to resort to Fibre Channel analyzers and SAN management tools to solve the problems indicated by this combination.

Table 9-1 summarizes the LED combinations.

Table 9-1   *The Port LED Status at a Glance*

Amber	Green	Status
Off	Off	The port is free.
Off/Blinking	On	A device has been attached to the port and has been recognized successfully.
On	Off/Blinking	GBIC connected to the port either is not seated properly or is malfunctioning.
Blinking	Blinking	The port is in maintenance mode.
On	On	Unmanaged device: The port has been bypassed because of the lack of proper signal.
		Managed device: Corrupt data received.

The next section discusses common problems you might face while accessing a storage device.

Storage Access Problems

After implementing a storage network, the biggest problem that you might come across is that either the entire storage system or a part of it is inaccessible to one or more servers. You can troubleshoot the problem by following these steps:

Step 1   Ensure that the given storage device(s) and server(s) are connected properly to the corresponding hub or switch.

Step 2   Some operating systems, such as Windows NT, require that the storage systems, especially disk arrays, must be booted before the servers running Windows NT boot up. It is quite possible that if a storage device is not operational before the servers are powered on, it might not be recognized by the servers. If this happens, shut down the Windows NT server. Then, reboot the connected storage device(s) and check if the storage device is still not being recognized by the server.

Step 3 If a single server consists of multiple Host Bus Adapters (HBAs), verify that the resource conflicts between the various HBAs is not preventing the server from recognizing one or more storage devices in the network. If so, you'll need to reconfigure the conflicting HBAs. Refer to the HBA manual provided by the vendor for more information on the correct configuration of HBAs.

Step 4 If the server still cannot recognize or access a particular storage system, verify that the appropriate device drivers are installed. Reinstall the device drivers, if necessary, and reboot the server.

If a server fails to recognize and access a storage device after following the previous steps, you might need to replace the HBAs, which might be faulty. Contact your vendor for more information if necessary.

Upper-Level Protocol Problems

Identifying problems that are related to physical connectivity or access to storage devices might be relatively easy. However, troubleshooting protocol-related problems on your own can prove to be very difficult. You might need a specialized diagnostic product known as a *Fibre Channel analyzer* for the purpose.

Fibre Channel analyzers are small (may be handheld) devices that are generally shipped with their own monitors. These devices are used to capture traffic generated by a port or a pair of ports engaged in a data transaction. After capturing the required data, Fibre Channel analyzers decode and analyze the data and display the resulting information in a manner that is easily understandable. You can use this information to isolate the protocol-related problem and troubleshoot the given problem with the help of facilities provided by the analyzer.

In addition, Fibre Channel analyzers can also provide performance statistics about a particular application. You can use this data to study the impact of the given application on the overall performance of the storage network. Some Fibre Channel analyzers also provide information about the presence of valid signals and transmission words on a port, and errors related to Cyclic Redundancy Check (CRC) in a frame.

Many vendors offer a wide range of Fibre Channel analyzers. These include Xyratex's Fibre Channel Investigator, Ancot's FCAccess 2000A and FCAccess 1000A series, and Finisar's GTX Protocol Analyzers, which are some of the commonly used Fibre Channel analyzers.

NOTE	Because of the advanced troubleshooting facilities that they provide, Fibre Channel analyzers are expensive devices. Their costs range from $30,000 to $50,000.

Managing SANs

A SAN is a complex environment. Therefore, after a SAN has been designed and deployed, you need to manage it effectively to ensure its smooth functioning. Also, its effective management ensures that the heterogeneous devices that make up the SAN are integrated seamlessly and that the complexity of the storage network is simplified.

Effective management must encompass a wide variety of activities ranging from the simplest to the most advanced management activities. Common SAN management activities include the following:

- Storage network planning
- Implementation and configuration of SAN components and storage devices
- Automatic discovery of a SAN topology and its components
- Security management
- Performance monitoring
- Event logging and notification
- Traffic management

The previously listed SAN management activities can be divided into four categories—network management, Storage Resource Management (SRM), data management, and performance management. These activities are discussed in the following sections.

Network Management

Sometimes also referred to as *Fabric management*, management activities related to this category control the SAN infrastructure and the flow of traffic across the Fabric. As a result, network management deals with the management of SAN components and the ensuing communication between these components. Network management consists of two types—in-band management and out-of-band management.

Generally, the workstation on which the management software is installed is referred to as a *management console*. When a SAN device communicates with the management console over the same Fibre Channel link that is used for data transport using SCSI Enclosure Services (SES) specification, the corresponding SAN management strategy is referred to as *in-band management*. Figure 9-1 shows the in-band management setup.

Figure 9-1 *Setup for In-Band Management*

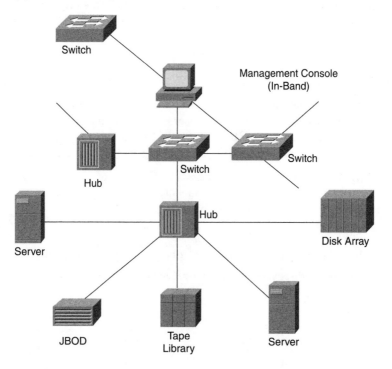

Proposed by ANSI, the SES specification defines commands, such as device service request (a SCSI command issued by an application server to a device server), for retrieving device-status information. This information includes fan speed, power supply status, device temperature, and other parameters that provide information on the status of the SCSI device. Implementation of SES in Fibre Channel hubs and switches can effectively reduce network traffic and can therefore help in the maximum utilization of network bandwidth.

The most sensitive point of this management strategy is the Fibre Channel link. If the link fails, the network cannot be managed because the management data is transmitted over the Fibre Channel links. As a result, detection, isolation, and troubleshooting faults and failures become difficult.

This link-related problem can be easily avoided by provisioning for redundant paths between the management console and managed devices. However, setting up a redundant path between the management console and each device can considerably increase the cost of implementation of the storage network.

In the out-of-band management strategy, the management console is connected to the storage network through a separate interface, such as Ethernet. As a result, although the management console might be a physical part of the Fibre Channel storage network, it is logically segregated from the SAN. Figure 9-2 depicts the setup for out-of-band management.

Figure 9-2   *Setup for Out-Of-Band Management*

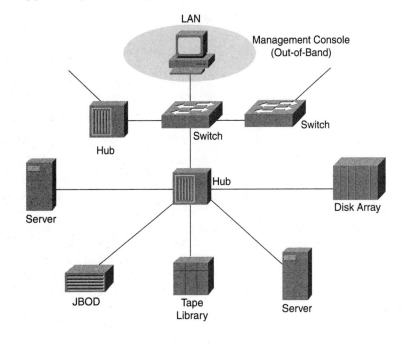

NOTE	Most Fibre Channel vendors provide a serial RS-232 or an Ethernet port in their products. You can use this port to connect the management console to a Fibre Channel switch or a hub.

The advantages offered by out-of-band management are the following:

- In the case of Fibre Channel link and Fabric failure, managing devices, such as Fibre Channel hubs, switches, and bridges, is possible through the Ethernet link.

- Out-of-band management facilitates the implementation of enterprise networks, where SAN devices can be managed locally and remotely.

- Out-of-band management uses IP-based protocols, such as Simple Network Management Protocol (SNMP), Hypertext Transfer Protocol (HTTP), and Telnet. This helps in the integration of storage networks with IP-based networks.

The out-of-band management strategy is also associated with a disadvantage. Because the management console can be logically (and also physically) segregated from the storage network, management functions, such as the automatic discovery of SAN topology and the implementation and configuration of SAN devices, are not possible.

Storage Resource Management

Storage devices are the backbone of any organization because they store a valuable asset—data. Storage Resource Management (SRM) provides the efficient management of storage devices in a SAN. SRM activities include the following:

- Configuration, support, and maintenance of the storage resources in the network

- Creation and management of logical units in the storage resources in the network

- Implementation of alternate data paths between storage resources and servers

- Implementation of RAID levels

- Scheduling of data defragmentation routines that do not interrupt regular operations

Various SRM applications, such as Sun's HighGround Storage Resource Manager Software, IBM's ADSM ADSTAR, and Computer Associate's BrightStor Storage Resource Manager, are available in the market. These applications allow administrators to view and manage the physically scattered storage devices and systems as one huge logical resource instead of as individual devices. As a result, an administrator can easily consolidate information about storage devices in the network. SRM applications also facilitate the regular retrieval of status information from storage resources. Therefore, the administrator has constant access to the latest information about the status of each and every device in the storage network.

SRM applications also help the administrator to set policies related to usage threshold. If the usage threshold of a storage device is exceeded, the administrator is instantly notified about the situation, thus preventing storage crashes and other storage-related problems.

Data Management

Apart from physical assets, data is one of the biggest assets of an organization. Unavailability or inaccessibility of data can lead to disruption in the normal functioning of the organization. Data management applications ensure that critical data is available and accessible at any given point in time.

Data management applications should provide for the following features:

- A strategy for data backup and restoration. At the same time, data management applications must ensure the optimal performance of the storage network.

- The efficient administration of logical units (LUs) in the storage network.

- The implementation and administration of file policies, such as file access.

- Access control to shared resources, such as disk arrays and tape libraries.

- Management and integration of various file systems.

Performance Management

Performance is an important criterion of any storage network. Only a high-performance SAN can ensure a good Return On Investment (ROI). To ensure good SAN performance, it is important to monitor SAN traffic and applications constantly. Constant and efficient monitoring of the storage network provides early notification of faults and failures before they become a disaster.

Performance management includes monitoring of the following:

- **Bandwidth usage**—Monitoring bandwidth usage allows the network administrator to determine actual, average, and peak usage of available network bandwidth. This helps the administrator to determine the bandwidth baseline, which if reached indicates the possibility of traffic congestion.

- **Storage usage**—Monitoring the usage of storage devices allows the administrator to identify the storage devices that are accessed most frequently and to take steps to reduce user-response time.

- **Traffic patterns**—Monitoring traffic patterns helps the administrator to identify those situations where network traffic does not comply with specified network policies or when it exceeds defined thresholds.

- **Events**—Monitoring events, such as exceeding the bandwidth threshold, by logging them helps the administrator of a storage network to identify a possible problem and to take action before it is blown out of proportion.

A careful choice of management tools is important to setting up a stable storage network. You will now learn about the features that you should look for in SAN management tools.

SAN Management Tool Features

A wide range and variety of SAN management tools and applications are available in the market. These tools offer a varying range of management capabilities. Because your organization has already invested a great deal of time, expertise, and money into the storage network, it makes good sense to buy a management tool or application to ensure the high-availability and high-performance of your SANs.

Although the following list is not exhaustive, you should look for the following features in a SAN management tool or application:

- **Backup sizing and planning**—Although the backup activity carried out in a storage network does not affect the users in the attached LAN, it might slow down access to the storage devices located in the SAN. This feature helps in determining the average backup window and identifying when to take backups so that access to these storage devices is least affected.

- **Asset tracking and configuration management**—This feature helps the SAN administrator to keep track of the status and the performance of all the devices that make up the SAN.

- **Event notification**—This feature helps in tracking events that could lead to a catastrophe and takes proactive action. These events might include unauthorized access into the network or reaching the bandwidth-usage threshold.

- **Partition space threshold**—This feature allows the administrator to identify when a partition reaches its maximum capacity.

- **Traffic monitoring**—This feature allows the network administrator to identify traffic patterns and to identify when the specified network policies are being violated or the network traffic threshold is being exceeded.

- **Storage monitoring**—This feature allows the SAN administrator to identify when a storage device reaches its maximum capacity. Also, storage monitoring allows the administrator to keep track of the usage of all the storage devices in the storage network and to set access rights so that the data stored on the storage device is not harmed in any way.

- **Load monitoring**—The load-monitoring feature allows the network administrator to determine the actual, average, and peak usage of available network bandwidth. This helps the administrator to determine the bandwidth baseline, which if reached indicates the possibility of traffic congestion.

- **Application monitoring**—This feature allows the SAN administrator to identify the application (or applications) that create bottlenecks and take preventive measures to curb network congestion.

- **Automated polling intervals**—This feature sets the optimum interval for polling the constituent SAN devices automatically on the basis of network policies, thresholds, and baselines, without the network administrator. This regular polling of devices helps in gathering the status information of the overall SAN and modifying the thresholds and baselines, if necessary.

- **QoS and performance metering**—This feature allows the administrator of the storage network to track the overall performance of the SAN and to take required measures if the performance level reaches below the set average.

- **Trend analysis and capacity planning**—This feature allows the administrator to analyze various trends, such as storage usage and link usage. These trends can then be used for setting baselines and thresholds.

- **Billing and cost management**—This feature helps the administrator in determining the cost of maintenance and management of the SAN. In the case of commercial organizations, such as application service providers (ASPs) that provide external data storage facilities, this feature helps in evaluating the total amount accrued by a customer.

- **Support to a wide range of platforms and operating systems**—The wider the range of platforms and operating systems supported by a management tool, the better the options it provides for the administrator to mix and match SAN products from various vendors. This helps in bringing down the Total Cost of Ownership (TCO) of the SAN considerably, while increasing its efficiency at the same time.

Some of the latest SAN management products available in the market today include Compaq's SANworks Network View, Sun's Sun Management Center 3.0, IBM's Tivoli NetView, Tivoli Storage Manager, and Tivoli Storage Network Manager, InterSAN's Pathline, SANavigator Inc's SANavigator version 1.5, and BakBone's NetVault.

In the next section, you learn about disaster management and how to handle situations, such as data loss.

Disaster Management

Data, especially business data, is one of the most valuable assets of any organization. Therefore, all necessary steps must be taken to ensure the safety of this data even in case of disastrous situations, such as storage crashes, virus attacks, and so on.

Data backups done on a regular basis are one of the most effective measures of disaster recovery. Timely restoration of business data can prevent a business from prolonged standstill situations. Corporations are struggling not only to cope with huge amounts of data and full-time, on-demand access to data, but also with the complex infrastructure that supports this data. As a result, backups seem to have taken a backseat because network administrators are busy with protecting the networks and ensuring full-time, high-speed availability of data. In fact, many administrators feel that they cannot back up their data as regularly and as cost-effectively as they would prefer. Therefore, many have been forced to adopt makeshift strategies, such as cloning and data replication to ensure the safety of mission-critical data.

In the following section, the traditional backup and restoration model will be discussed. You'll learn about this model and its advantages and disadvantages.

Traditional Backup and Restoration

The following backup and restoration models have been used traditionally:

- Servers with dedicated storage resources
- Backup and restoration over LAN

The model that represents servers with dedicated storage resources features dedicated storage devices connected directly to the application servers in the LAN, as shown in Figure 9-3. The problem with this setup is that as the number of LAN servers increases, the number of corresponding storage devices increases proportionally. As a result, the management of storage resources becomes a time-consuming and tedious task. The other disadvantages associated with this model are the following:

- Under-utilization of storage resources because one server cannot access and use storage resources attached to another server, even if it urgently requires disk space.

- Different platforms and operating systems use different backup and restoration applications and tools, such as Veritas' Backup Exec, BEI Corp's UltraBac, and Computer Associate's ARCServe 6.5. These tools and applications might not necessarily be compatible. This not only complicates SRM, but also increases the TCO of the storage network.

The backup and restoration over the LAN model features a centralized backup system that consists of a primary backup server. All the storage resources in the network are directly attached to this backup server. Figure 9-4 shows the setup of this model.

Figure 9-3   *LAN Servers with Dedicated Storage Resources*

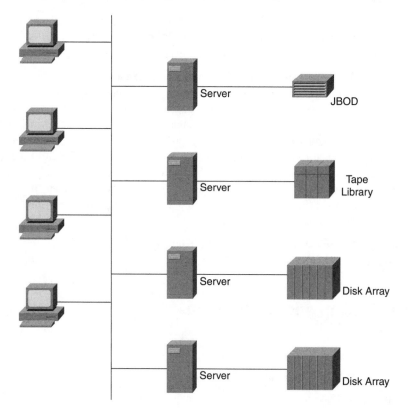

Figure 9-4   *Backup and Restoration over a LAN*

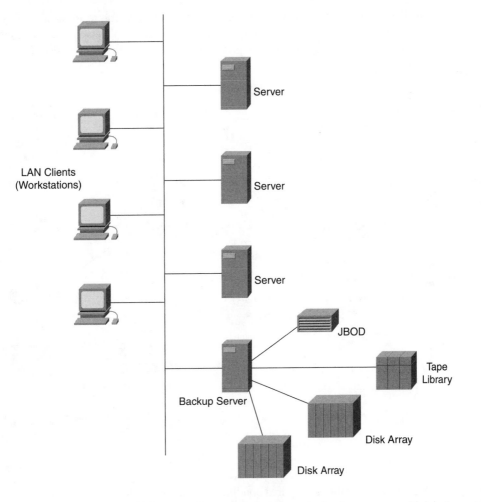

In this setup, the LAN servers forward their data to the backup server, which in turn stores this data on one of the attached storage devices. This approach alleviates some of the drawbacks posed by the previous direct-attached storage approach. This model offers better disk utilization, faster deployment, and cost-effective backup and restoration opportunities to network administrators. However, the use of LAN bandwidth for the transportation of huge amounts of bandwidth-intensive backup data can prove to be a major bottleneck and can degrade the overall performance of the LAN.

In the next section, you'll learn how the SAN backup and restoration model overcomes the problems generally faced in the traditional model.

SAN Backup and Restoration

The design of a SAN is such that the data can be backed up and restored efficiently and regularly, without bringing down the performance of the local network to which the SAN is attached. Figure 9-5 depicts the typical SAN backup and restoration model.

Figure 9-5 *Backup and Restoration over a SAN*

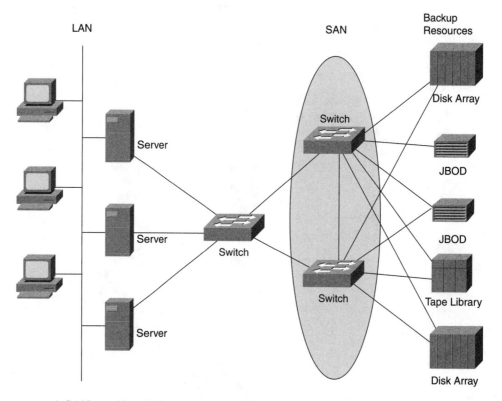

A SAN provides all the required conditions to perform efficient backup and restoration activities. These include the following:

- 100 Mbps or above full-duplex links that bring down the total time required for the backup or restoration of huge amounts of data.

NOTE The total time that is required to complete a backup process is commonly referred to as a *backup window*. Generally, the length of the backup window in LANs for an average of 1 TB of data is 12–18 hours. However, SAN-based backups reduce the length of backup windows for 1 TB of data to a mere 4–6 hours. This vast difference in the backup windows of LANs and SANs is because backups in SAN are LAN-free. As a result, the available bandwidth is not shared between users and the backup window, which greatly decreases the size of the backup window. More importantly, fiber-optic links that are used in SANs support transmissions at the rate of several gigabits. This is another reason why the backup windows in SANs are practically half the size of backup windows in LANs.

- High-performance infrastructure that is designed to transmit large chunks of data more efficiently and reliably as compared to IP-based networks.
- Segregation of the storage network from the primary LAN, which allows anytime data backups and restorations.

You will now examine the various SAN backup and restoration models.

SAN Backup and Restoration Models

Two models for SAN-based backup and restoration processes exist. These include the following:

- LAN-free backup and restoration model
- Server-free backup and restoration model

In the LAN-free backup and restoration model, the LAN infrastructure is not used for the transportation of backup and recovery traffic. Each server sends its own backup data directly to the concerned storage device. The entire process is controlled by the backup and restoration application on the server and shared storage device.

Because the LAN infrastructure is not burdened with bandwidth-intensive traffic, the performance of the LAN is not degraded. Backup and restoration processes are fast, efficient, and reliable. The biggest advantage is that the need for overnight backups or restorations is eliminated completely because data can be backed up or restored any time, when necessary.

The server-free backup and restoration model is sometimes referred to as the *automated backup and restoration* model. In this yet to be fully developed model, the data backup and restoration is done directly between the concerned storage resource and the backup resource. As a result, the role of servers in backup and restoration activities is reduced to a bare minimum.

This SAN-based model is realized with the help of an evolving technology known as Third Party Copy. This technology needs to be implemented in the various SAN components and storage resources. Because the participation of servers in CPU-intensive backup and restoration processes is practically nothing, the performance of servers is improved significantly. However, this is an evolving technology and has yet to gain industry-wide acceptance.

Summary

Problems in a SAN can be categorized as the following:

- Problems related to the physical connectivity of devices
- Problems related to the access of storage devices
- Problems related to the upper-layer protocols

In this chapter, you learned about basic techniques that are the groundwork for isolating and troubleshooting these problems in a storage network.

You learned that the management of a storage network can be widely categorized into four subcategories. These four categories, which help you to maintain and support a stable storage network, include the following:

- Network management
- Storage Resource Management (SRM)
- Data management
- Performance management

You also learned about important features that you must look for in a SAN management tool or application.

Finally, you learned about one of the most critical aspects of any network—disaster management. Data backup and restoration are the two techniques that help you in recovering data without potential corruption or loss if you have to face network failure or data loss. There are two models of data backup and recovery:

- Traditional data backup and recovery model
- SAN-based backup and recovery model

Over time, the traditional backup and recovery model has failed to keep up with demands. As a result, the SAN-based model has emerged as the most efficient, reliable, and fastest means of backup and restoration, irrespective of the time the backup or data recovery is conducted.

In this chapter, you will learn about the following:

- The emergence of iSCSI technology
- iSCSI concepts
- iSCSI design considerations and security requirements

CHAPTER 10

iSCSI Technology

Since the advent of storage networks, Fibre Channel has been the mainstay of storage area networks (SANs). In fact, for most of us, Fibre Channel is synonymous with SANs. However, the unrivaled reign of Fibre Channel technology might not entirely be due to the fact that it provides high-performance solutions. Fibre Channel has never had to face any serious competition because of the significant lack of options in the field of SAN products.

Fibre Channel has been, and still is, a market on its own. However, the Fibre Channel market is now facing a serious challenge for the first time in its history. A small group of SAN vendors have come up with a new standard called *Internet Small Computer System Interface (iSCSI)* that is creating waves in the SAN arena.

The Emergence of iSCSI Technology

Although Fibre Channel products form the backbone of most of the SAN solutions that are being implemented today, Fibre Channel technology poses a few problems. These include high cost and difficulty of implementation, necessity of retraining staff or of hiring additional staff, incompatibility with other technologies, and relatively immature management tools. Each of these problems is examined in the following section.

Problems Faced by Fibre Channel Technology

Typical Fibre Channel products are implemented at an average cost of $1000 for each port. Until now, the Fibre Channel market has been virtually without competition. Therefore, the cost of per-port implementation is not estimated to go down in the near future. To some extent, the high cost of implementation has limited the popularity of SANs. This is because medium- and small-sized companies either cannot afford the staggering cost of Fibre Channel implementation or cannot be convinced about the viability of implementing expensive Fibre Channel solutions.

Most corporations and companies have their own local-area network (LAN) and wide-area network (WAN) setups and the expertise to support these networks efficiently. This is because Transmission Control Protocol/Internet Protocol (TCP/IP) networks have been around for about three decades. In contrast to well-established TCP/IP technology, Fibre Channel is comparatively new and is based on an entirely different infrastructure. Therefore, sufficient expertise is not available to implement and support Fibre Channel-based SANs. As a result, most companies find it difficult to implement SAN solutions.

Being entirely different from existing networking technologies, corporations and companies that implement Fibre Channel SANs either need to hire expensive experts or retrain the existing support staff. Both solutions can drain extra money from a company's budget.

Because Fibre Channel uses a different infrastructure, it is incompatible with many popular networking technologies such as TCP/IP. This fact has made many corporations hesitant about the implementation of Fibre Channel SANs.

Although a few Fibre Channel products can extend Fibre Channel links well over 100 kilometers, they are extremely expensive. The general category of Fibre Channel products available in the market can usually span distances up to 10 kilometers. Therefore, Fibre Channel links prove to be good solutions for campus networks. However, they cannot be extended across WANs because they are incompatible with the Internet, which is TCP/IP-based. Therefore, setting up long-distance Fibre Channel connectivity is an extremely expensive and impractical exercise.

Again, being a new technology, management tools for Fibre Channel SANs are relatively immature in comparison to the management tools offered by time-tested and popular networking technologies such as TCP/IP.

In summary, problems posed by Fibre Channel technology have made experts look for cheaper and easier methods for connecting devices to a SAN. Various industry organizations are working to make SAN solutions less expensive and extend the reach of SANs geographically, and at the same time not compromising the performance of storage networks. The Internet Engineers Task Force (IETF) is one of these organizations.

IETF

One of the most active organizations involved in the advancement of SANs is the IETF. Because of the ubiquitous presence of TCP/IP networks and the availability of considerable expertise in TCP/IP technology, the IETF is working on two approaches to transfer speed- and storage-intensive data over IP networks. These approaches are the following:

- Tunneling Fibre Channel control information and data inside IP streams
- iSCSI

In the first approach, where data needs to be tunneled inside IP streams, extensions using IP protocols are added to the SCSI control codes and data. These packets are then tunneled from one remote SAN to another over TCP/IP networks. However, this approach is not being considered as a major breakthrough because it is a complex approach and doesn't effectively address other issues, such as cost considerations and support requirements related to SANs.

NOTE   Also known as encapsulation, *tunneling* is the technology where data packets of one protocol are encapsulated (or hidden) within the packets of a second protocol, which are then transmitted to the recipient. The latter protocol, within which the original data packets are hidden, provides the routing information for these packets to be successfully transmitted to the destination. For example, Cisco's Layer Two Tunneling Protocol (L2TP) allows organizations to transfer data across their Virtual Private Networks (VPNs) by using the Internet (and therefore TCP/IP) as the transmission medium. However, the one major disadvantage associated with tunneling technology is that tunneling is always slower than running the protocol natively.

The next approach—iSCSI—is attracting a lot of attention in industry circles because it promises the reuse of existing IP networks for the transmission of storage data between remote SANs. As per the iSCSI specification, Fibre Channel storage blocks are encapsulated into IP packets before being transmitted over IP-based LANs and WANs. In this manner, iSCSI promises the elimination of SANs' dependence on Fibre Channel technology, which allows SANs to be built on the basis of the popular and cost-effective Ethernet infrastructure.

iSCSI promises many benefits that make it a lucrative solution. The main benefits offered by iSCSI include the following:

- **Lower Total Cost of Ownership (TCO)**—By using the existing TCP/IP infrastructure, the need to set up extremely expensive Fibre Channel devices and links is eliminated. This significantly reduces the TCO of a SAN implementation, thereby allowing small- and medium-sized companies to employ SAN solutions that fit in their budgets.

- **Extended connectivity**—By allowing the transfer of SCSI input/output (I/O) blocks over the existing LAN, metropolitan-area network (MAN), and WAN infrastructure and native protocols (such as TCP/IP), iSCSI helps in implementing connections and data transfers between storage devices that are located thousands of miles apart. Therefore, iSCSI helps in extending the boundaries of conventional SANs to Storage WANs (SWANs).

- **Ease of implementation**—By allowing the reuse of existing network infrastructures, iSCSI makes the implementation of SANs an easy exercise. At the same time, considerable expertise is available in the field of TCP/IP. This simplifies the support and maintenance of iSCSI-based SANs.

- **No need to retrain staffs or hire experts**—By using the existing skills and knowledge of Ethernet and other TCP/IP-based networks, iSCSI technology eliminates the expensive exercise of retraining the existing staff or hiring additional staff.

- **Compatibility and interoperability with IP-based networking technology**—Unlike Fibre Channel, which is incompatible with most of the existing networking technologies, iSCSI offers a high degree of compatibility and interoperability with other existing technologies, especially TCP/IP. In fact, the entire concept of iSCSI is based on the use of existing TCP/IP networks to transfer storage data between devices that might be remotely located.

iSCSI is discussed in full in the next section.

iSCSI Concepts

iSCSI is an industry standard jointly proposed by a group of vendors led by IBM and Cisco along with HP, Quantum, Adaptec, Intel, and so on. Although the proposal is still in its draft stages, it is estimated that iSCSI's future will be much clearer by mid-2002.

iSCSI, which is often referred to as *SCSI over IP networks*, is a next generation SCSI standard. In other words, iSCSI derives its roots from SCSI. SCSI is one of the most popularly used interfaces (or protocols) to facilitate data movement on a storage network. To understand iSCSI, you will briefly review the concept of SCSI.

SCSI—An Overview

Initially, SCSI was developed to enable faster and more efficient communication between the processor(s) of a PC and the peripheral devices attached to it. Some of these peripheral devices include printers, scanners, hard drives, CD drives, tape drives, and so on. With the gradual increase in the amount of data to be stored by companies, SCSI evolved as a popular storage protocol that enables successful communication between storage devices.

SCSI is based on client/server architecture in the following cases:

- Any individual I/O device is referred to as a *logical unit (LU)*.

- Each LU is associated with a unique address called a *Logical Unit Number (LUN)*.

- Any LU that starts a service request to another LU is known as an *initiator*.

- An LU or a set of LUs to which a service request is targeted is referred to as the *target*.

- The service request is popularly referred to as a *SCSI task* or a *SCSI command*. LUs can support multiple tasks by queuing them. Each task is associated with a *task tag*, which uniquely identifies the given task.

- Each LU is associated with a *device server* that accepts SCSI commands (or tasks) and processes them.

- SCSI data transfers are associated with two phases—*data phase* and *response phase*. SCSI commands might or might not lead to a data phase. This phase is optional, where the initiator can direct the information to the target (Write operation), the target can direct information to the initiator (Read operation), or the initiator and target can direct information to each other (Read/Write operation). The response phase is a required phase, where the target informs the initiator about the final status of the service request (whether the command was completed successfully) and terminates the ongoing SCSI command.

SCSI uses *block I/O* technology. In block I/O technology, when a server (or an initiator) requests data from a storage device in a SAN, the storage device retrieves the required data and formats the data into blocks. Each SCSI block indicates the location and address of the LU from which it was retrieved. The blocks are then placed on a SCSI or Fibre Channel link to be sent to the initiator (that is, the server that started the data request). On receiving the blocks, the initiator formats these blocks into corresponding packets of the native network protocol, such as TCP/IP, IEEE 802.5, IPX/SPX, so that these packets can be successfully transmitted to the network clients.

Similar to Read operations, when a server needs to save (that is, Write) data to a storage device, the server's operating system or the application, such as the database that started the save request, formats the data into blocks and forwards these blocks to the target storage device. On receiving the data blocks, the storage device maps these blocks to a block table, which is located in the I/O bus of the storage device. Ultimately, the block is forwarded to the destination sector on the storage disk of the storage device. Figure 10-1 depicts the SCSI block I/O process.

Now that you are familiar with SCSI, you need to consider iSCSI and the role it will play in storage networks of the future.

Figure 10-1 *SCSI Block I/O Process*

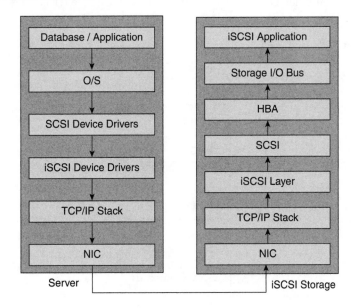

iSCSI Basics

iSCSI is a SCSI-based protocol. Therefore, the common terminology used in iSCSI is almost the same as its predecessor—SCSI. However, slight differences have been proposed in iSCSI, which include the following:

- The initiator and target communicate with each other in the form of messages. These messages are referred to as iSCSI *Protocol Data Units (PDUs)*.

- Instead of separate data and response phases in SCSI, iSCSI proposes to combine the two. Instead of sending commands and data separately, the initiator sends the SCSI command and data simultaneously to the target. Similarly, the target can send the requested data and response status together. This change offers enhanced performance by iSCSI when compared to SCSI.

The following sections describe various aspects of iSCSI.

iSCSI Protocol Stack

As previously discussed, the idea behind iSCSI is to enable the transport of SCSI-based commands reliably over the TCP/IP protocol. As a result, the iSCSI protocol stack links the two sets of protocols (SCSI and TCP/IP) together for the successful transmission of data. Figure 10-2 depicts the iSCSI protocol stack.

The *link layer* is also known as the physical network. The link layer is a combination of the physical and data link layers. This layer supports parallel SCSI, Fibre Channel, Ethernet, and Gigabit Ethernet for local networks, and ATM and SONET networks for wide-area connectivity.

Figure 10-2 *The iSCSI Protocol Stack*

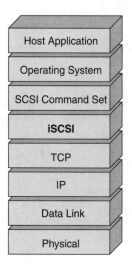

The *network transport layer* represents the two universally deployed protocols—TCP and IP. In addition to flow control, TCP facilitates the reliable transmission of data to the recipient by providing guaranteed in-order delivery of data packets. IP, on the other hand, is responsible for routing data packets to the destination network.

The *iSCSI layer* is the most important layer of the stack aside from the network layer. The main function of the iSCSI layer is to provide compatibility between a storage network and the IP-based network. The most important function of this layer is to encapsulate SCSI commands into TCP/IP packets so that the packets can be transmitted over the IP-based environment. In addition, this layer provides mechanisms for authenticating logins, checking the integrity of received data, and mapping storage devices to the corresponding IP-based environment.

The *SCSI command set layer* is shared by Fibre Channel, iSCSI, and parallel SCSI interfaces. This layer provides data commands and device-type commands—stream commands and block commands for the transportation of SCSI-data over the TCP/IP infrastructure.

The *operating system layer* represents the operating system of the host storage device. Windows 2000, NT, UNIX, Linux, AIX are a few examples of host operating systems.

Finally, the *host application layer* represents the application or the program that originated the data-access request from a storage device. File systems and databases are the applications commonly associated with this layer.

NOTE   Most servers and storage systems generally support the upper three layers of the iSCSI protocol stack—host application, operating system, and SCSI command set. This is because these three layers are a legacy from the original SCSI interface and protocol.

In the next section, you learn about the format of iSCSI packets.

iSCSI Packet Format

The iSCSI packet consists of the following fields:

- **Preamble**—This 8-byte long data pattern is transmitted before every iSCSI PDU and allows the receiver to recognize the beginning of a frame. The preamble also helps the receiver to synchronize its clock with the sender device.

- **Destination Address**—This 6-byte long field contains the address of the destination device.

- **Source Address**—This 6-byte long field contains the address of the sender device.

- **Type**—This field contains information about the protocol that is associated with the information carried in the Data field. The length of the field is 3 bytes.

- **IP**—This 32-byte long field represents the IP header that is appended to the iSCSI data.

- **TCP**—This 32-byte long field represents the TCP header that is appended to the iSCSI data.

- **Data**—The length of this field is variable and cannot exceed 1500 bytes. The Data field contains the data that is being exchanged between the two communicating ends.

- **Frame Check Sequence (FCS**—This 4-byte long field contains an algorithm to detect transmission errors.

Figure 10-3 depicts the format of an iSCSI packet.

Figure 10-3 *The iSCSI Packet Format*

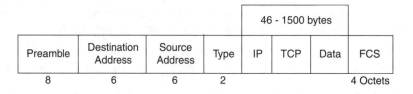

The next section briefly highlights the basic components of an iSCSI-based storage network.

iSCSI-Based Network and Its Components

The basic components that are used to build an iSCSI-based network can be divided into three basic categories—*end nodes*, *interface cards*, and *iSCSI/IP storage switches and routers*.

End nodes, such as servers and storage devices, act as the basic iSCSI devices. In the iSCSI terminology, servers that request data transfers and encapsulate SCSI commands into TCP/IP packets are referred to as *iSCSI initiators*. Storage devices that receive iSCSI commands and exchange data over an IP-based LAN or WAN are also known as *iSCSI targets*.

Unlike the restriction of only using Fibre Channel devices in a Fibre Channel-based SAN, the servers that are used in LANs (and WANs), you can upgrade to support the iSCSI capability by installing an iSCSI network interface card (NIC). *iSCSI/Ethernet Host Bus Adapters (HBAs)*, also known as *storage NICs (SNICs)*, provide the required iSCSI/Fibre Channel interface. SNICs are Gigabit Ethernet adapters that support iSCSI and TCP/IP protocols natively. As a result, they handle protocol-related processing (such as the encapsulation of SCSI data into TCP/IP packets) without the interference of the host CPU. This reduces the processing load from the host CPU, which results in increased performance of iSCSI servers and storage devices.

Another category of NICs, *iSCSI/Ethernet NICs*, is also used to provide the iSCSI interface. In addition to the Gigabit Ethernet interface, these NICs support the iSCSI/ TCP/IP protocol stack as system software. Therefore, unlike SNICs, this category of NICs is dependent on the host-system CPU for protocol-related processing, which makes them comparatively slower than SNICs.

NOTE   NICs used in LANs and WANs can also be upgraded to support the iSCSI interface by installing iSCSI software drivers. However, the performance of these NICs might not be up to the mark, as is required in storage networks.

Because the basic idea of iSCSI is to build a storage network over an IP-based network, standard IP-based Gigabit Ethernet switches can be used to build the Fabric of a local iSCSI-based SAN. Similarly, IP-based routers that are used in WANs can also be used effectively to build storage WANs (SWANs).

Figure 10-4 depicts the typical setup of an iSCSI-based SAN.

Most storage networks are based on Fibre Channel technology. Therefore, for iSCSI to be successful in the current scenario, it is important that iSCSI devices communicate successfully with Fibre Channel devices.

Figure 10-4   *The iSCSI-Based Storage Network*

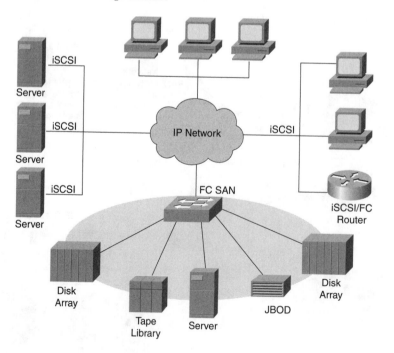

Bridging Fibre Channel to iSCSI

The integration of iSCSI and Fibre Channel storage networks offers many benefits. Besides the obvious reuse of the existing Fibre Channel infrastructure with its proven performance and reliability, storage devices can be accessed universally, regardless of the interface. Also, the organization can work out a viable and long-term storage strategy by chalking out a migration path to the IP environment. As a result, this bridging capability of iSCSI to Fibre Channel also maximizes the market potential of iSCSI.

The iSCSI/Fibre Channel (FC) routers and switches are used to connect a Fibre Channel-based storage network to iSCSI devices. These devices support both interfaces— Fibre Channel and iSCSI. Therefore, iSCSI/FC switches can perform IP/Gigabit Ethernet switching and Fibre Channel switching. Nishan's 3000 IPS series' switches belong to this category. iSCSI/FC routers, however, can support protocol conversion effectively. Cisco's SN5420 is an example of an iSCSI/FC router.

NOTE   Refer to Chapter 4, "Fibre Channel Products," for more information on SN5420 routers.

Figure 10-5 depicts an iSCSI device integrated with a Fibre Channel storage network over an IP-based network.

You now learn about the iSCSI data exchange and encapsulation process.

Figure 10-5 *Bridging iSCSI with Fibre Channel*

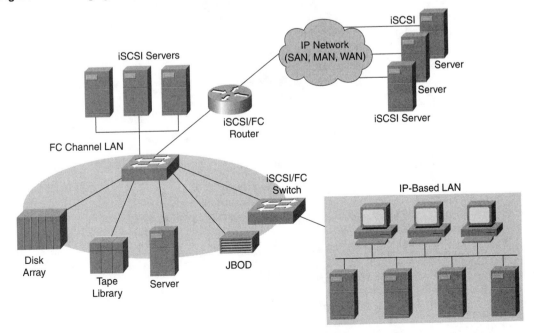

iSCSI Data Exchange and Encapsulation

In the iSCSI environment, when a Fibre Channel device located in the storage network needs to communicate with an IP-based device, the data is exchanged between the two in the following manner:

1 The Fibre Channel device encapsulates the data as a Fibre Channel frame and forwards it to the nearest Fibre Channel switch in the Fabric.

2 On the basis of the destination address, the Fibre Channel switch forwards the data to the nearest iSCSI/FC-bridging device.

3 The iSCSI/FC-bridging device then strips the Fibre Channel header and adds the iSCSI header to the Fibre Channel frame. In addition, a TCP, an IP, and an Ethernet header are added to the frame. The bridging device then forwards the data packet to the destination IP-based device.

4 The IP device strips off all the headers and retrieves the request sent by the Fibre Channel device. The device then processes the request, encapsulates the response as an IP-based data packet, and forwards it to the iSCSI/FC-bridging device.

5 The bridging device strips off the Ethernet, IP, and TCP headers, adds the Fibre Channel header, and forwards the resulting Fibre Channel frame to the recipient.

NOTE   Refer to Chapter 3, "Fibre Channel Basics," for more information on Fibre Channel frames.

The entire exchange process is shown in Figure 10-6.

iSCSI Naming and Addressing Scheme

Similar to IP, iSCSI allows logical units in the network to be assigned a name and an address. As a result, each iSCSI device is assigned two types of identifiers—an *iSCSI name* and an *iSCSI address*. This dual identification of iSCSI devices ensures that a storage device in the network can be uniquely identified, regardless of its location or the IP address in the network.

NOTE   iSCSI names are assigned permanently to the LUs. However, iSCSI addresses are subject to change if the location of the iSCSI device is changed in the network.

The following sections discuss these two iSCSI identifiers in more detail.

Figure 10-6   *The iSCSI Data Exchange and Encapsulation Process*

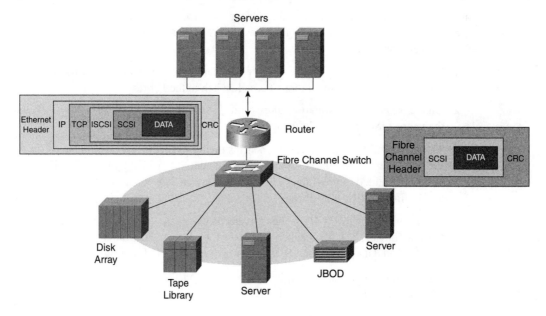

iSCSI Names

Also known as *World-Wide Unique Identifier (WWUI)*, an iSCSI name is a 255-byte long identifier that provides unique human-readable identity to iSCSI devices.

An iSCSI name comprises the following three parts:

- **Type designator**—This part simply acts as the prefix of the iSCSI name. Generally, the value of this part is iSCSI or fqn, where *fqn* stands for fully qualified name.

- **Naming authority**—Similar to the World-Wide Names (WWNs) used in Fibre Channel technology, iSCSI names are assigned by an existing naming authority. A corporation that maintains a Domain Name System (DNS) server, OS vendors, NIC or driver vendors, device vendors, service providers, and sometimes even customers can act as the naming authority.

- **Unique Identifier**—As the name suggests, this is the unique identity of the given device. The format of this part is designated by the naming authority.

For example, suppose a device, tapelibrary.3456789, needs to be assigned an iSCSI name by a naming authority called storage-vendor.com. In this case, the fully qualified iSCSI name of the device would be the following:

fqn.com.storage-vendor.tapelibrary.3456789

Another example of a valid iSCSI name is the following:

iscsi.com.some-isp.jbod3.fin.177

In this example, iscsi is the designator type, some-isp.com represents the naming authority, and jbod3.fin.177 is the device's unique identity.

Fibre Channel WWNs can also be accommodated by the iSCSI naming scheme. Here, the Fibre Channel WWN is prefixed by eui, which is an IEEE format. As a result, the corresponding iSCSI name of a Fibre Channel device with WWN 0312234AC4122E10 is represented as the following:

eui. 0312234AC4122E10

NOTE   Refer to Chapter 3 for more information on Fibre Channel WWNs.

The iSCSI names are permanent. This means that even if a device is relocated in the network, its iSCSI name remains the same. This allows the device to be rediscovered by other devices in the network. Another benefit of iSCSI names is that they are hardware-independent. As a result, an iSCSI device driver can be assigned a single name, even if multiple SNICs are used to attach the storage device (or server) to the network. Also, even if an iSCSI device is connected to the network through multiple connections to maintain redundant paths, the device is always identified as a single entity because of the iSCSI name.

The next section sheds light on the iSCSI addressing scheme.

iSCSI Addresses

iSCSI target devices are also associated with an individual iSCSI address, which is a combination of the DNS name (or the IP address), the target TCP port address, and the iSCSI name. This iSCSI address is presented in a URL-like format, which is shown here:

<Domain name> :<Port>/<WWUI>

For example, the iSCSI address of a target iSCSI device whose name is fqn.com.storage-vendor.tapelibrary.3456789 and whose IP address is 108.2.45.56, needs to be contacted at TCP port 2667. In this case, the corresponding iSCSI address is the following:

iscsi://108.2.45.56:2667/fqn.com.storage-vendor.tapelibrary.3456789

If iSCSI names or addresses were used to route information, they would generate a huge amount of traffic and overload network-parsing engines because of the length of iSCSI names and addresses. Therefore, neither iSCSI names nor addresses are used for routing purposes. As a result, after the IP address and the TCP port of the target LU has been established, only an IP address/TCP port combination is used during the transaction.

iSCSI Sessions and Data Transfers

iSCSI data transfers are connection-oriented. To exchange data and commands with the target, a *session* must be established between the initiator and target LUs. A session is a set of one or more TCP connections, which carry control messages, SCSI commands, parameters, and iSCSI PDUs between the two communicating LUs.

Each TCP connection within a session is associated with a *connection ID (CID)*. The CID helps in uniquely identifying the connection within a given iSCSI session if the session consists of more than one connection. Similarly, each session is uniquely identified with the *help of a session ID (SID)*, which is partly contributed by the initiator and target LUs. When an initiator logs on to a target, it supplies an *Initiator Session ID (ISID)*. The target responds to the successful login request with its own *Target Session ID (TSID)*. This TSID/ISID pair is referred to as a SID.

Being a connection-oriented technology, a persistent iSCSI session between the target and the initiator is set in the following phases:

- Login phase
- Text-mode negotiation phase
- Full-feature phase
- ISCSI connection termination phase

NOTE   In much of iSCSI-related literature, an iSCSI data transfer is considered to be outbound (or outgoing) if the direction of data transfer is from initiator to target. On the other hand, data transfer from the target to the initiator is considered to be inbound (or incoming).

Each of the phases is discussed in the following sections.

Login Phase

The Login phase starts with the initiator issuing the login command to the target. The login command signals that the initiator needs to communicate with the intended target. This phase is responsible for the following actions:

- Establishing a TCP connection over which the session will take place
- Authenticating the two communicating devices
- Negotiating the session parameters

After the two sides have been authenticated and session parameters have been mutually agreed upon, the target responds with the *accept login* response. If the session cannot be established successfully for some reason, the target sends the *reject login* response to the initiator. On receiving a negative response from the target, the initiator must restart the Login phase. The login response concludes the Login phase.

Text-Mode Negotiation Phase

The Text-Mode phase is optional and can occur anytime—at the start of the session or during the session—when data exchange parameters need to be negotiated. As the name suggests, the parameter negotiation takes place through the exchange of text information.

Text-Mode negotiation can be of two types—*list negotiation* or *numerical negotiation*.

In List Negotiation Mode, the communicating end that started the negotiation sends a list of values of the required parameter(s) in the order of preference. The other end can either respond with a value from the list or respond with none to indicate that it does not support the given parameter.

In Numerical Negotiation Mode, the two communicating ends exchange numerical values of the parameter being negotiated.

Full-Feature Phase

After the initiator has successfully completed the Login phase and has been authorized by the target to send SCSI commands, the iSCSI session enters the Full-feature phase. In this phase, SCSI commands issued by the initiator are encapsulated as SCSI PDUs and are passed to the TCP layer. The TCP layer breaks the PDUs into packets that can be transmitted over the network or the WAN, which is usually the Internet. The data being exchanged by the two ends can also be encrypted, if security is an issue. Popular security protocols, such as IP Security (IPSec), Transport Layer Security (TLS), Public Key Infrastructure (PKI), and Kerberos V5 are used for encrypting iSCSI PDUs.

NOTE   Developed by the IETF, IPSec is a set of protocols that facilitates secure data exchanges at the IP layer. This protocol is widely implemented in VPNs. TLS is used to ensure secure, authenticated, and private data exchanges for other protocols, such as HTTP, which run at the TCP layer. TLS is also popularly referred to as Secure Sockets Layer (SSL). PKI is a system of digital certificates that are used to authenticate the participants of data exchange over the Internet. Kerberos V5 is a network authentication protocol developed at Massachusetts Institute of Technology (MIT) to provide the strong authentication of parties involved in data exchange in insecure environments, such as the Internet.

At the target-end, packets are recombined and decrypted, if necessary, into the original SCSI commands and data. These commands are then processed. The target device must respond to each command with its completion status, Ready To Transfer (R2T).

iSCSI Connection Termination Phase

After all the outstanding tasks of a connection are completed, the initiator sends a logout request to the target. The target must conclude its outstanding tasks, send the status of each task to the initiator, and then respond to the logout request. When the corresponding TCP connection is terminated, the iSCSI session is also considered to be successfully completed. If one end assumes the connection to be terminated while the other end still has outstanding tasks, or the end that started the connection termination does not receive the status of completed tasks, recovery actions are started.

iSCSI Ordering and Numbering

iSCSI supports three numbering schemes to maintain the ordered delivery of SCSI commands and to enable fast recovery in case of session failure or the abrupt disruption of a connection. The iSCSI ordering and numbering schemes include the following:

- **Command numbering**—Each command issued by the initiator to the target is allocated a unique number known as the *Command Reference Number (CmdRN)*. This number ensures the ordered delivery of commands within a specified session. This number is viable only for a given session. After the command has been delivered to the target, the number loses its significance. Command numbering is also used as a command flow-control mechanism for a given session.

- **Status numbering**—Each response from the target to the initiator is allocated a unique number called the *Status Reference Number (StatRN)*. If a response fails to reach the initiator, status numbering helps in recovering and retransmitting the response to the initiator. Status numbering is valid for a given connection only.

NOTE   This iSCSI numbering scheme is also popularly referred to as *Response numbering* and is similar to numbering schemes used in any other connection-oriented protocol, which uses sequences and positive or negative acknowledgments of transmissions.

- **Data numbering**—Each data PDU sent by the target to the initiator is allocated a unique number referred to as the *Data Reference Number (DataRN)*. This number helps in the fast and efficient recovery of lost data PDUs sent by the target. PDUs known as *NOP-Out PDUs* carry the same initiator tag as the original data PDUs. Therefore, the NOP-Out PDUs are used to acknowledge data PDUs. The maximum number of unacknowledged PDUs is negotiated during the Login phase.

NOTE	For detailed information on iSCSI concepts and basic functions, refer to the Internet draft called draft-ietf-ips-iscsi-07.txt at the site www.haifa.il.ibm.com/satran/ips/draft-ietf-ips-iSCSI-07.txt.

iSCSI Design Considerations and Security Requirements

The iSCSI requirements and design considerations draft (draft-ietf-ips-iscsi-07.txt) presented by the IETF defines the most important requirements that should be fulfilled by the proposed iSCSI protocol, as shown in Table 10-1.

Table 10-1   *iSCSI Requirements*

Definition	Requirements	Description
Performance/ cost	MUST allow implementations to equal or improve the current state of SCSI interconnects MUST enable cost competitive implementations MUST have low host CPU uses, equal to or better than current technology MUST be possible to build I/O adapters that handle the entire SCSI task MUST provide for the full use of the available link bandwidth	To make iSCSI a viable and marketable solution, there should be a balance between the performance and the cost of implementation and the maintenance of iSCSI-based networks. Although reusing most of the existing IP-based infrastructure, it should be able to meet the basic requirements of high speed and high availability. Use of SNICs can help meet most of these requirements because these adapters handle protocol-related processing, such as encapsulation, CRC checks, and so on, and therefore offload the burden of processing from the host CPU.
Flow control and synchronization	MUST be able to support existing flow-control mechanisms MUST be able to synchronize the transaction between iSCSI and non-iSCSI devices	The iSCSI protocol must incorporate additional information in PDU headers or data streams so that implementations can locate the boundaries of iSCSI PDUs within the TCP byte stream.

continues

Table 10-1   *iSCSI Requirements (Continued)*

Definition	Requirements	Description
High bandwidth/ bandwidth aggregation	MUST operate over a single TCP connection	To be able to compete with Fibre Channel technology, which offers high-bandwidth solutions, iSCSI must be able to facilitate the full use of the available link bandwidth while minimizing the use of TCP connections. This is because if one session were to operate over multiple TCP connections, it would slow down the network considerably, especially during peak hours because other devices would have to wait for an availabile TCP connection. Also, it is important that iSCSI must not jeopardize the performance of simultaneous connections within the interconnect Fabric.
Ease of implementation/ complexity of protocol	SHOULD keep the protocol simple MUST operate correctly when no optional features are negotiated and when individual option negotiations are unsuccessful	For the protocol to be marketable, it should be simple to understand and easy to implement. This makes it simple for network administrators to diagnose problems. To diagnose faults and failures, the protocol must provide parameter negotiation during the Login phase. Also, its default parameters must be such that successful transactions can be handled if optional features were not negotiated during transaction.
Detection of data corruption	MUST support a data integrity check format for use in digest generation	Data might be corrupted while in transit. Therefore, the iSCSI protocol must support data integrity check formats for the early detection of data corruption. Also, the iSCSI data corruption detection mechanism must support other detection methods, such as checksum and Cyclic Redundancy Checks (CRCs).

Table 10-1   *iSCSI Requirements (Continued)*

Definition	Requirements	Description
Recovery	MUST specify mechanisms to recover in a timely fashion from failures on the initiator, target, or connecting infrastructure SHOULD take into account failover schemes for mirrored targets or highly available storage configurations SHOULD provide a method for sessions to be gracefully terminated and restarted by either the initiator or target	In case of network failures, iSCSI should support recovery mechanisms. Also, it should support failover strategies that ensure the availability of data, even if the primary source is down.
Internet infrastructure	MUST be compatible with both IPv4 and IPv6 MUST use TCP connections conservatively, keeping in mind that there might be many other users of TCP on a given machine MUST NOT require changes to the existing Internet protocols SHOULD minimize required changes to existing TCP/IP implementation.	Because it operates over IP-based infrastructures, ISCSI must be compatible with the current version of IP—IPv4. IPv6 is likely to take over from IPv4 in the near future. Therefore, iSCSI technology should be worked out in such a manner that no major issues related to infrastructure arise during the transition from IPv4 to IPv6.
Interoperability	iSCSI protocol document MUST be clear and unambiguous	Incompatibility with contemporary network technologies has forced the industry to look for other solutions. The iSCSI protocol must be simple and unambiguous so that it can be seamlessly integrated with other popular networking technologies, such as the Internet, SCSI, and Fibre Channel.

continues

Table 10-1 *iSCSI Requirements (Continued)*

Definition	Requirements	Description
Extensible security	SHOULD require minimal configuration and overhead in an insecure operation SHOULD provide for strong authentication when increased security is required SHOULD allow integration of new security mechanisms without breaking backward compatible operations	Because iSCSI stresses data transfers over insecure media, such as the Internet, extensible security measures, such as strong authentication, should be implemented in case of iSCSI data exchanges to ensure integrity and confidentiality of the data being transmitted over the iSCSI infrastructure. At the same time, these measures should also be compatible with existing security mechanisms and must not require major reconfiguration.
Authentication	MUST support private authenticated login CAN support various levels of authentication security iSCSI authenticated login MUST be resilient against passive attacks.	To ensure secure transactions over insecure media, iSCSI must support strong authentication mechanisms.
SCSI	SHOULD track changes to SCSI and the SCSI architecture model MUST reliably transport SCSI commands from the initiator to the target MUST correctly deal with iSCSI packet drops, duplication, correction, stale packets, and re-ordering	Because it is the next-generation, SCSI-based technology, iSCSI must be able to accommodate future changes in the existing SCSI model.
Data integrity	SHOULD NOT preclude the use of additional data integrity protection protocols (for example, IPSec and TLS)	In addition to strong authentication, additional security measures will only improve the reliability of iSCSI-based transactions.
Management	SHOULD be manageable by using standard IP-based management protocols (for example, SNMP, RMI, and so on)	Because iSCSI transactions are carried over the IP-based infrastructure, the iSCSI protocol must be manageable by using the standard IP-based management protocols. For this, iSCSI specifications must ensure that the iSCSI resources are uniquely identifiable, and also can be located by using IP-based standard resource location methods, such as DNS.

Table 10-1   *iSCSI Requirements (Continued)*

Definition	Requirements	Description
Naming	The means by which an iSCSI resource is located MUST use or extend existing Internet standard resource location methods. MUST provide a means of identifying iSCSI targets by a unique identifier that is independent of the path on which it is found An iSCSI name should be a human-readable string in an international character set encoding Standard Internet lookup services SHOULD be used to resolve iSCSI names.	The iSCSI naming scheme must be human-readable and compatible with both IP and Fibre Channel. This ensures the smooth discovery of iSCSI devices regardless of the interface.
Discovery	MUST have no impact on the current IP network discovery techniques	The iSCSI specification must ensure that iSCSI devices and services can be discovered by standard discovery methods, such as DNS, which are used in IP-based networks.
Internet accessibility	SHOULD be scrutinized for denial of service issues and the issues should be addressed	The iSCSI protocol specifications must be able to protect the storage network from unauthorized and malicious attacks without hampering the security of the entire network. For this, the iSCSI implementation must be able to seamlessly support Network Address Translators (NATs), proxy servers, and firewalls without disturbing the existing network setup.
Firewalls and proxy servers	SHOULD allow deployment where functional and optimizing middle-boxes such as firewalls, proxy servers, and NATs are present Use of IP addresses and TCP ports SHOULD be firewall friendly.	As an added security mechanism, iSCSI should be able to seamlessly support the current breed of network security devices, such as firewalls, proxy servers, and NATs.

continues

Table 10-1 *iSCSI Requirements (Continued)*

Definition	Requirements	Description
Congestion control and transport selection	MUST be a good network citizen with TCP-compatible congestion control (as defined in RFC 2309) iSCSI implementations MUST NOT use multiple connections as a means to avoid transport layer congestion control.	During peak hours, iSCSI must be able to handle transport layer network congestions so that situations leading to traffic congestions do not occur or their after-effect is minimized if congestion does occur.

Now that you are aware of how iSCSI can simplify the life of storage network administrators, you must also learn the challenges that you might come across while dealing with the iSCSI technology.

iSCSI—The Challenges

Standards come and go. The biggest challenge iSCSI has to overcome is that it has still not undergone the acid test of practicality. Although industry leaders, such as IBM and Cisco, are actively involved in the enhancement of the technology, it has still not been implemented and tested on a wide scale.

Most of the SANs today are Fibre Channel-based. Although highly expensive, Fibre Channel is a proven technology and organizations have invested millions of dollars in their storage networks. Even if iSCSI proves itself as a stable and viable alternative over time, migrating to the iSCSI environment from the pure Fibre Channel environment will mean extra investment. Because of this trade, pundits predict slow movement towards iSCSI.

Another problem with iSCSI is that it operates over SCSI and IP-based environments. The SCSI protocol demands data integrity, whereas data transmission in IP networks is unreliable. The possibility of loss or corruption of data packets is high.

Although the TCP layer is meant to deal with this instability of IP-based transactions, TCP-based processing overhead is imposed on the iSCSI infrastructure. As a result, many experts fear that the performance of an iSCSI-based network could be compromised. On an average, data amounting to several terabytes is transacted over a storage network. If this slow-performance factor is not taken care of, iSCSI might still lose to Fibre Channel.

In addition, because of the high number of transactions over IP-based networks at any point of time, traffic congestion is another common problem. This results in variable bandwidth in IP networks. This is a problem because SCSI-based transactions demand high network bandwidth.

Security is another area where experts are skeptical about the performance of iSCSI. This is because mission-critical organization data is transacted over untrusted networks, such as the Internet. If iSCSI is to compete with Fibre Channel technology successfully, it has to ensure that an organization's data is not compromised while in transit.

iSCSI has much to offer, but it also has a lot to prove. It has to prove itself to be stable, fast, and able to meet all the requirements of a storage network. Most of all, it has a formidable competitor in the form of Fibre Channel technology. Fibre Channel has its own drawbacks, but it has been around for some time. It has proven itself, which iSCSI has yet to do because iSCSI is an emerging technology. However, whether iSCSI will lose its battle to Fibre Channel, supplant it, or end up as a complementary technology is yet to be decided.

Summary

SANs of today are Fibre Channel-based. There are certain drawbacks of Fibre Channel, however, which include high cost and difficulty of implementation, necessity of retraining staff or of hiring additional staff, and incompatibility with other technologies. These drawbacks have led to the emergence of iSCSI.

iSCSI is an open-standard approach that promises to transport SCSI data and commands over IP-based networks, such as the Internet. This allows storage networks to be extended worldwide, making the possibility of cost-effective SWANs an achievable reality.

However, iSCSI is still in the draft stages, and although it is the emerging darling of the industry right now, it still has to overcome a few hurdles to prove itself to be stable and marketable. As of yet, nobody can predict the future of iSCSI. Whether it will surpass Fibre Channel, lose to Fibre Channel, or end up as a complementary storage technology has yet to be decided.

In this chapter, you will learn about the following:

- The need for change
- SAN technology developments
- Non-SAN technologies

CHAPTER 11

Future of SANs

Storage networking is a powerful technology and its potential is staggering. As companies and organizations all over the world struggle with huge amounts of mission-critical data, the storage area network (SAN) has emerged as an extremely reliable solution. SANs offer a high-performance means of ensuring that data is always available, which has brought a new lease on life to e-commerce and online businesses. However, a few hurdles still remain. SANs are a costly venture, and the in-depth, technical know-how necessary to implement SANs is scarce. The emergence of other storage technologies, such as Internet Small Computer System Interface (iSCSI), Internet Protocol (IP), and Storage over Internet Protocol (SoIP) have further challenged the coveted position of SANs in the field of storage technology.

In this chapter, you learn why SAN technology is being challenged by new arrivals in the storage arena. You learn about the need for change in the present storage scenario. You learn about various SAN technology developments, such as optical storage networking (OSN), IP SANs, and the emergence of storage service providers. These developments address several issues and problems faced in traditional SANs. Finally, you learn about technology developments other than SANs, including SoIP, Network Data Management Protocol (NDMP), virtual interface (VI) architecture, Direct Access File System (DAFS), and InfiniBand. Some of these, such as SoIP, are rival technologies, whereas others, such as NDMP, DAFS, VI, and InfiniBand, when augmented with the existing SAN technology, enhance the performance, reach, and popularity of SANs.

The Need for Change

SAN technology has, slowly but surely, gained acceptance in the networking industry. In fact, many experts vouch for its high-speed transactions, adaptability to future growth, reliability, high availability of data, and faultless performance. However, SANs are entirely dependent on the Fibre Channel technology, which can pose a few problems that are propelling vendors and customers to look into other alternatives. The major reasons for this heightened interest for other alternatives include the following:

- Fibre Channel's high cost of implementation

- The difficulty of Fibre Channel's implementation

- A lack of expertise and technical know-how

- The necessity for retraining staff or for hiring additional staff

- Incompatibility with other popular technologies (such as TCP/IP)

- Inability to support long-distance data transfers

- A lack of mature management tools

These reasons have heralded the need for change in the existing SAN technology. If most of these problems are not resolved in the immediate future, the predictions of some pessimists might come true about the imminent doom of SAN technology. Many vendors and industry organizations have taken heed of the signs and are actively working to solve the shortcomings. Various potential solutions have emerged. However, these have yet to pass practicality tests and gain industry-wide acceptance. You learn more about these emerging technologies in the following sections.

SAN Technology Development

Similar to other technologies, many advancements have been made in the arena of storage networks. Several organizations are actively involved in extending the capabilities of SANs and the reach of Fibre Channel technology. Technologies are being developed to incorporate multicasting, virtual circuits, and enhance upper-layer protocol support. In addition, present-day SAN technology is gearing up to accommodate the increasing future requirements of bandwidth, security, and scalability.

SAN technology has stepped into the next phase of its evolution. The latest trends in the field of storage networking include the following:

- OSN

- IP SANs

- Storage service providers

These trends are discussed in the following sections.

OSN

Technically referred to as *dense wavelength-division multiplexing* (*DWDM*), OSN technology offers a fast, simple, and efficient solution to the distance, capacity, and speed limitations posed by present-day storage networks. DWDM combines the strengths of existing SAN, fiber-optic, and Fibre Channel technologies to deliver long-distance and high-bandwidth storage networks.

A typical Fibre Channel link can be extended to a maximum distance of 10 kilometers. If properly optimized, a Fibre Channel link can be stretched to 15 kilometers. On the other hand, by implementing the DWDM technology, a Fibre Channel link can easily be extended to a minimum distance of 100 kilometers, without the need to regenerate signals. In addition, by allowing more traffic through a single fiber-optic link, DWDM can double the capacity of a SAN.

The DWDM technology increases the capacity of the existing fiber-optic links by multiplexing (combining and transmitting) multiple protocol-independent light streams at different wavelengths (referred to as *lambdas* and represented by the symbol *l*) on a single fiber-optic cable. In other words, one fiber-optic link behaves as a set of multiple virtual fibers that carry many signals of different wavelengths simultaneously. For example, by combining eight OC-48 signals into a single fiber-optic link of 2.5 Gbps, you can achieve an aggregate bandwidth of 20 Gbps. Similarly, by using DWDM technology, you can combine a Gigabit Ethernet signal, three Fibre Channel signals, and three FICON channels on a single fiber-optic link.

NOTE   OC stands for Optical Carrier, which is a standard for fiber-optic transmissions. Various signal versions of OC are available. These include OC-1 (supports a transmission speed of 51.85 Mbps), OC-3 (supports a transmission speed of 152.52 Mbps), OC-12 (supports a transmission speed of 622.08 Mbps), OC-24 (supports a transmission speed of 1.24 Gbps), and OC-48 (supports a transmission speed of 2.48 Gbps).

Before the introduction of DWDM technology, connecting storage networks across a metropolitan was a challenge because most fiber-optic cabling extends to an average of 10 kilometers. Long-haul, fiber-optic devices can stretch the maximum distance to 100 kilometers. However, they can increase the implementation cost of the storage network considerably. In addition, a separate fiber-optic link has to be established for each individual connection. This might not be a problem for a small number of connections. However, installing and managing a large number of long-distance fiber cables is not only a severe management headache, but also extremely expensive. Figure 11-1 depicts the connectivity of a metropolitan storage network where DWDM technology has not been implemented.

By implementing DWDM technology, multiple data streams are multiplexed over a single connection at different speeds. As a result, each connection is assigned a separate wavelength as opposed to a separate fiber pair, which helps the organization save considerable expense. Figure 11-2 depicts a metropolitan SAN with DWDM connectivity.

Figure 11-1 *Metropolitan SAN Without DWDM Connectivity*

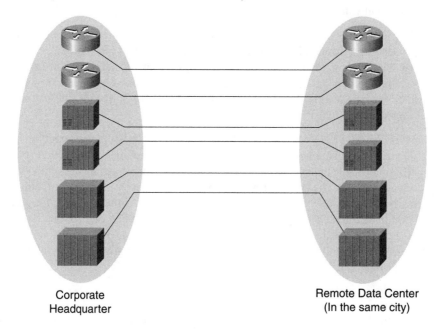

Corporate
Headquarter

Remote Data Center
(In the same city)

Figure 11-2 *Metropolitan SAN with DWDM Connectivity*

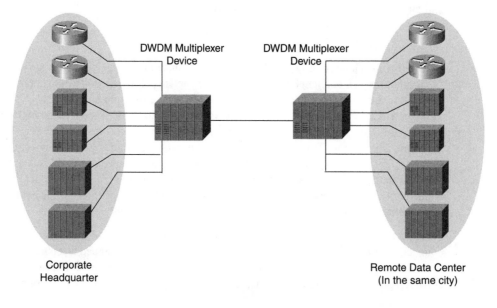

Corporate
Headquarter

Remote Data Center
(In the same city)

OSN is heralded as the future of SANs for the following reasons:

- **Enhanced performance**—Optical storage networking bolsters the performance of a SAN significantly in terms of distance, capacity, and speed. By implementing a high-speed optical infrastructure, OSN-based storage networks can easily handle large volumes of data traffic while successfully avoiding bottlenecks. As a result, network administrators do not face any problems during the deployment of extremely time-sensitive applications, such as remote mirroring. Because of the elimination of distance constraints, OSN also allows an organization to connect its existing SAN- or IP-based network to a storage service provider without having to worry about upgrading or replacing the existing storage infrastructure.

- **Simple and low-cost implementation**—Despite the obvious advantages it has to offer, DWDM technology does not demand an additional high-cost infrastructure. In fact, the only thing that SAN builders need to take care of are the power levels between Fibre Channel devices and DWDM interconnects. These power levels need to be the same. This is easily achieved by the addition or subtraction of attenuators.

NOTE   Apart from DWDM multiplexer devices, OSN technology does not require additional devices or infrastructure because it doesn't propose any change in the signaling technology that is used in Fibre Channel-based SANs. Cisco's Metro 1500 Series, Alidian's Metro DWDM System, and Optix's BWS1600G are some of the commonly used DWDM multiplexers.

- **Support to a wide range of technologies**—Being protocol-independent, DWDM can support Fibre Channel, fiber-optic, and LAN-based technologies. Therefore, it can support SANs, network attached storage (NAS), direct attached storage (DAS), and mainframe-based devices seamlessly. In addition, the OSN infrastructure can also support future technologies, such as SoIP, Fibre Channel over Internet Protocol (FCIP), Internet Fibre Channel Protocol (iFCP), and InfiniBand.

- **Ease of reconfiguration**—Implementing DWDM interconnects and devices allows the reconfiguration of an existing SAN without unnecessarily disturbing the rest of the storage network components. As a result, the entire SAN topology can be changed with minimal expense and effort. This makes DWDM-based networks highly scalable and adaptive to future growth.

In the next section, you learn more about another upcoming SAN technology: IP SANs.

IP SANs

According to an estimate, $10.5 billion was spent during the Christmas season of 1999. The figure rose to an estimated $20 billion in the same season of year 2000. As e-commerce continues to grow globally, it is extremely important that businesses scattered all over the globe remain interconnected. This is where Fibre Channel SANs fail to deliver and IP SANs come into the picture.

IP SANs use IP as the primary protocol in a storage network. As a result, IP SANs allow tunneling of Fibre Channel traffic from storage switches and devices into IP-based links. Figure 11-3 depicts how Fibre Channel SANs can be extended globally with the implementation of IP SANs.

Figure 11-3 *IP SAN Implementation*

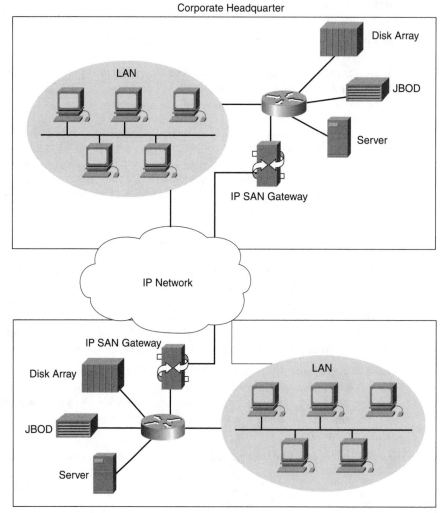

IP SANs are attracting much attention from vendors, industry organizations, and customers for the following reasons:

- **Absence of distance constraints**—IP is a proven technology for long-distance wide-area network (WAN) connections. Therefore, the incorporating IP technology in storage networks helps eliminate the distance constraint that is the bane of present-day SANs.

- **Low cost of implementation**—IP is a low-cost technology that doesn't demand an expensive infrastructure. Therefore, IP-based SANs allow even small-scale companies to adopt storage networks that are currently out of their reach.

- **Maturity of the IP technology**—IP is a long-standing, mature technology. As a result, technical know-how and expertise for IP-based networks is abundantly available. In contrast, most organizations sorely lack the expertise and the technical know-how to construct, deploy, and maintain Fibre Channel SANs. Implementing IP technology in storage networks allows for easier deployment and maintenance of SANs, which in turn will boost the interest of many organizations in storage networks.

- **High-availability of data in the form of redundant paths**—Another factor that makes IP SANs a worthwhile solution for most organizations is that implementing redundant paths to the storage devices in the SAN is not as expensive as in the case of the pure Fibre Channel environment.

Despite the advantages, many experts are skeptical about the future of IP SANs because IP doesn't offer high data security during transmissions. Most of the data traveling over a SAN is highly mission-critical. As a result, IP SANs have yet to achieve a balance between practicality and performance.

Storage Service Providers

SAN technology has steadily gained popularity over the years. With the possibility of the implementation of storage WANs (SWANs), more and more organizations are gearing up to adopt this technology. As a result of this growing interest, storage service providers are appearing on the scene.

Because storage service providers offer off-premises storage, backup, and restoration facilities, they allow an organization to outsource its storage network. E-commerce and Web-based businesses, Internet service providers (ISPs), application service providers (ASPs), and any other organization with high storage demands and a low budget can avail the advantage of high-performance storage networks without having to worry about future requirements, upgrades, and replacement of the existing infrastructure.

Analysts estimate that the hidden and visible costs of managing a storage system can be as much as half of an organization's IT budget. This cost of implementation and management is so high that it comes out to be roughly 10 times the cost of a storage device. By outsourcing its storage network to a Selective Storage Presentation (SSP), an organization can cut its IT budget in half because it becomes the responsibility of the SSP to handle all issues concerning hardware interoperability, upgrades, expertise and staffing, and incorporating the latest technologies. As a result, the prospect of spending between $20,000 to $200,000, as compared to millions of dollars a year, is more appealing to organizations.

NOTE   According to an estimate by Morgan Stanley Dean Witter & Co. quoted in the article, "All Eyes on Cisco" at www.byteandswitch.com, the storage service provider market is estimated to grow from $273 million in 2000 to a staggering $15 billion by the year 2005.

Increased security risk, however, still remains a major concern in outsourcing mission-critical data to an SSP because an SSP might serve multiple clients at the same time. Another problem in outsourcing storage to an outsider is the possibility of data-loss during off-site transactions. In addition, SSPs also continue to struggle for skilled personnel.

Despite the rosy future being predicted by some experts, SSPs can flourish only if they manage to overcome these problems and gain the necessary seal of approval from IT market giants and users. However, the silver lining in this case is that most of these issues are similar to the ones that cropped up initially with the viability of using ASPs. The ASP market flourished despite the same issues, and therefore, experts are hopeful about the future of SSPs.

Table 11-1 sums up the SAN technologies and solutions discussed thus far.

Table 11-1   *SAN Technologies at a Glance*

SAN Technology	Advantages	Disadvantages
Fibre Channel	High-availability of data	Extremely expensive
	High-performance	Non-compatibility with other existing network technologies, such as TCP/IP
	Extremely secure transactions	
	LAN-less backups and restorations	Difficult to implement
		Lack of expertise
		Inability to support long-distance transactions
DWDM	High-availability	Difficulty of implementation
	High-performance	Relatively expensive (though cheaper than Fibre Channel)
	Secure transactions	
	Support to long-distance connectivity	
	Cost-effective	

Table 11-1   *SAN Technologies at a Glance (Continued)*

SAN Technology	Advantages	Disadvantages
IP SANs	Long-distance connectivity	Extremely high security risks
	Availability of expertise	
	Low-cost implementation	
	High-availability of data	
SSPs	Removes headaches related to data-management	High security risk
		Possibility of data-loss during off-site transactions with the SSP
	Extremely cost-effective	Lack of skilled professionals

Non-SAN Technologies

As a result of varying customer demands and diverse networking environments, a lot of development work is being carried out in the field of storage networks. Many of these developments complement the existing SAN technology. A few developments, however, display the potential to develop into full-fledged storage solutions in the near future. All these developments, along with the existing SAN solutions, provide the customer with a wide range of choices according to their individual requirements.

Some of the fast-emerging technologies that are gaining wide acceptance include the following:

- SoIP
- NDMP
- FCIP
- iFCP
- DAFS
- VI
- InfiniBand

The following sections discuss these technologies in more detail.

SoIP

Proposed by Nishan Systems, the concept of SoIP merges the traditional storage and Fibre Channel technologies with the popular IP technology. The result is a high-availability and high-performance storage solution that can span vast geographical distances. Thus, SoIP overcomes the distance limitations commonly faced in traditional storage networks.

As the name suggests, SoIP is an IP-based technology that uses a wide range of standard protocols used in IP-based networks. These protocols include Simple Network Management Protocol (SNMP), Open Shortest Path First (OSPF), Routing Information Protocol (RIP), and Simple Mail Transfer Protocol (SMTP). As a result, SoIP is also highly compatible with existing IP and Gigabit Ethernet infrastructures. This compatibility and long-distance connectivity makes SoIP seem similar to the iSCSI technology. However, this is not the case. Where iSCSI is based on TCP/IP, SoIP is User Datagram Protocol (UDP)-based.

SoIP uses *metro Fibre Channel Protocol* (*mFCP*), which is based on UDP. Because UDP is a connectionless transfer protocol, SoIP transactions are much faster, albeit less reliable than iSCSI transactions. mFCP works on the assumption that error control, flow control, and reliability issues will be handled by the underlying (encapsulated) Fibre Channel protocol. As the primary protocol of the SoIP SAN, the main objective of mFCP is to provide a common interface between the storage interfaces (Fibre Channel and SCSI) and network interfaces (Gigabit Ethernet and IP).

Figure 11-4 depicts the implementation of SoIP-based storage networks.

NOTE   The term connectionless refers to the absence of acknowledgments between the sender and receiver device during a transaction.

Due to its compatibility and interoperability with existing IP and Ethernet technologies, SoIP allows seamless interconnection between typical storage interfaces, such as SCSI and Fibre Channel and IP-based devices. The focus of SoIP is on being able to use the existing SAN infrastructure in the SoIP-based storage networks with a minimal amount of additional hardware and low-cost modifications, if required at all. This low-cost implementation of long-reaching storage networks makes SoIP a lucrative technology.

NOTE   For more information on SoIP, refer to the Web site at www.ietf.org/internet-drafts/draft-monia-ips-ifcparch-00.txt.

In the next section, you learn about NDMP, the open standard protocol for enterprise-wide backup of heterogeneous storage devices.

Figure 11-4   *SoIP SAN Implementation*

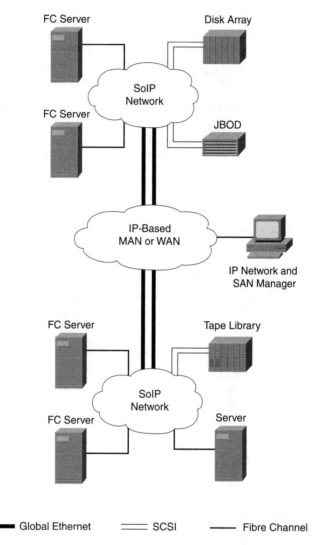

NDMP

Backing up and restoring information in enterprise storage networks is a management nightmare. Because of the increasingly heterogeneous environment in present-day networks, the data that is extremely important for an organization's proper functioning might be stored across multiple hardware and software (operating systems) that might be spread across the globe. In these situations, security, cost-effectiveness, and performance

are major concerns. The NDMP protocol offers a centralized enterprise-wide backup and restoration solution for large-scale storage networks.

According to the traditional backup architecture, the entire process of data backup, from a server to a backup device, is controlled and managed by the backup software. The common backup architecture is depicted in Figure 11-5. Because backup protocols are not standardized, vendors offer vendor-specific backup solutions.

Compared to the traditional backup architecture, the NDMP-based backup architecture standardizes the backup interface. In other words, the data flows from the server's file system to the backup device through the common interface, irrespective of the vendor of the backup product or hardware/software platform being used. Figure 11-6 depicts the NDMP backup architecture.

Figure 11-5 *Traditional Backup Architecture*

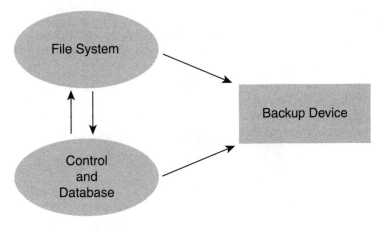

Figure 11-6 *NDMP-Based Backup Architecture*

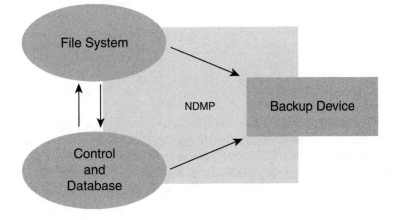

Pioneered by Network Appliance and Intelliguard, NDMP is based on two protocols—
TCP/IP and External Data Representation (XDR). Developed by Sun Microsystems Inc.,
XDR is a machine-independent standard that is used by Remote Procedure Calls (RPCs) in
remote transactions. Although TCP/IP ensures that NDMP-based storage networks can be
extended over large distances, XDR takes care of the remote functionality required in
remote backup and restoration operations. In addition, XDR is responsible for data
transfers between primary and secondary devices. The focus of NDMP technology is to
ensure interoperability and compatibility between existing SAN and IP infrastructures.

NOTE   A primary device stores the original data. A secondary device stores a backup copy of the
original data.

NDMP is a client/server architecture, which consists of three components: *NDMP host*,
NDMP server, and *NDMP client*.

The NDMP host is a primary device that holds original data. The NDMP server runs on the
NDMP host. The NDMP server is a virtual machine on the NDMP host that controls the
NDMP operations. Finally, the NDMP client is a set of backup and restoration manage-
ment software that controls the NDMP server. The NDMP client runs on a backup host.
Figure 11-7 depicts the simplest implementation of the NDMP configuration.

Figure 11-7   *NDMP Configuration*

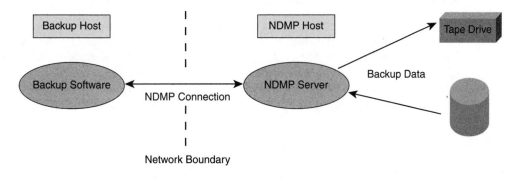

NOTE   For more information on the NDMP specification, refer to the Web site at www.ndmp.org/
wp/wp.shtml. Additional information on NDMP is available at www.ndmp.org/info.

In the next section, you learn about the next trend in non-SAN technology development: FCIP.

FCIP

The FCIP protocol uses IP-based networks as the backbone for long-distance transmissions between distributed SANs. To facilitate these transmissions and connectivity, FCIP is responsible for TCP encapsulation and IP routing of Fibre Channel frames. FCIP is sometimes also referred to as *tunneling*. This is because it provides dedicated point-to-point links between two SANlets in a distributed storage network. Dedicated point-to-point links are an expensive solution. Therefore, the focus of FCIP technology is on the capability of reusing existing metropolitan-area network (MAN) and WAN connections to interconnect SANlets separated by huge distances.

FCIP merges the features of IP and Fibre Channel technologies to connect distributed SANs, where TCP/IP technology tends to prevail over Fibre Channel technology. As a result, all Fibre Channel frames are known as datagrams by FCIP. Here, the responsibility of TCP is to provide flow control. At the same time, Fibre Channel, along with TCP, is responsible for error control and recovery from losses during transactions.

The implementation of FCIP technology requires the use of FCIP devices. These devices encapsulate Fibre Channel frames into TCP segments during transmission. At the receiver end, FCIP devices re-assemble the received TCP segments into original Fibre Channel frames. FCIP devices are available as standalone devices or they can be integrated with IP devices, such as IP routers and switches. These devices are transparent to both technologies. As a result, the IP-based network is not aware of the Fibre Channel traffic that passes through it. Similarly, the Fibre Channel network is equally unaware of the existence of the TCP/IP-based network.

Figure 11-8 shows a sample FCIP-based storage network configuration.

The FCIP protocol is a powerful networking technology that offers many advantages. The foremost advantage is that it offers the best of Fibre Channel and IP technology. As a result, it offers high-speed and highly reliable data transfers over long distances. In addition, it is cost effective because it can be implemented with minimum changes to the existing infrastructure. Also, FCIP allows the use of existing SAN management applications, which highly reduces the management cost of a SANlet or storage island across an IP-based infrastructure.

NOTE   For more information on FCIP, refer to the Web site at www.ietf.org/internet-drafts/draft-ietf-ips-fcip-slp-01.txt. Another great site for detailed reference on FCIP is www.snia.org/English/Colletrals/ Forum_Docs/ IP_Storage_FCIP.html.

The next section discusses iFCP, another standard that uses the IP infrastructure to extend a storage network.

Figure 11-8 *A Sample FCIP-Based SAN*

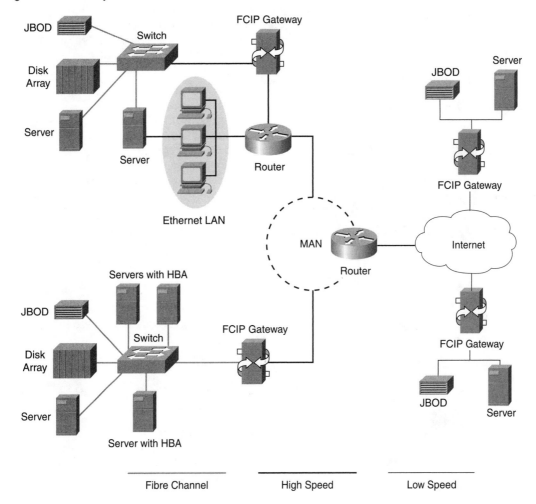

iFCP

iFCP is a gateway-to-gateway protocol, which allows Fibre Channel frames to be switched and routed over a storage network by using IP technology. An iFCP gateway (or edge switch) is used to interconnect a Fibre Channel-based storage network with an IP-based network. The gateway is transparent to both networks. Therefore, the SAN configuration and topology is hidden from the IP-based network. At the same time, the Fibre Channel storage network remains unaware of the connected IP network.

All the traffic directed by the IP network toward the Fibre Channel network is intercepted by the iFCP gateway. The iFCP gateway supports a set of Fabric services, which are required by Fibre Channel devices in the Fibre Channel network. When intercepting the incoming traffic, the gateway de-encapsulates the received segments into Fibre Channel frames. It also emulates Fabric services required by the Fibre Channel devices. Similarly, iFCP gateways also intercept the traffic directed toward the IP network and encapsulate the frames into corresponding TCP segments.

Figure 11-9 depicts a typical iFCP-based SAN.

Figure 11-9 *A Typical iFCP-Based SAN Setup*

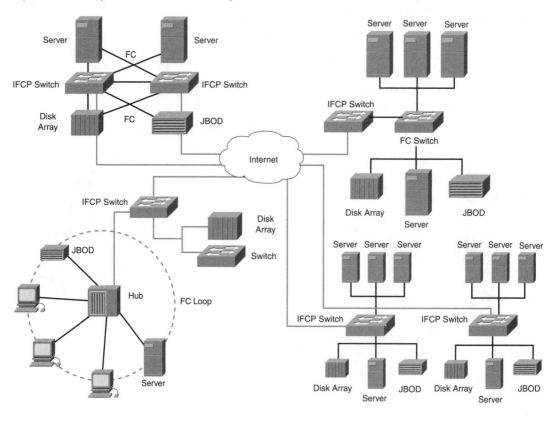

NOTE	iFCP is an expensive technology because iFCP gateways, which are required, are expensive devices. For more information on iFCP, refer to the Web site at www.ietf.org/internet-drafts/draft-monia-ips-ifcp-00.txt.

DAFS has emerged as the latest fast and lightweight technique of accessing data from a server. The next section discusses this new file access method that promises to make file transactions much faster, thus further improving the performance of networks, especially SANs.

DAFS

Based on the Network File System (NFS) version, DAFS is a mechanism for accessing data from application servers. DAFS is a memory-to-memory transaction mechanism that allows clusters of application servers to share data speedily and efficiently, while avoiding the traffic overhead generated by operating systems.

In conventional file-access methods, such as local NFS-based file accesses over the network, an additional data copy is created at every intermediary protocol stack on the way to the connectivity cable (see Figure 11-10). Copies of the data are created at the levels of application buffer, NFS, TCP/IP, and NIC driver. This practice slows down network transactions because the data copy needs to be processed at every underlying protocol stack and operating system.

Figure 11-10 *The Conventional File Access Method*

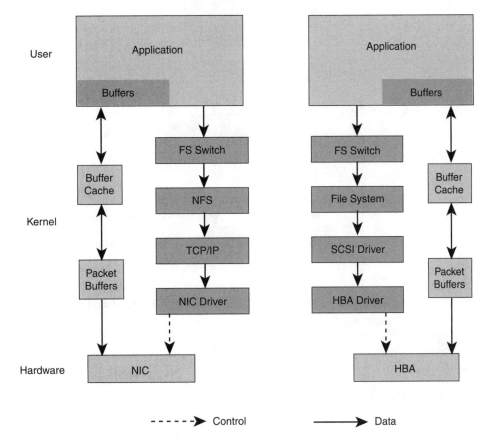

Contrary to local and network file accesses, applications supporting the DAFS can bypass the underlying protocol stacks and operating systems to directly place their data on the network link. This takes a huge load off the processor and makes the input/output (I/O) subsystem much faster, which leads to fast and reliable data transfers. In addition, DAFS reduces the overhead generated by system started interrupts, loss recovery operations, and intermediary context switches. It also increases the availability and integrity of mission-critical data and provides high fail-over from device failures.

Figure 11-11 depicts the implementation of DAFS.

Figure 11-11 *The DAFS File Access Method*

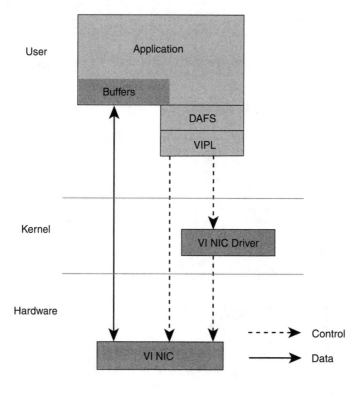

NOTE   For more information on DAFS, refer to the Web site at www.dafscollaborative.org/press/ dafs_whitepaper.shtml.

DAFS is based on transaction technologies, such as VI and InfiniBand. These technologies are discussed in the following sections.

VI

VI focuses on eliminating system overhead generated during communication over a network. This improves the performance of distributed applications. As per the VI technology, each process is allocated a direct interface to the device to which the process needs to communicate. This interface is not accessible to other ongoing processes and is referred to as *VI*.

The VI architecture consists of four components:

- **VI**—This is the direct and protected interface between the communicating process and the destination hardware device.

- **VI provider**—The NIC and operating system's kernel agent together are known as the VI provider. The VI provider implements the VI and completion queue upon connection establishment, and is responsible for data transactions between the communicating process and the destination hardware device.

- **VI consumer**—The end user of the virtual interface and the initiator of data transaction requests. The requesting application and the underlying operating system on the consumer machine are together referred to as the VI consumer.

- **Completion queue**—This queue contains the completion notifications for all the completed tasks in the request. The completion queue is created during the establishment of VI and is destroyed with the end of VI.

Figure 11-12 depicts the VI architectural model.

The network adapter plays an important role in the VI technology because it actually realizes the establishment of the VI. In addition, the network adapter is also responsible for multiplexing, de-multiplexing, and scheduling data transfers. All these activities, which are handled by the network adapter in VI architecture, are the responsibility of the operating system in normal networking architectures. However, the network adapter can also take the additional responsibility of ensuring the reliability of communication between two VIs. The data transfers supported by the network adapter can either be point-to-point or bi-directional, depending on the request.

NOTE   For more information on VI architecture, download the VI Architecture specification from the Web site at www.viarch.org/html/Spec/vi_specification_version_10.htm. Another site that provides detailed information on VI is www.dell.com/us/en/gen/topics/vectors_2001-via_sql2000.htm.

Besides VI, DAFS is also based on the InfiniBand architecture. The following section discusses this architecture.

Figure 11-12 *The VI Architecture Model*

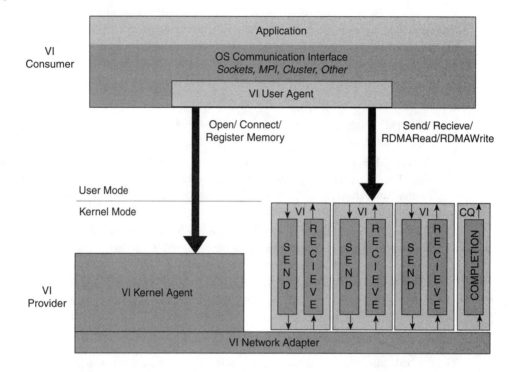

InfiniBand Architecture

Previously known as System I/O, the InfiniBand architecture seeks to eliminate the processing overhead on processors by limiting the transaction between the I/O subsystem and the memory of a device. This architecture offers greater bandwidth and high-level adaptability to future computer architectures. In fact, trade pundits expect InfiniBand to gradually replace the shared bus-based Peripheral Component Interconnect (PCI) architecture, which is prevalent in today's PCs.

InfiniBand offers a connection speed of 2.5 Gbps with 1, 4, or 12 cable link widths. In addition, the InfiniBand architecture offers built-in security and increased data reliability during transactions. Because of these advantages, InfiniBand is also destined to become the standard I/O specification for application servers. It not only facilitates connections between local servers and other devices, but also offers reliable connections with remote servers and storage devices.

NOTE   You can download more information related to the InfiniBand architecture from the Web site at www.infinibandta.org/estore.html. If you are not a member of Infinita, you are prompted to register yourself at the site.

Summary

SANs are here to stay. They have shown big e-commerce businesses a way to handle mountains of data, while ensuring $24 \times 7 \times 365$ availability of data and secure transmissions that are extremely difficult to tap into. Most of today's SANs are based on Fibre Channel technology. However, despite the high-performance and high-availability that Fibre Channel offers, it has failed to deliver in the field of ease of implementation and interoperability with other existing networking technologies. The industry is searching hard for personnel who are experts in the field of Fibre Channel SANs. More importantly, extending a Fibre Channel-based SAN across a metropolitan remains mostly un-chartered waters where only a few dare to tread simply because this is an extremely expensive and difficult affair. These issues have made the future of Fibre Channel SANs a topic of wide speculation.

Better and faster file access technologies, such as DAFS, VI, and InfiniBand architecture promise to enhance the performance of storage access further.

IT industry leaders and experts are coming up with various advancements that ensure that SANs do not disappear. Various technologies are being developed. Most prominent of these is iSCSI, about which you learn in Chapter 10, "iSCSI Technology." Other promising advancements include DWDM-based optical networking technology, SoIP, FCIP, and iFCP.

Whether the proposed advancements will survive the stiff competition from the time-tested Fibre Channel technology or emerge as supplementary technologies to Fibre Channel, making SAN an achievable goal for even small-sized companies, is yet to be seen. These technologies have yet to prove themselves.

RAID Technology and Fibre Channel Vendors

"Redundant Array of Independent Disks, or RAID, has revolutionized the way online data is stored in computers. Spanning the entire spectrum, from personal computers to supercomputers, RAID technology offers significant improvements in reliability, availability, and serviceability of data."

—Joe Molina, Chairman, RAID Advisory Board

Originally referred to as Redundant Array of Inexpensive Disks, the concept of RAID was first developed in the late 1980s by Patterson, Gibson, and Katz of the University of California at Berkeley. (The RAID Advisory Board has since substituted the term Inexpensive with Independent.)

RAID is a disk subsystem that is composed of multiple, independent, and high-performance disk drives. These disk drives are generally of similar capacity and are referred to as an *array*. Although made up of multiple disk drives, the entire disk subsystem appears as a single high-speed and reliable logical disk drive.

A typical RAID subsystem offers the following features:

- The same data is stored redundantly on multiple disks of the subsystem. As a result, failure of one disk does not render the data completely inaccessible. This makes the system highly fault-tolerant and reliable.

- A failed disk can be replaced while the array is still operational, which increases the accessibility and availability of data.

- RAID allows the creation of hard disk partitions that are much larger than the size of the largest physical disk available in the market.

- RAID offers high data transfer and Input/Output (I/O) rates, which are attributed to the parallel access of data from multiple disks.

Against popular belief, the focus of RAID technology is not on the security of data, but on maximizing the availability and accessibility of data. In other words, RAID technology does not make the data more secure. It just makes the data more accessible and reliable. Implementation of RAID can significantly reduce system downtime that is caused by hardware failures. The disks in a RAID subsystem can sustain disk problems ranging from bad sectors on the member disks of the array to entire disk failures without the end user feeling the affect of these failures.

Although a RAID subsystem can contain any number of disks, typical RAID arrays are made up of two to eight disk drives. Initially, RAID subsystems required that all the component disks be of similar capacity. However, the advancement in disk technology today allows a RAID set to be composed of disks with dissimilar capacities.

The main drawback associated with the use of dissimilar disks is that the smallest capacity in the set is considered as the default capacity of all the disks in the RAID set. For example, if a RAID set comprises six 9-GB disks, one 2-GB disk, and one 1-GB disk, the RAID controller adapter treats all the other high-capacity disks as 1 GB disks.

There are six commonly implemented RAID levels. These include Level 0, Level 1, Level 2, Level 3, Level 4, and Level 5. The popular misconception is that the higher the level number, the superior its performance. However, this is not true. Each level has unique benefits and drawbacks associated with it. You must understand each level and its implementation to choose the correct RAID level for your organization's requirements. The following sections describe each level.

RAID Level 0

Despite the name, RAID Level 0 is not actually a RAID. This is because it does not employ any type of redundancy while saving data. It is a non-redundant disk array that provides high I/O performance at the lowest cost of implementation. It employs the *spanning* or *data striping* technique, which is depicted in Figure A-1. According to this technique, data from a file or a database is split across multiple disk drives within the array.

Figure A-1   *Data Striping in RAID Level 0*

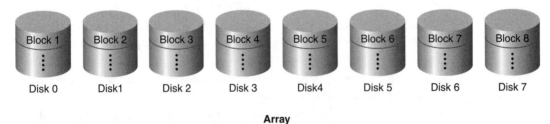

The high performance of this level is attributed to the following reasons:

- **Data is not saved redundantly**—Therefore, any change in data does not need to be updated or replicated at multiple locations.

- **A single copy of data is striped across multiple disks in the array**—As a result, data can be read from or written to all disks in the array in parallel.

The lowest cost of implementation of Level 0 is attributed to the lack of redundancy. However, the same lack of redundancy makes it the least reliable and fault-tolerant of all RAID levels. This is because the failure of one single disk in the array can lead to data loss.

This level is best suited for environments where performance and disk storage capacity are the main concerns, instead of reliability and full-time accessibility of data. Therefore, this level is commonly implemented in supercomputing environments, where the focus is on maximized data transfer rates and file sizes.

RAID Level 1

RAID Level 1 is one of the oldest and most commonly implemented RAID levels. It offers simplicity, the highest reliability, and the maximum data availability of all the levels. It employs the *mirroring* or *shadowing* technique. In this technique, data is duplicated on at least one or more disks in the array. In other words, while being written to the primary disk, data is also written to one or more redundant disks. As a result, there are always at least two or more copies of the same data at any given point in time. Figure A-2 depicts the mirroring technique used in RAID Level 1.

Figure A-2   *Mirroring in RAID Level 1*

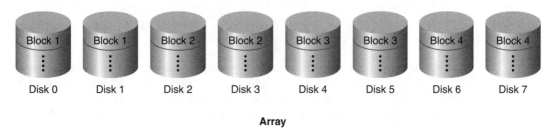

Other reasons for the high-performance of Level 1 are the following:

- Data is retrieved from the disk that has the shortest queue, seek, and rotational delays.
- Data is accessed simultaneously from multiple disks during read operations.

Because of the high redundancy factor, Level 1 is one of the most reliable and fault-tolerant setups. If a disk fails, data is accessed from other operational disks. The entire process is transparent to end-users. However, the high level of data redundancy also makes it one of the most expensive RAID implementations. This RAID level is most commonly implemented in database applications, in which accessibility and reliability of data are extremely important.

RAID Level 2

RAID Level 2 is one of the most rarely implemented levels. This is because it requires special disk features that make its implementation more expensive than the implementation of other RAID levels.

In RAID Level 2, data from a file or a database is interleaved across multiple disks in the array. In addition, extra disks are needed to store error-detecting code and parity information. The parity information and error-detection code is used to identify a disk failure or a part of a disk that contains errors. Both the parity information and error-detecting code are generated by using *Hamming code*. Hamming code is a binary code, which adds three check bits after every four data bits. These check bits detect and correct single-bit and double-bit transmission errors at the receiver end. Figure A-3 depicts the technique used in the RAID Level-2 setup.

Figure A-3   *Hamming Code Parity in RAID Level 2*

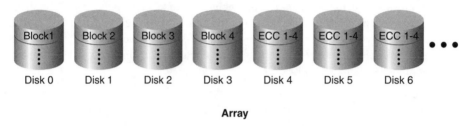

Array

ECC = Error Detection Code

Although this level offers high data availability and reliability, it is considered to be an impractical solution. This is because four disks in the array require three additional error-detection disks, which increases the cost of implementation considerably (refer to Figure A-3). Another reason that makes the implementation of RAID Level 2 impractical is that due to the advancement in disk technology, most of the disk drives today are shipped with an internal error-control mechanism. As a result, implementation of an external error-control mechanism that involves additional disk drives is not an intelligent solution.

NOTE   RAID Level 2 is generally implemented in memory systems because it provides high-speed data transfers, in addition to high data availability.

RAID Level 3

RAID Level 3 attempts to address the disadvantages of RAID Level 2. Instead of a set of additional parity disks that help in recovering lost data, a single parity disk is used to identify failed disks in the array and to recover lost information.

In this RAID level, data from a file or a database is interleaved byte-by-byte across multiple disk drives. Then, the disk controllers generate a parity byte from all the corresponding data disks that contain the data. The parity information is written to an additional disk, which is used to store this information. Figure A-4 depicts the technology used in the RAID Level-3 setup.

Figure A-4   *Byte-Level Parity in RAID Level 3*

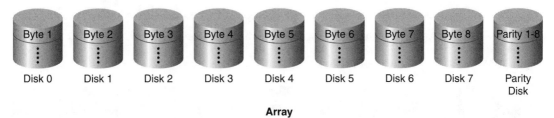

The performance of RAID Level 3 is slightly lower than the rest of the RAID levels for the following reasons:

- Any read request must access all the data disks in the array. On the other hand, a write request must involve the parity disk in addition to all the data disks in the array. As a result, only one request—read or write—can be served at a time.

Note   The parity disk does not take part in write requests, as it does not contain any data.

- The RAID Level-3 scheme can detect data errors, but lacks the mechanism to correct these errors. This is because the information to determine which byte contains incorrect information is lacking.

- Parity information is calculated during write operations. This negatively affects the overall performance of the array.

Despite the low performance, this level is popular. It offers high redundancy in case of disk failures, it's easier to implement, and it can be implemented at inherently lower costs than mirroring or interleaving data across multiple disks and and maintaining disks for parity information.

RAID Level 3 is generally implemented for those applications that demand high bandwidths and large data transfers, but do not focus on high data transfer rates. Therefore, this level is popular for transferring large graphic and imaging files.

RAID Level 4

RAID Level 4 is similar to RAID Level 3. However, there are certain differences between the two levels:

- Instead of byte interleaving, which is employed in RAID Level 3, Level 4 interleaves data in the form of blocks across multiple disks in the array. These blocks are known as *striping units*.

- The member disks of the array, unlike Level 3, can be accessed independently.

Figure A-5 depicts the technology used in the RAID Level-4 setup.

Figure A-5 *Block-Level Parity in RAID Level 4*

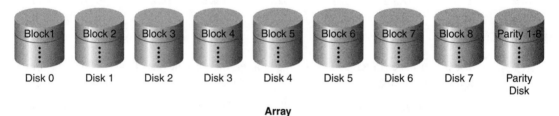

Disk 0   Disk 1   Disk 2   Disk 3   Disk 4   Disk 5   Disk 6   Disk 7   Parity Disk

Array

RAID Level 4 allows small read requests to be restricted to a single disk in the array. This makes the read operations fast. Write requests, on the other hand, even if small in size, require a minimum of four disk operations. These operations are popularly known as *read-modify-write procedures*.

NOTE   Read requests that are smaller in size than striping units are referred to as small read requests.

Four operations are a part of read-modify-write procedures:

- Reading the old data
- Reading the old parity information

Note   The two read operations compute the new parity.

- Writing the new data to the destination disk(s)
- Writing the new parity information to the parity disk

Although this RAID level offers higher redundancy and better performance than Level 3, there is a major disadvantage associated with it. The parity disk must be updated for every write operation. However, there is only one parity disk, which can easily become a performance bottleneck in case of write-intensive applications and environments. Because of this reason, RAID Level 4 is implemented in combination with other complimentary technologies, such as a write-back cache.

NOTE   Also referred to as copy-back cache, write-back cache is a caching technique, in which a write-request is considered complete as soon as the data is written to the cache. The actual writing of data to permanent storage occurs later. In this manner, the write-back cache technique offers better system performance by reducing the number of writes to the main memory.

RAID Level 5

RAID Level 5 offers considerable improvement over RAID Level 4 in terms of performance. In RAID Level 5, the data is interleaved in the form of blocks across some or all the disk drives in the array. A parity disk is singularly lacking in this setup. In contrast to Level 4, where parity information is written onto a dedicated parity disk, the parity information in RAID Level 5 is written onto the next available disk. Distribution of data and parity information in RAID Level 5 is depicted in Figure A-6.

Figure A-6   *Interleave Parity in RAID Level 5*

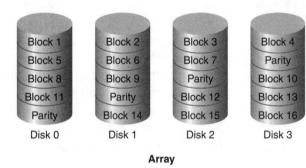

Major advantages of RAID Level 5 include the following:

- Allows concurrent read and write operations, which improves the performance of this level considerably over other levels.

- Distribution of parity information across multiple disk drives eliminates the need for an additional parity disk. This helps bring down the cost of implementation of the setup. Distribution of parity information across multiple disks also eliminates write bottlenecks caused by a single parity disk.

Because of these advantages, RAID Level 5 offers the best small-read and large-write performance. However, small-write requests are still inefficient because the regular read-modify-write procedures need to be performed to update parity information. These long update cycles can cause write operations to last much longer than they should. For this reason, RAID Level 5 is often used with other augmenting technologies, such as caching and parallel multiprocessing.

NOTE	A small-read/write request is one whose size is smaller than the stipulated size of a request. Similarly, the size of a large-read/write request is larger than the stipulated size of a request.

Table A-1 summarizes the six popular RAID levels. In this table, N represents the number of disk drives in the RAID array and C represents the default capacity of the disks in the array.

NOTE	In case of disk drives with dissimilar capacity, the default capacity of a RAID array is determined by the lowest-capacity disk in the array.

Table A-1   *The Six RAID Levels at a Glance*

RAID Level	Technique Employed	Capacity	Advantage	Disadvantage
0	Striping	$N \times C$	Maximum data transfer rates and sizes	No redundancy
1	Mirroring	$(N/2) \times C$	High performance and fastest write operations	Highest cost of implementation
2	Hamming-code parity	$(N-1) \times C$	Highest redundancy and data availability	Impractical
3	Byte-level parity	$(N-1) \times C$	Easy to implement and high error recoverability	Low performance
4	Block-level parity	$(N-1) \times C$	High redundancy and better performance than Level 3	Write-related bottlenecks
5	Interleave parity	$(N-1) \times C$	High performance, less expensive than Level 4, and eliminates write-related bottlenecks to some extent	Comparatively low performance in case of small-sized write operations

Fibre Channel Vendors

With the growing popularity of Fibre Channel technology and storage networks, many vendors have ventured into the arena of Fibre Channel products. Table A-2 presents a comprehensive list of these vendors.

Table A-2   *Fibre Channel Vendors at a Glance*

Vendor	Product(s)	URL
AMP	Transceivers	www.amp.com
ADIC	RAID, Just a Bunch of Disks (JBOD), Tape Subsystems, SAN Management Solutions	www.adic.com
AmDahl Corporation	SAN Solutions, Host Bus Adapters (HBAs), Fibre Channel Hubs, Fibre Channel Bridges, Fibre Channel Switches	www.amdahl.com
ATL Products	RAID, JBOD, Tape Subsystems, SAN Solutions	www.atlp.com
Atto Technology	HBAs, Fibre Channel (Loop) Hubs, Fibre Channel-Small Computer System Interface (SCSI) Bridges	www.attotech.com
Avid Technology	SAN Solutions, RAID, JBOD, Tape Subsystems	www.avid.com
BoxHill Systems Corporation	RAID, JBOD, Tape Subsystems	www.boxhill.com
Brocade Communications System	Fibre Channel Switches, Fabric Management Software	www.brocade.com
Chaparral Technologies	Fibre Channel-SCSI Bridges, RAID Controllers, Fibre Channel Routers	www.chaparraltech.com
Ciprico	RAID, JBOD, Tape Subsystems	www.ciprico.com
Compaq Computer Corporation	SAN Solutions, RAID, JBOD, Tape Subsystems, HBAs	www.compaq.com
Crossroads System	Fibre Channel-SCSI Bridges, Fibre Channel Routers, Fibre Channel Solutions, Tape Subsystems	www.crossroads.com
Dell Computer Corporation	SAN Solutions, RAID, JBOD, Tape Subsystems	www.dell.com
Dot Hill Systems Corporation	SAN Solutions, Fibre Channel Hubs, RAID, JBOD, Tape Subsystems, SAN Management Software	www.dothill.com

continues

Table A-2   *Fibre Channel Vendors at a Glance (Continued)*

Vendor	Product(s)	URL
EMC Corporation	RAID, JBOD, Tape Subsystems, Fibre Channel Switches, SAN Management Software	www.emc.com
Emulex Corporation	HBAs, Fibre Channel Hubs, Fibre Channel Solutions	www.emulex.com
Eurologic	RAID, JBOD, Tape Subsystems	www.eurologic.com
Exabyte Corporation	RAID, JBOD, Tape Subsystems	www.exabyte.com
Finisar Corporation	HBAs, Transceivers, Protocol Analyzers	www.finisar.com
Fujikura	HBAs and Transceivers	www.fujikura.com
Gadzoox Networks	Fibre Channel Hubs, Fibre Channel Switches, SAN Management Software	www.gadzoox.com
Hitachi Data Systems	RAID, JBOD, Tape Subsystems	www.hds.com
Hewlwtt Packard	HBAs, Transceivers, RAID, JBOD, Tape Subsystems, Fibre Channel Hubs, Fibre Channel Switches	www.hp.com
IBM Corporation	Transceivers, Fibre Channel Hubs, Fibre Channel Switches, Fibre Channel-SCSI Bridges, Fibre Channel Routers, RAID, JBOD, Tape Subsystems, Fibre Channel Solutions	www.ibm.com
Jaycor Networks	HBAs, Tape Subsystems, ASICs, SAN Management and Configuration Software, Drivers	www.jni.com
Legato Systems Inc.	SAN Solutions, SAN Management Software	www.legato.com
LSILogic	HBAs, Application Specific Integrated Circuits (ASICs), Storage Management Software, Drivers	www.lsilogic.com
Mcdata Corporation	Fibre Channel Switches and Directors	www.mcdata.com
Methode Electronics	Transceivers, Media Interface Adapters (MIAs)	www.methode.com
MTI Technology Corporation	RAID, JBOD, Tape Subsystems, SAN Management Software	www.mti.com
Mylex	RAID, JBOD, Tape Subsystems	www.mylex.com
Prisa Networks	HBAs, SAN Configuration and Management Software	www.prisa.com

Table A-2   *Fibre Channel Vendors at a Glance (Continued)*

Vendor	Product(s)	URL
Qlogic	HBAs, SAN Management Software, Fibre Channel Switches, Tape Subsystems	www.qlogic.com
Quantum Corporation	SAN Solutions, Tape Subsystems	www.quantum.com
RaidTec Corporation	RAID, JBOD, Tape Subsystems, SAN Solutions, Fibre Channel Bridges	www.raidtec.com
Seagate Technology	RAID, JBOD, Tape Subsystems	www.seagate.com
StorageTek	RAID, JBOD, Tape Subsystems	www.storagetek.com
StorNet Inc.	SAN Solutions, RAID, Tape Subsystems, SAN Management Software solutions	www.stornet.com
Sun Microsystems	RAID, JBOD, Tape Subsystems, SAN Solutions, SAN Management Software	www.sun.com
Troika Networks	HBAs, Fibre Channel Solutions	www.troikanetworks.com
Veritas	SAN Management Software, Tape and Backup Subsystems	www.veritas.com
Vixel Corporation	HBAs, Transceivers, Fibre Channel (Loop) Hubs, Fabric Switches, Fibre Channel Management Solutions	www.vixel.com
Vicom Systems Inc.	Fibre Channel Routers, SAN Management Software, SAN Solutions	www.vicom.com

NUMERICS

568SC connectors. Color-coded, push-pull type duplex connectors that allow for easy connections and reconnections.

8B/10B encoding. The native data encryption method of Fibre Channel technology.

A

AL-PA (Arbitrated Loop-Physical Address). An address dynamically assigned to FC-AL devices.

ANSI (American National Standards Institute). Rather than actively developing standards, ANSI acts as a middleman between the various organizations, such as the IETF, FCIA, and SNIA.

ATM (Asynchronous Transfer Mode). ATM is a fast packet-switching technology that uses fiber-optic cables for data transmissions at rates of 600 Mbps and above. Data is transmitted in the form of fixed-length cells, whose length is 53 bytes. ATM can transport a wide range of data that includes text, voice, imaging, and video.

AVVID (Architecture for Voice, Video, and Integrated Data). Cisco's scalable and manageable solutions for both SAN- and NAS-based networks.

B

B2B transactions (business-to-business transactions). B2B represents commerce between two or more commercial setups, such as companies.

B2C transactions (business-to-consumer transactions). B2C represents online transactions between a commercial setup (company) and individuals (buyers) or other consumers.

Backbone. The common transmission medium that interconnects network devices in the bus topology.

Backup window. The total time that is required to complete a backup process.

BER (bit error rate). The ratio of total bits received to bits received in error.

Bridge. Network devices that help to break a large-scale network into smaller segments. Fibre Channel bridges facilitate communication between Fibre Channel interfaces (such as FICON and ESCON) and SCSI interfaces, which enables communication between the primary LAN and SAN.

Brouter. A combination of a router and bridge. Brouters can handle communication within a network, and between different networks or subnets.

Bus and Tag interfaces. Interfaces that allow SAN servers with PCI bus slots to directly connect to the mainframe channel at a data transfer speed of 4.5 MB.

Bus topology. In this topology, all network devices are connected to a common cable called the backbone in a multi-point connection. The network devices have to contend with each other to gain access to the transmission medium, if they need to transmit data to another network device.

C

CD (compact disc). A read-only optical storage technology that can store up to 650 MB of data.

Channel. A point-to-point connection between two communicating entities.

Cluster. A set of network devices used as a single entity.

Collision. The simultaneous placement of two or more signals on the transmission medium. Signals collide and result in corruption of both the signals and the subsequent disruption of the normal network functioning.

Contention. Media access method where two or more network devices need to contend to place data on the transmission medium.

CoS (class of service). Data delivery scheme across the Fibre Channel infrastructure. There are six classes of service that range from Class-1 to Class-6.

CRC (Cyclic Redundancy Check). CRC algorithms are implemented by many protocols and transmission technologies to verify the correct reception of data during a transmission.

D

DAFS (Direct Access File System). A high-speed and reliable memory-to-memory transaction mechanism for accessing data from application servers.

DAS (Directly Attached Storage). An external storage device that is connected directly to the server through the SCSI interface.

DASD (Direct Access Storage Device). Any storage device that is directly attached to an application server. Disk and CD drives are examples of DASDs.

DC (Direct Current). Current that is produced by batteries and that flows steadily in one direction. Computers and other electronic devices operate on DC.

Director. A high-bandwidth, high-availability (99.999%), and high-performance category of switches.

Disk array. A set of high-performance storage disks that can store several terabytes of data.

Disk mirroring. The method of simultaneously writing data to two disks that share the same disk controller. This is a fault-tolerance technique.

Disk pooling. In disk pooling, the disk storage resources are allocated to multiple hosts instead of being dedicated to a single host.

DVD (digital versatile disc). Originally referred to as digital video discs, DVDs are high-capacity optical discs that are similar in physical size and appearance to a compact disc. However, compared to 650 MB stored by a CD-ROM, a standard single-layer, single-sided DVD can store 4.7 GB of data. A two-layer standard DVD can store up to 8.5 GB, and a double-sided DVD can store 17 GB.

DWDM (dense wavelength-division multiplexing). Optical technology that is used to combine the optical signals from several laser devices in a single optical fiber. DWDM allows each transmitting laser device to operate at a different wavelength. Despite multiplexing several signals in a single optical fiber, each signal can be separated at the output of the fiber.

E

E_Port. Used to connect Fibre Channel switches to other Fibre Channel switches and routers. These ports can only be attached to other E_Ports.

EMI (electromagnetic interference). The phenomenon that occurs during transmission when a data signal is affected by an external electromagnetic field or by other undesirable electromagnetic waves.

EOF (end of frame). The group of ordered sets that indicates the end of a transmitted frame to the recipient end.

ERP (Enterprise Resource Planning). ERP is a resource management technology that integrates the enterprise-wide resources of a company. These operations include human resources, financial operations, manufacturing, and distribution. ERP also connects an organization to its customers and suppliers.

ESCON (Enterprise Systems Connection). This interface is used to connect ESCON directors to the other SAN components in half-duplex mode at a comparatively low speed of 17 MB.

Extenders. Devices that allow the extension of Fibre Channel media beyond their maximum length.

F

F_Port (Fabric ports). These act as middlemen by facilitating communication between two entities. These ports can only be attached to other N_Ports.

Fabric. A SAN that implements hubs, switches, gateways, and routers.

FC-AL (Fibre Channel Arbitrated Loop). A Fibre Channel protocol, topology, and interface.

FC-AL topology. A Fibre Channel topology that allows the connection of up to 126 nodes to form a complete loop.

FCIA (Fibre Channel Industry Association). The international organization of Fibre Channel product vendors, industry professionals, system integrators, and consumers whose main focus is to establish a broad and successful market for the Fibre Channel infrastructure in the field of SAN.

FCOIP (Fibre Channel over Internet Protocol). FCOIP uses IP-based networks as the backbone for long-distance transmissions between distributed SANs.

FCP (Fibre Channel Protocol). Developed by the X3T10 committee, FCP is the serial SCSI-command protocol used in Fibre Channel networks.

Fibre Channel layers. The Fibre Channel standard has been structured as a stack of five layers—FC-0, FC-1, FC-2, FC-3, and FC-4.

FICON. A high-speed (100 Mbps) interface that is used to connect FICON directors to other SAN components in full-duplex mode.

FL_Port (Fabric-Loop ports). These ports are used to connect the FC-AL loop to the rest of the SAN Fabric. Similar to F_Ports, these ports also act as middlemen between the communicating ports. They can only be attached to other NL_Ports.

FLOGI (Fabric LOGIn). This procedure helps a Fabric switch to identify N_Ports and NL_Ports that are attached directly or indirectly to it.

FSPF (Fabric Shortest Path First). The protocol for path selection in Fibre Channel networks.

FTP (File Transfer Protocol). FTP is a TCP-based protocol that ensures the error-free transmission and downloading of program and data files across remote networks and the Internet.

Full duplex. In full-duplex mode, the receiver and the sender can transmit and receive data simultaneously.

G

Gateway. A device to interconnect two networks that use dissimilar protocols.

GBIC (Gigabit Interface Converter). Small interface modules that are used to connect copper or fiber-optic devices to hubs, switches, and adapters. Media Interface Adapters (MIAs) handle the conversion of copper-based connections into Fiber-based connections and vice versa.

Gigabyte. 2^{30} bytes or 1024 Megabytes (1,073,741,824 bytes.)

GLM (Gigabit Link Module). Fibre Channel transceiver units that are used to connect MIAs to Fibre Channel devices.

H

Half duplex. In half-duplex mode, the communicating entity (sender or receiver) can either receive data or transmit data, but not both at one time.

HBA (Host Bus Adapter). Provides a physical interface between the host bus and other SAN interfaces.

HIPPI (High Performance Parallel Interface). HIPPI is an ANSI standard interface that provides a point-to-point link for transferring data at speeds ranging between 100 Mbps and 200 Mbps over Fibre Channels.

HSSDC (High-Speed Serial Data Connector). Copper-based connectors that are used to connect 1 GB and 2 GB Fibre Channel devices to the copper media.

HTTP (Hyptertext Transfer Protocol). The standard protocol that supports data transfers over the Web (WWW). Each HTTP-based transaction consists of an ASCII request from the client-side browser and a server-side response.

Hubs. Hubs act as a central point of connection in a network by allowing multiple devices to be connected to them.

I

IETF (Internet Engineering Task Force). One of the most important and active communities of the networking industry. The IETF is an active player in the evolution and implementation of networking standards. It is also actively involved in the development of SAN technology and standards.

IFCP (Internet Fibre Channel Protocol). A gateway-to-gateway protocol that allows Fibre Channel frames to be switched and routed over a storage network by using IP technology.

In-band management. Communication between a Fibre Channel device and the management console over a Fibre Channel link by using the SCSI Enclosure Services (SES) specification.

InfiniBandTA (InfiniBand Trade Association). Founded by IBM, this organization is currently working on the development of new I/O specifications to facilitate high-speed data transfers on the switched Fabric technology.

Intercabinet GBICs. GBICs that allow long-distance (up to 33 meters) connectivity between cabinets.

Interconnect. A device that interconnects local or remote storage interfaces. Hubs, bridges, routers, gateways, and connectors are some of the interconnects used in a SAN.

Intracabinet GBIC. GBICs that allow short-distance (up to 25 meters) connectivity within a cabinet.

IP SAN. A SAN that is based on IP technology instead of the popular Fibre Channel technology used in SANs.

IPX (Internetwork Packet Exchange). Novell's proprietary, unreliable, and connectionless internetwork protocol. It facilitates data transfers between two devices that are located in different networks. Although functionally IPX is similar to IP, the difference between the two is that IPX uses 10-byte addresses in comparison to 4-byte addresses used by IP.

iSCSI (Internet SCSI). This technology eliminates the sole dependency of SANs on Fibre Channel technology, which allows SANs to be built on the popular and cost-effective Ethernet infrastructure.

ISDN (Integrated Services Digital Network). Technology that provides high-speed (156 Mbps) end-to-end digital connectivity by using digital telephone systems. ISDN can easily support bandwidth-intensive services, such as video on demand, live television, full-motion multimedia, and high-quality audio signals, in addition to text-based data signals.

ISL (Inter-Switch Link). A Fibre Channel link that interconnects two switches in a SAN.

J

JBOD (Just a Bunch of Disks). JBOD is a collection of disks that may or may not be configured on a RAID. As a subsystem of disks, JBODs provide high fault tolerance and performance.

Jumper cabling. Jumper cables are used to connect one Fibre Channel device directly to another. Because individual cables are used to connect Fibre Channel devices, the number of cables in this system is very large.

L

L_Port (Loop port). Basic ports that are used in the Fibre Channel-Arbitration Loop (FC-AL) topology and that are a part of FC-AL nodes. These ports can be of two types—NL_Ports or FL_Ports.

LILP (Loop Initialization Loop Position). This frame allows each loop port to know its position on the loop on the basis of information collected by the LIRP frame.

LIP (Loop Initialization Primitive). A set of three identical ordered sets that trigger the loop initialization process.

LIRP (Loop Initialization Report Position). This frame determines the position of all NL_Ports in relation to the position of the loop master.

LISM (Loop Initialization Select Master). This frame is used to start the selection process of a temporary loop master.

Loop master. A FC-AL device that is responsible for the initialization, management, and closure of a FC-AL loop.

LU (logical unit). Any individual I/O device in Fibre Channel technology.

LUN (Logical Unit Number). The unique address of an LU in a storage network.

LUN masking. A selective storage presentation technique where those LUNs that a particular server does not have rights to access are effectively masked. The server can view only those LUNs to which it has accessibility rights.

M

MAC (Media Access Control). The sublayer of the data link layer in the Open System Interconnection (OSI) model.

MAC standards. These standards include the rules and guidelines to prevent data collisions by controlling when a network device can transmit data.

Media connectors. Provide network devices with a point of connectivity to the network's transmission medium.

Megabyte. Approximately one million bytes (1,048,576 bytes).

Mesh topology. An extremely reliable but expensive network topology in which each device is connected to every other device on the network.

MIAs (Media Interface Adapters). Handles the conversion of copper-based connections into fiber-based connections and vice versa.

MIS (Management Information System). Also known as Business Intelligence (BI), MIS is the process of gathering, managing, and analyzing data on which future business decisions and operational processes are based.

MMF (Multi-Mode Fiber). Fiber-optic cables that are used in connections that span up to two kilometers.

Modem (modulator-demodulator). Converts analog signals received from a telephone line into digital signals that a computer can process and vice versa.

N

N_Port (Node port). These ports are used to connect two Fibre Channel nodes to the rest of the Fabric. These ports can only be attached to other N_Ports and Fabric ports (F_Ports).

NAS (network attached storage). A storage device that is connected directly to the network, instead of being connected to a server.

NAT (Network Address Translation). A mechanism for conserving registered IP addresses in large networks and for simplifying IP addressing management tasks. Implementation of NAT also provides cost-effective protection from unauthorized access from outside, without requiring any elaborate setup, such as firewalls.

NDMP (Network Data Management Protocol). Facilitates enterprise-wide backup and restoration solutions for large-scale storage networks.

NFS (Network File System). Developed by Sun Microsystems, NFS allows a computer to access files over a network as if they were on local disks.

NIC (network interface card). Also known as network adapter cards, NICs provide network connectivity to a device. They are also the source of the hardware address of a network device.

NL_Port (Node-Loop ports). These ports can only be attached to other NL_Ports and FL_Ports.

Node level. A Fibre Channel upper level that includes layers FC-3 and FC-4 and plays an important role in providing services and in mapping upper-level protocols and applications.

NSPOF (No Single Point Of Failure). Represents the connection strategy, where a single device or point of connection cannot bring down the entire network.

O

OFC (Open Fiber Control). An open-fiber port safety mechanism that is employed in Fibre Channel networks to control the intensity of laser radiations in cases where an optical cable is broken or damaged.

OSI model (Open System Interconnect). The seven-layer model whose main aim is to establish open standards for current and future developments in the field of networking. The seven layers include the following: physical layer, data link layer, network layer, transport layer, session layer, presentation layer, and application layer.

OSN (optical storage networking). Also referred to as DWDM technology, OSN combines the strengths of the existing SAN, fiber-optic, and Fibre Channel technologies to deliver long-distance and high-bandwidth storage networks.

Out-of-band management. Communication between the management console and the Fibre Channel device through an Ethernet interface, such as RS-232.

P

PLOGI (Port Login). This procedure establishes a session between two N_Ports before the two can communicate.

Point-to-point topology. Fibre Channel topology where two Fibre Channel nodes are directly connected to each other through N_Ports.

Polling. Media access method where a primary device polls all the network devices at regular intervals to check whether they need to transmit data.

Port level. Physical and signaling level that includes the three lowest layers from FC–0 through FC–2 and that facilitates communication between devices.

PRLI (Process Login). This procedure establishes the environment between two communicating processes that are located at the respective ports.

Protocol. A set of standards to facilitate communication between two network devices.

R

RAID (Redundant Array of Independent [Inexpensive]) Disks). RAID is the method of distributing data across several storage disks. Five levels of RAID help in the efficient usage of the available bandwidth. The RAID levels also provide efficient methods of data recovery in the case of server crashes.

Repeaters. Extend the length of a transmission medium by amplifying the signal to its original strength.

Ring topology. In this topology, all the network devices are connected to their neighboring device to form a ring.

Router. The network device that is used to connect separate networks or subnets. Routers also facilitate the communication between different networks.

RSCN (Registered State Change Notification). A Fibre Channel switch function that notifies registered nodes of any change that occurs in the Fabric.

S

SAN (storage area network). The latest storage solution technology that was developed to deal with large amounts of data securely and reliably without hampering overall network performance.

SAN application. The applications that allow you to configure, manage, maintain, and exploit the SAN.

SCN (State Change Notification). A Fibre Channel function that notifies a Fibre Channel node about any change that occurs with another node.

SCSI (Small Computer System Interface). An ANSI standard parallel interface that provides high-speed connectivity to peripheral devices, such as printers and CD-ROMs.

SCSITA (SCSI Trade Association). An organization of various vendors of Small Computer System Interface (SCSI) products. The main aim of SCSITA is to promote SCSI technology in the field of SANs.

SES (SCSI Enclosure Services). A subset of the SCSI protocol that is used to monitor and manage the power, temperature, and the fan status of SCSI-based devices.

SMF (Single-Mode Fiber). Fiber-optic cables that are used over longer distances that span up to 10 kilometers.

SNIA (Storage Networking Industry Association). The primary organization for the development of SAN standards. As a forum of major SAN vendors, the main aim of SNIA is to develop and promote efficient and compatible SAN solutions in the market.

SNMP (Simple Network Management Protocol). The application layer protocol that is used to manage devices in an IP-based network without the need of continual polling.

SNS (Simple Name Server). Components of Fabric switches that contain the table that maps 24-bit addresses of all the ports that have logged into the switch, with the corresponding WWPN and WWN of the node to which the ports belong.

SOF (start of frame). The group of ordered sets that indicates the beginning of a transmitted frame to the recipient-end of the transmission.

SoIP (Storage over IP). Facilitates building long-distance SANs by merging Fibre Channel and IP technologies.

SSP (Selective Storage Presentation). Synonym of LUN masking.

Star topology. In this topology, all network devices are connected to a central device called the hub through drop cables in a point-to-point connection. This is a highly cost-effective, commonly used topology.

Structured cabling. Fibre trunk cables, patch panels, and patch cables are used extensively to reduce the number of individual cables running under the floor. As a result, the system requires few cables.

Subnet. Logical divisions of a network.

SWAN (storage wide-area network). A SAN that extends over a broad geographic area (hundreds and thousands of kilometers).

Switched Fabric topology. Fibre Channel topology where the Fabric—a set of one or more interconnected switches—is used to interconnect nodes to form a virtual mesh.

T

Tape library. A set of tape cartridges that are used to store from 10 GB to 1 TB of data.

TCO (Total Cost of Ownership). TCO is a non-standard measurement of the total cost of a network. It includes the costs of hardware and software used in the setup, the cost of maintenance of the entire system, and the costs of direct support and end user support.

Terabyte. 2^{40} bytes or approximately one trillion bytes (1,099,511,627,776).

Token. A special frame that continuously keeps circulating in a ring-based network.

Topology. The physical arrangement of the transmission medium in a network, and the manner in which network devices are connected to the medium.

U–V

UDP (User Datagram Protocol). Similar to Transmission Control Protocol (TCP), UDP also relates to the transport layer of the OSI reference model. However, UDP is a connectionless protocol where data packets are not acknowledged.

VI (virtual interface). Technology that seeks to eliminate system overheads generated during communication over a network by establishing virtual interfaces between the communicating process and destination hardware device.

VPN (Virtual Private Network). A private network that extends over open public transmission systems, such as the Internet. Because transmissions are carried across insecure public systems, VPNs use encryption and secure protocols such as PPTP to ensure that data transmissions are not intercepted by unauthorized parties.

W–Z

WWN (World Wide Name). 64-bit address hard-coded in a Fibre Channel device's HBA.

WWPN (World Wide Port Name). 64-bit port address that facilitates the accessibility of a Fibre Channel port.

WWUI (World-Wide Unique Identifier). The unique name used by an initiator to identify itself and the target with which it needs to establish the session.

Zoning. The method of dividing SAN ports into separate groups so that ports belonging to one group cannot access the ports that belong to other groups.

INDEX

Numerics

A

B

G

J-L

M

N

O

P

Q-R

S

T

U

V-Z

Hey, you've got enough worries.

Don't let IT training be one of them.

Get on the fast track to IT training at InformIT,
your total Information Technology training network.

 www.informit.com

■ Hundreds of timely articles on dozens of topics ■ Discounts on IT books from all our publishing partners, including Cisco Press ■ Free, unabridged books from the InformIT Free Library ■ "Expert Q&A"—our live, online chat with IT experts ■ Faster, easier certification and training from our Web- or classroom-based training programs ■ Current IT news ■ Software downloads ■ Career-enhancing resources